THE TALE OF

Despereaux

*being the story of a
mouse, a princess,
some soup, and
a spool of thread*

⌐⌐

Kate Di Camillo

illustrated by Timothy Basil Ering

The Tale of Despereaux

Text © 2003 by Kate Dicamillo

Illustrations © 2003 by Timothy Basil Ering

Published by arrangement with Walker Books Limited, London SE11 5HJ.

For information about permission, write to editor@ltinc.net

ISBN 979-11-91343-95-3 14740

Longtail Books

For Luke, who asked for
the story of an unlikely hero

Contents

—∞—

—∞—

The world is dark, and light is precious.
Come closer, dear reader.
You must trust me.
I am telling you a story.

Book
THE FIRST

A Mouse Is Born

Chapter One *ᐓ*
the last one

THIS STORY BEGINS within the walls of a castle, with the birth of a mouse. A small mouse. The last mouse born to his parents and the only one of his **litter** to be born alive.

"Where are my babies?" said the **exhaust**ed mother when the **ordeal** was through. "Show to me my babies."

The father mouse held the one small mouse up high.

"There is only this one," he said. "The others are dead."

"*Mon Dieu*,★ just the one mouse baby?"

"Just the one. Will you name him?"

★ mon Dieu [감탄사] 어머나, 저런. 'my God'의 프랑스어이다.

"All of that work **for nothing**," said the mother. She sighed. "It is so sad. It is such the disappointment." She was a French mouse who had arrived at the castle long ago in the **luggage** of a visiting French **diplomat**. "Disappointment" was one of her favorite words. She used it often.

"Will you name him?" repeated the father.

"Will I name him? Will I name him? Of course, I will name him, but he will only die like the others. Oh, so sad. Oh, such the **tragedy**."

The mouse mother held a **handkerchief** to her nose and then waved it in front of her face. She **sniffed**. "I will name him. Yes. I will name this mouse Despereaux, for all the sadness, for the many **despairs** in this place. Now, where is my mirror?"

Her husband handed her a small **shard** of mirror. The mouse mother, whose name was Antoinette, looked at her **reflection** and **gasped** aloud. "Toulèse," she said to one of her sons, "get for me my **makeup** bag. My eyes are a **fright**."

While Antoinette touched up her eye makeup, the mouse father put Despereaux down on a bed made of blanket **scraps**. The April sun, weak but **determined**, **shone** through a castle window and from there **squeezed** itself through a small hole in the wall and placed one

10

Despereaux's eyes should not have been open.

golden finger on the little mouse.

The other, older mice children gathered around to stare at Despereaux.

"His ears are too big," said his sister Merlot. "Those are the biggest ears I've ever seen."

"Look," said a brother named Furlough, "his eyes are open. Pa, his eyes are open. They shouldn't be open."

It is true. Despereaux's eyes should not have been open. But they were. He was staring at the sun reflecting off his mother's mirror. The light was shining onto the ceiling in an oval of brilliance, and he was smiling up at the sight.

"There's something wrong with him," said the father. "Leave him alone."

Despereaux's brothers and sisters stepped back, away from the new mouse.

"This is the last," proclaimed Antoinette from her bed. "I will have no more mice babies. They are such the disappointment. They are hard on my beauty. They ruin, for me, my looks. This is the last one. No more."

"The last one," said the father. "And he'll be dead soon. He can't live. Not with his eyes open like that."

But, reader, he did live.

This is his story.

Chapter Two
such a disappointment

DESPEREAUX TILLING LIVED.

But his existence was cause for much speculation in the mouse community.

"He's the smallest mouse I've ever seen," said his aunt Florence. "It's ridiculous. No mouse has ever, ever been this small. Not even a Tilling." She looked at Despereaux through narrowed eyes as if she expected him to disappear entirely. "No mouse," she said again. "Ever."

Despereaux, his tail wrapped around his feet, stared back at her.

"Those are some big ears he's got, too," observed his uncle Alfred. "They look more like donkey ears, if you ask me."

"They are **obscenely** large ears," said Aunt Florence.

Despereaux **wiggled** his ears.

His aunt Florence **gasped**.

"They say he was born with his eyes open," **whispered** Uncle Alfred.

Despereaux stared hard at his uncle.

"Impossible," said Aunt Florence. "No mouse, no matter how small or obscenely large-eared, is ever born with his eyes open. It simply isn't done."

"His pa, Lester, says he's not well," said Uncle Alfred.

Despereaux **sneezed**.

He said nothing in **defense** of himself. How could he? Everything his aunt and uncle said was true. He *was* ridiculously small. His ears *were* obscenely large. He *had* been born with his eyes open. And he was **sickly**. He **cough**ed and sneezed so often that he carried a **handkerchief** in one **paw** at all times. He ran **temperature**s. He **faint**ed at loud noises. Most **alarm**ing of all, he showed no interest in the things a mouse should show interest in.

He did not think **constant**ly of food. He was not **intent** on **track**ing down every **crumb**. While his larger, older **siblings** ate, Despereaux stood with his head **cocked** to one side, holding very **still**.

"Do you hear that sweet, sweet sound?" he said.

"I hear the sound of cake crumbs falling out of people's mouths and hitting the floor," said his brother Toulèse. "That's what I hear."

"No . . . ," said Despereaux. "It's something else. It sounds like . . . um . . . honey."

"You might have big ears," said Toulèse, "but they're not attached right to your brain. You don't *hear* honey. You *smell* honey. When there's honey to smell. Which there isn't."

"Son!" barked Despereaux's father. "Snap to it. Get your head out of the clouds and hunt for crumbs."

"Please," said his mother, "look for the crumbs. Eat them to make your mama happy. You are such the skinny mouse. You are a disappointment to your mama."

"Sorry," said Despereaux. He lowered his head and sniffed the castle floor.

But, reader, he was not smelling.

He was listening, with his big ears, to the sweet sound that no other mouse seemed to hear.

Chapter Three
once upon a time

DESPEREAUX'S **SIBLINGS** tried to educate him in
the ways of being a mouse. His brother Furlough took
him on a tour of the castle to **demonstrate** the art of
scurrying.

"Move from side to side," **instruct**ed Furlough,
scrabbling across the **waxed** castle floor. "Look over your
shoulder all the time, first to the right, then to the left.
Don't stop for anything."

But Despereaux wasn't listening to Furlough. He was
staring at the light pouring in through the **stained-glass***
windows of the castle. He stood on his **hind** legs and

---

* stained-glass 교회의 창 등에 쓰는 착색 유리.

held his handkerchief over his heart and stared up, up, up into the **brilliant** light.

"Furlough," he said, "what is this thing? What are all these colors? Are we in heaven?"

"**Cripes!**" shouted Furlough from a far corner. "Don't stand there in the middle of the floor talking about heaven. Move! You're a mouse, not a man. You've got to scurry."

"What?" said Despereaux, still staring at the light.

But Furlough was gone.

He had, like a good mouse, disappeared into a hole in the **molding**.

Despereaux's sister Merlot took him into the castle library, where light came **stream**ing in through tall, high windows and landed on the floor in bright yellow **patch**es.

"Here," said Merlot, "follow me, small brother, and I will instruct you on the fine points of how to **nibble** paper."

Merlot scurried up a chair and from there **hop**ped onto a table on which there sat a huge, open book.

"This way, small brother," she said as she **crawl**ed onto the pages of the book.

And Despereaux followed her from the chair, to the

table, to the page.

"Now then," said Merlot. "This **glue**, here, is tasty, and the paper **edge**s are **crunch**y and yummy, like so." She nibbled the edge of a page and then looked over at Despereaux.

"You try," she said. "First a bite of some glue and then follow it with a crunch of the paper. And these **squiggle**s, they are very tasty."

Despereaux looked down at the book, and something **remarkable** happened. The marks on the pages, the "squiggles" as Merlot called them, **arranged** themselves into shapes. The shapes arranged themselves into words, and the words **spell**ed out a delicious and wonderful **phrase**: *Once upon a time.*

"'Once upon a time,'" **whisper**ed Despereaux.

"What?" said Merlot.

"Nothing."

"Eat," said Merlot.

"I couldn't possibly," said Despereaux, backing away from the book.

"Why?"

"Um," said Despereaux, "it would **ruin** the story."

"The story? What story?" Merlot stared at him. A piece of paper **trembled** at the end of one of her **indignant whiskers**. "It's just like Pa said when you were

"'Once upon a time,'" whispered Despereaux.

singing to his daughter, the Princess Pea, every night before she fell asleep.

Hidden in a hole in the wall of the princess's bedroom, the mouse listened with all his heart. The sound of the king's music made Despereaux's soul grow large and light inside of him.

"Oh," he said, "it sounds like heaven. It smells like honey."

He **stuck** his left ear out of the hole in the wall so that he could hear the music better, and then he stuck his right ear out so that he could hear better still. And it wasn't too long before one of his paws followed his head and then another paw, and then, without any real planning on Despereaux's part, the whole of him was on display, all in an effort to get closer to the music.

Now, while Despereaux did not **indulge** in much of the normal behavior of mice, he did **adhere** to one of the most basic and **elemental** of all mice rules: Do not ever, under any **circumstances**, **reveal** yourself to humans.

But . . . the music, the music. The music made him lose his head and act against the few small mouse **instincts** he was in **possession** of, and because of this he revealed himself; and **in no time** at all, he was **spied** by the sharp-eyed Princess Pea.

"Oh, Papa," she said, "look, a mouse."

The king stopped singing. He **squint**ed. The king was **near-sighted**; that is, anything that was not right in front of his eyes was very difficult for him to see.

"Where?" said the king.

"There," said the Princess Pea. She pointed.

"That, my dear, is a bug, not a mouse. It is much too small to be a mouse."

"No, no, it's a mouse."

"A bug," said the king, who liked to be right.

"A *mouse*," said the Pea, who knew that she was right.

As for Despereaux, he was beginning to realize that he had made a very **grave** error. He **trembled**. He shook. He sneezed. He **considered fainting**.

"He's **frightened**," said the Pea. "Look, he's so afraid he's shaking. I think he was listening to the music. Play something, Papa."

"A king play music for a *bug*?" King Phillip **wrinkled** his **forehead**. "Is that proper, do you think? Wouldn't that make this into some kind of **topsy-turvy**, wrong-headed world if a king played music for a bug?"

"Papa, I told you, he's a *mouse*," said the Pea. "Please?"

"Oh, well, if it will make you happy, I, the king, will play music for a bug."

"A *mouse*," corrected the Pea.

The king **adjust**ed his heavy gold crown. He cleared

his **throat**. He **strum**med the guitar and started to sing a song about stardust.* The song was as sweet as light shining through stained-glass windows, as **captivating** as the story in a book.

Despereaux forgot all his fear. He only wanted to hear the music.

He **crept** closer and then closer still, until, reader, he was sitting right at the foot of the king.

★ stardust 소성단(小星團). 우주의 군데군데 모여있는 작은 별들의 집단.

Chapter Five
what Furlough saw

THE PRINCESS PEA looked down at Despereaux. She smiled at him. And while her father played another song, a song about the deep purple falling over sleepy garden walls, the princess reached out and touched the top of the mouse's head.

Despereaux **stared** up at her in **wonder.** The Pea, he decided, looked just like the picture of the **fair maiden** in the book in the library. The princess smiled at Despereaux again, and this time, Despereaux smiled back. And then, something **incredible** happened: The mouse fell in love.

Reader, you may ask this question; in fact, you *must* ask this question: Is it **ridiculous** for a very small, **sickly,**

Despereaux stared up at her in wonder.

big-eared mouse to fall in love with a beautiful human princess named Pea?

The answer is . . . yes. Of course, it's ridiculous.

Love is ridiculous.

But love is also wonderful. And powerful. And Despereaux's love for the Princess Pea would prove, in time, to be all of these things: powerful, wonderful and ridiculous.

"You're so sweet," said the princess to Despereaux. "You're so tiny."

As Despereaux looked up at her adoringly, Furlough happened to scurry past the princess's room, moving his head left to right, right to left, back and forth.

"Cripes!" said Furlough. He stopped. He stared into the princess's room. His whiskers became as tight as bowstrings.

What Furlough saw was Despereaux Tilling sitting at the foot of the king. What Furlough saw was the princess touching the top of his brother's head.

"Cripes!" shouted Furlough again. "Oh, cripes! He's nuts! He's a goner!"

And, executing a classic scurry, Furlough went off to tell his father, Lester Tilling, the terrible, unbelievable news of what he had just seen.

Chapter Six
this drum

"HE CANNOT, he simply cannot be my son," Lester said. He **clutch**ed his whiskers with his front paws and shook his head from side to side in **despair**.

"Of course he is your son," said Antoinette. "What do you mean he is not your son? This is a ridiculous statement. Why must you always make the ridiculous statements?"

"You," said Lester. "This is your fault. The French blood in him has made him crazy."

"*C'est moi?*★" said Antoinette. "*C'est moi?* Why must it always be I who takes the **blame**? If your son is such the

---

★ c'est moi? [프랑스어] (= It's me?) 그게 나라구요?

disappointment, it is as much your fault as mine."

"Something must be done," said Lester. He pulled on a whisker so hard that it came loose. He waved the whisker over his head. He pointed it at his wife. "He will be the end of us all," he shouted, "sitting at the foot of a human king. **Unbelievable!** Unthinkable!"

"Oh, so **dramatic**," said Antoinette. She held out one paw and studied her painted nails. "He is a small mouse. How much of the harm can he do?"

"If there is one thing I have learned in this world," said Lester, "it is that mice must act like mice or else there **is bound to** be trouble. I will call a special meeting of the Mouse **Council**. Together, we will decide what must be done."

"Oh," said Antoinette, "you and this council of the mouse. It is a waste of the time in my opinion."

"Don't you understand?" shouted Lester. "He must be **punish**ed. He must be **brought up** before the **tribunal**." He pushed past her and **dug furious**ly through a **pile** of paper **scraps**, until he **uncover**ed a **thimble** with a piece of **leather stretch**ed across its open end.

"Oh, please," said Antoinette. She covered her ears. "Not this drum of the council of the mouse."

"Yes," said Lester, "the drum." He held it up high above his head, first to the north and then to the south,

and then to the east and the west. He lowered it and
turned his back to his wife and closed his eyes and took a
deep **breath** and began to **beat** the drum slowly, one long
beat with his tail, two staccato* beats with his paws.

Boom. Tat-tat. Boom. Tat-tat. Boom. Tat-tat.

The **rhythm** of the drum was a signal for the
members of the Mouse Council.

Boom. Tat-tat. Boom. Tat-tat. Boom.

The beating of the drum let them know that an
important decision would have to be made, one that
affected the safety and **well-being** of the **entire** mouse
community.

Boom. Tat-tat. Boom. Tat-tat.

Boom.

★ staccato 스타카토. 악보상에서 음을 연주하거나 부를 때 한 박자를 절반 정도의 길이로
끊어서 연주하거나 부르도록 하는 용어.

Chapter Seven
a mouse in love

AND WHAT WAS OUR OWN favorite member of the mouse community doing while the sound of the Mouse **Council** drum **echo**ed through the walls of the castle?

Reader, I must report that Furlough had not seen the worst of it. Despereaux sat with the princess and the king and listened to song after song. At one point, gently, oh so gently, the Pea picked up the mouse in her hand. She **cup**ped him in her **palm** and **scratch**ed his **oversize** ears.

"You have lovely ears," the Pea said to him. "They are like small pieces of velvet.*"

★ velvet 벨벳. 표면에 부드러운 보풀이 촘촘히 난 직물.

Despereaux thought that he might **faint** with the pleasure of someone **refer**ring to his ears as small and lovely. He **laid** his tail against the Pea's **wrist** to **steady** himself and he felt the princess's **pulse**, the **pound**ing of her heart, and his own heart **immediately** took up the **rhythm** of hers.

"Papa," the Pea said when the music was over, "I am going to keep this mouse. We are going to be great friends."

The king looked at Despereaux cupped in his daughter's hands. He **narrow**ed his eyes. "A mouse," he muttered. "A *rodent.*"

"What?" said the Pea.

"Put it down," the king **command**ed.

"No," said the Pea, who was a person not at all used to being told what to do. "I mean, why should I?"

"Because I told you to."

"But why?" **protest**ed the Pea.

"Because it's a mouse."

"I know. I'm the one who told you he was a mouse."

"I wasn't thinking," said the king.

"Thinking of what?"

"Your mother. The queen."

"My mother," said the Pea sadly.

"Mice are rodents," said the king. He **adjust**ed his

crown. "They are related to . . . rats. You know how we feel about rats. You know of our own dark history with rats."

The Pea **shudder**ed.

"But Papa," she said, "he is not a rat. He's a mouse. There's a difference."

"**Royalty**," the king said, "has many **responsibilities**. And one of them is not becoming involved **personally** with even the **distant relatives** of one's **enemies**. Put him down, Pea."

The princess put Despereaux down.

"Good girl," said the king. And then he looked at Despereaux. "**Scat**," he said.

Despereaux, however, did not scat. He sat and stared up at the princess.

The king **stamp**ed his foot. "Scat!" he shouted.

"Papa," said the princess, "please, don't be mean to him." And she began to **weep**.

Despereaux, seeing her tears, broke the last of the great, **ancient** rules of mice. He spoke. To a human.

"Please," said Despereaux, "don't cry." He held out his handkerchief to the princess.

The Pea **sniff**ed and **lean**ed down close to him.

"*Do not speak to her!*" **thunder**ed the king.

Despereaux dropped his handkerchief. He backed

away from the king.

"Rodents do not speak to princesses. We will not have this becoming a **topsy-turvy**, wrong-headed world. There are rules. Scat. **Get lost**, before my **common sense** returns and I have you killed."

The king stamped his foot again. Despereaux found it **alarm**ing to have such a big foot brought down with so much force and anger so close to his own small head. He ran toward the hole in the wall.

But he turned before he entered it. He turned and shouted to the princess, "My name is Despereaux!"

"Despereaux?" she said.

"I **honor** you!" shouted Despereaux.

"I honor you" was what the **knight** said to the fair maiden in the story that Despereaux read every day in the book in the library. Despereaux had muttered the **phrase** often to himself, but he had never before this evening had **occasion** to use it when speaking to someone else.

"Get out of here!" shouted the king, stamping his foot harder and then harder still so it seemed as if the whole castle, the very world, were shaking. "Rodents know nothing of honor."

Despereaux ran into the hole and from there he looked out at the princess. She had picked up his handkerchief and she was looking at him . . . right, directly into his soul.

"Despereaux," she said. He saw his name on her lips.

"I honor you," **whisper**ed Despereaux. "I honor you." He put his **paw** over his heart. He **bow**ed so low that his whiskers touched the floor.

He was, **alas,** a mouse deeply in love.

Chapter Eight
to the rats

THE MOUSE COUNCIL, thirteen honored mice and one Most Very Honored Head Mouse, heeded the call of Lester's drum and gathered in a small, secret hole off King Phillip's throne room. The fourteen mice sat around a piece of wood balanced on spools of thread and listened in horror while Despereaux's father related the story of what Furlough had seen.

"At the foot of the king," said Lester.

"Her finger right on top of his head," said Lester.

"He was looking up at her, and . . . it was not in fear."

The Mouse Council members listened with their mouths open. They listened with their whiskers drooping and their ears flat against their heads. They listened in dismay and outrage and fear.

When Lester finished, there was a silence dismal and deep.

"Something," intoned the Most Very Honored Head Mouse, "is wrong with your son. He is not well. This goes beyond his fevers, beyond his large ears and his lack of growth. He is deeply disturbed. His behavior endangers us all. Humans cannot be trusted. We know this to be an indisputable fact. A mouse who consorts with humans, a mouse who would sit right at the foot of a man, *a mouse who would allow a human to touch him*"—and here, the entire Mouse Council indulged in a collective shiver of disgust—"cannot be trusted. That is the way of the world, our world.

"Fellow mice, it is my most fervent hope that Despereaux has not spoken to these humans. But obviously, we can assume nothing. And this is a time to act, not wonder."

Lester nodded his head in agreement. And the twelve other members of the Mouse Council nodded their heads too.

"We have no choice," said the Head Mouse. "He must go to the dungeon." He pounded his fisted paw on the table. "He must go to the rats. Immediately. Members of the council, I will now ask you to vote. Those in favor of Despereaux being sent to the dungeon, say 'aye.★'"

There was a **chorus** of sad "ayes."

"Those **opposed** say 'nay.✻'"

Silence **reign**ed in the room.

The only noise came from Lester. He was crying.

And thirteen mice, **ashamed** for Lester, looked away.

Reader, can you imagine your own father not voting against your being sent to a dungeon full of rats? Can you imagine him not saying one word in your **defense**?

Despereaux's father **wept** and the Most Very Honored Head Mouse **beat** his paw against the table again and said, "Despereaux Tilling will appear before the mouse community. He will hear of his **sins**; he will be given a chance to **deny** them. If he does not deny them, he will be allowed to **renounce** them so that he may go to the dungeon with a pure heart. Despereaux Tilling is **hereby** called to sit with the Mouse Council."

At least Lester had the **decency** to weep at his act of **perfidy**. Reader, do you know what "perfidy" means? I have a feeling you do, based on the little **scene** that has just **unfold**ed here. But you should look up the word in your dictionary, just to be sure.

★ aye (= yes) 예, 그렇소. 의회 등에서 찬성 투표를 할때 하는 말.
✻ nay (= no) 아니, 아니요.

38

Chapter Nine
the right question

THE MOUSE COUNCIL sent Furlough to collect Despereaux. And Furlough found his brother in the library, standing on top of the great, open book, his tail wrapped tightly around his feet, his small body shivering.

Despereaux was reading the story out loud to himself. He was reading from the beginning so that he could get to the end, where the reader was assured that the knight and the fair maiden lived together happily ever after.

Despereaux wanted to read those words: *Happily ever after.* He needed to say them aloud; he needed some assurance that this feeling he had for the Princess Pea, this love, would come to a good end. And so he was reading the story as if it were a **spell** and as if the words of it, spoken aloud, could make magic happen.

"See here," said Furlough out loud to himself. He looked at his brother and then looked away. "This is just the kind of thing I'm talking about. This is exactly the kind of thing. What's he doing here, **for cripes' sake**? He's not eating the paper. He's *talking* to the paper. It's wrong, wrong, wrong."

"Hey," he said to Despereaux.

Despereaux kept reading.

"Hey!" shouted Furlough. "Despereaux! The Mouse Council wants you."

"**Pardon**?" said Despereaux. He looked up from the book.

"The Mouse Council has called you to sit with them."

"Me?" said Despereaux.

"You."

"I'm busy right now," said Despereaux, and he **bent** his head again to the open book.

Furlough **sighed**. "Geez,*" he said. "Cripes. Nothing **makes sense** to this guy. Nothing. I was right to **turn him in**. He's sick."

★ geez [감탄사] 이런, 이크. 놀랐을 때 내는 소리. 예수님을 뜻하는 'Jesus'에서 나온 말이다.

40

Furlough **crawl**ed up the chair leg and then **hop**ped onto the book. He sat next to Despereaux. He **tap**ped him on the head once, twice.

"Hey," he said. "The Mouse Council isn't asking. They're telling. They're *commanding.* You have to come with me. Right now."

Despereaux turned to Furlough. "Do you know what love is?" he said.

"Huh?"

"Love."

Furlough shook his head. "You're asking the wrong question," he said. "The question you should be asking is why the Mouse Council wants to see you."

"There is somebody who loves me," said Despereaux. "And I love her and that is the only thing that **matter**s to me."

"Somebody who loves you? Somebody who you love? What difference does that make? What matters is that you're in a lot of trouble with the Mouse Council."

"Her name," said Despereaux, "is Pea."

"What?"

"The person who loves me. Her name is Pea."

"Cripes," said Furlough, "you're missing the whole point of everything here. You're missing the point of being a mouse. You're missing the point of being called to sit with the Mouse Council. You've got to come with me. It's the law. You've been called."

Despereaux sighed. He reached out and touched the words *fair maiden* in the book. He traced them with one paw. And then he put his paw to his mouth.

"Cripes," said Furlough. "You're making a fool of yourself. Let's go."

"I honor you," whispered Despereaux. "I honor you."

And then, reader, he followed Furlough over the book and down the chair leg and across the library floor to the waiting Mouse Council.

He allowed his brother to lead him to his fate.

Chapter Ten
good reasons

THE **ENTIRE** MOUSE **COMMUNITY,** as **instruct**ed by the Most Very **Honor**ed Head Mouse, had gathered behind the wall of the castle **ballroom.** The members of the Mouse **Council** sat **atop** three **bricks piled** high, and **spread** out before them was every mouse, old and young, foolish and wise, who lived in the castle.

They were all waiting for Despereaux.

"Make way," said Furlough. "Here he is. I've got him. Make way."

Furlough pushed through the crowd of mice. Despereaux **clung** to his brother's tail.

"There he is," the mice **whisper**ed. "There he is."

"He's so small."

"They say he was born with his eyes open."

Some of the mice **pulled away** from Despereaux in **disgust**, and others, **thrill seeker**s, reached out to touch him with a whisker or a **paw**.

"The princess put a finger on him."

"They say he sat at the foot of the king."

"It is simply not done!" came the **distinctive** voice of Despereaux's aunt Florence.

"Make way, make way!" shouted Furlough. "I have him right here. I have Despereaux Tilling, who has been called to sit with the Mouse Council."

He led Despereaux to the front of the room. "Honored members of the Mouse Council," shouted Furlough, "I have brought you Despereaux Tilling, as you requested, to sit with you." He looked over his shoulder at Despereaux. "**Let go of** me," Furlough said.

Despereaux dropped Furlough's tail. He looked up at the members of the Mouse Council. His father met his **gaze** and then shook his head and looked away. Despereaux turned and faced the sea of mice.

"To the dungeon!" a voice cried out. "Straight to the dungeon with him."

Despereaux's head, which had been full of such **delightful phrase**s as "happily ever after" and "lovely ears" and "I honor you," suddenly cleared.

"Straight to the dungeon!" another voice shouted.

"Enough," said the Most Very Honored Head Mouse.

"This **trial** will be **conduct**ed in an **orderly** fashion. We will act **civilized**." He cleared his **throat**. He said to Despereaux, "Son, turn and look at me."

Despereaux turned. He looked up and into the Head Mouse's eyes. They were dark eyes, deep and sad and **frighten**ed. And looking into them, Despereaux's heart **thud**ded once, twice.

"Despereaux Tilling," said the Head Mouse.

"Yes, sir," said Despereaux.

"We, the fourteen members of the Mouse Council, have discussed your behavior. First, we will give you a chance to **defend** yourself against these **rumor**s of your **egregious** acts. Did you or did you not sit at the foot of the human king?"

"I did," said Despereaux, "but I was listening to the music, sir. I was there to hear the song that the king was singing."

"To hear the what?"

"The song, sir. He was singing a song about the deep purple falling over sleepy garden walls."

The Head Mouse shook his head. "Whatever you are talking about is beside the point. The question is this and only this: Did you sit at the foot of the human king?"

"I did, sir."

The community of mice shifted their tails and paws and whiskers. They waited.

"And did you allow the girl human, the princess, to touch you?"

"Her name is Pea."

"Never mind her name. Did you allow her to touch you?"

"Yes, sir," said Despereaux. "I let her touch me. It felt good."

A gasp arose from the assembled mice.

Despereaux heard his mother's voice. "*Mon Dieu*, it is not the end of the world. It was a touch, what of it?"

"It is simply not done!" came Aunt Florence's voice from the crowd.

"To the dungeon," said a mouse in the front row.

"Silence!" roared the Most Very Honored Head Mouse. "Silence." He looked down at Despereaux.

"Do you, Despereaux Tilling, understand the sacred, never-to-be-broken rules of conduct for being a mouse?"

"Yes, sir," said Despereaux, "I guess so. But . . ."

"Did you break them?"

"Yes, sir," said Despereaux. He raised his voice. "But . . . I broke the rules for good reasons. Because of music. And because of love."

"Love!" said the Head Mouse.

"Oh, cripes," said Furlough, "here we go."

"I love her, sir," said Despereaux.

"We are not here to talk about love. This trial is not about love. This trial is about you being a mouse," shouted the Most Very Honored Head Mouse from high atop the bricks, "and not *acting like one!!!*"

"Yes, sir," said Despereaux. "I know."

"No, I don't think that you do know. And because you do not **deny** the **charge**s, you must be **punish**ed. You are to be sent, as **ancient** castle-mouse law **decree**s, to the dungeon. You are being sent to the rats."

"That's right!" called out a mouse in the crowd. "That's the ticket."

The dungeon! The rats! Despereaux's small heart **sank** all the way to the **tip** of his tail. There would be no light in the dungeon. No **stain**ed-glass windows. No library and no books. There would be no Princess Pea.

"But first," said the Most Very Honored Head Mouse, "we will give you the chance to **renounce** your actions. We will allow you to go to the dungeon with a pure heart."

"Renounce?"

"**Repent**. Say that you are sorry you sat at the foot of the human king. Say that you are sorry you allowed the human princess to touch you. Say that you regret these actions."

Despereaux felt hot and then cold and then hot again. Renounce her? Renounce the princess?

"*Mon Dieu!*" shouted his mother. "Son, do not act the fool. Renounce! Repent!"

"What say you, Despereaux Tilling?"

"I say . . . I say . . . I say . . . *no,*" whispered Despereaux.

"What?" said the Head Mouse.

"No," said Despereaux. And this time, he did not whisper the word. "I am not sorry. I will not renounce my actions. I love her. I love the princess."

There was a **bellow** of **collective outrage**. The whole of the mouse community **surge**d toward Despereaux. The mice seemed to become one angry body with hundreds of tails and thousands of whiskers and one huge, hungry mouth opening and closing and opening and closing, saying over and over and over again, "To the dungeon. To the dungeon. To the dungeon."

The words **pound**ed through Despereaux's body with each beat of his heart.

"Very well," said the Most Very Honored Head Mouse. "You will die, then, with a black heart. **Threadmaster**," he called, "bring out the thread."

48

Despereaux **marvel**ed at his own **bravery.**

He **admired** his own **defiance.**

And then, reader, he **fainted.**

Chapter Eleven
the threadmaster cometh★

WHEN DESPEREAUX CAME TO, he heard the drum. His father was beating a **rhythm** that had much more *boom* and much less *tat*. Together, Lester and the drum produced an **ominous** sound that went something like this: *Boom-boom-boom-tat. Boom-boom-boom-tat.*

"Make way for the thread!" cried a mouse who was pushing a wooden **spool** of red thread through the crowd. "Make way for the thread!"

Boom-boom-boom-tat, went the drum.

"To the **dungeon!**" shouted the mice.

Despereaux lay on his back, **blink**ing his eyes. How,

★ cometh 'comes'의 고어.

50

he **wonder**ed, had things gone so terribly wrong? Wasn't it a good thing, to love? In the story in the book, love was a very good thing. Because the **knight** loved the fair **maiden**, he was able to **rescue** her. They lived happily ever after. It said so. In the book. They were the last words on the page. *Happily ever after.* Despereaux was certain that he had read exactly those words time and time again.

Lying on the floor with the drum beating and the mice shouting and the thread**master** calling out, "Make way, make way," Despereaux had a sudden, **chilling** thought: Had some other mouse eaten the words that spoke the truth? Did the knight and the fair maiden actually *not* live happily ever after?

Reader, do you believe that there is such a thing as happily ever after? Or, like Despereaux, have you, too, begun to question the **possibility** of happy endings?

"Happily ever after," whispered Despereaux. "Happily ever after," he said again as the spool of thread came to a stop beside him.

"The thread, the thread, the thread," **murmur**ed the mice.

"I'm sorry," said the mouse behind the spool, "but I have to ask you to stand up. I have to do my job."

Despereaux **got** slowly **to his feet.**

"On your **hind** legs, please," said the threadmaster.

"It's the rules."

Despereaux stood on his hind legs.

"Thank you," said the mouse. "I appreciate it."

While Despereaux watched, the threadmaster unwound a length of red thread from the spool and tied a loop.

"Just enough for the neck," muttered the mouse. "No more, no less. That's what the last threadmaster taught me: enough thread for the neck." He looked up at Despereaux and then back down at the loop of thread. "And you, my friend, have a small neck."

The threadmaster raised his arms and put them around Despereaux's neck. He leaned in close and Despereaux smelled celery. He could feel the threadmaster's breath in his ear as he worked at tightening the thread.

"Is she beautiful?" the threadmaster whispered.

"What?" said Despereaux.

"Shhhh. Is the princess beautiful?"

"The Princess Pea?"

"Yes."

"She is lovely beyond all imagining," said Despereaux.

"Just right," the threadmaster said. He drew back. He nodded his head. "A lovely princess, just so, like a fairy tale. And you love her, as a knight loves a maiden.

"Just enough for the neck," muttered the mouse.
"No more, no less."

You love her with a **courtly** love, a love that is based on **bravery** and **courtesy** and honor and **devotion**. Just so."

"How do you know that?" Despereaux said. "How do you know about fairy tales?"

"Shhhhh." The mouse leaned in close, and Despereaux smelled celery again, green and alive. "Be brave, friend," whispered the threadmaster. "Be brave for the princess." And then he stepped back and turned and shouted, "**Fellow** mice, the thread has been tied. The thread has been **knotted**."

A **roar** of **approval** went up from the crowd.

Despereaux **square**d his shoulders. He had made a decision. He would do as the threadmaster had suggested. He would be brave for the princess.

Even if (reader, could it be true?) there was no such thing as happily ever after.

Chapter Twelve
adieu

THE SOUND OF THE DRUM changed again. The final *tat* disappeared and it became nothing but *boom*.

Boom, boom, boom.

Boom, boom, boom.

Lester used only his tail, bringing it down with great force and seriousness upon the drum.

The threadmaster **retrea**ted.

The room full of mice fell silent, **expectant**, waiting.

And as Despereaux stood before them with the red thread around his neck and the fourteen members of the Mouse **Council perch**ed on the **bricks** above him, two **burly** mice came forward. Black pieces of cloth covered their heads. There were **slits** for their eyes.

"We," said the bigger of the two mice, "will **escort** you to the dungeon."

"Despereaux," Antoinette called out. "Ah, my Despereaux!"

Despereaux looked out into the crowd of mice and saw his mother. She was easy to **spot. In honor of** her youngest mouse being sent to the dungeon, she had put on a **tremendous** amount of **makeup**.

Each of the **hood**ed mice put a paw on Despereaux's shoulder.

"It's time," said the one on the left, the first hood.

Antoinette pushed her way through the crowd. "He is my son," she said. "I want to have a last word with my son."

Despereaux looked at his mother. He **concentrated** on standing before her without **trembling**. He concentrated on not being a disappointment.

"Please," said Antoinette, "what will happen to him? What will happen to my baby?"

"Ma'am," said the first hood. His voice was deep and slow. "You don't want to know."

"I want to know. I want to know. He is my child. The child of my heart. The last of my mice babies."

The hooded mice said nothing.

"Tell me," said Antoinette.

56

"The rats," said the first.

"The rats," said the second.

"Yes. Yes. *Oui.*★ The rats. What of them?"

"The rats will eat him," said the second hood.

"Ah," said Antoinette. "*Mon Dieu!*"

At the thought of being eaten by rats, Despereaux forgot about being brave. He forgot about not being a disappointment. He felt himself heading into another faint. But his mother, who had an excellent sense of **dramatic timing, beat** him **to it**; she **executed** a beautiful, **flawless swoon**, landing right at Despereaux's feet.

"Now you've done it," said the first hood.

"It doesn't **matter,**" said the second. "Step over her. We have a job to do. Nobody's mother is going to stop us. To the dungeon."

"To the dungeon," repeated the first hood, but his voice, so deep and certain a moment ago, now shook a tiny bit. He put a paw on Despereaux and **tugged** him forward, and the two hoods and Despereaux stepped over Antoinette.

The crowd **parted.**

The mice began again to **chant**: "To the dungeon. To the dungeon. To the dungeon."

★ oui 'yes'의 프랑스어.

The drumbeat continued.

Boom, boom, boom. Boom, boom, boom.

And Despereaux was led away.

At the last moment, Antoinette came out of her faint and shouted one word to her child.

That word, reader, was *adieu*.★

Do you know the **definition** of *adieu?* Don't **bother** with your dictionary. I will tell you.

Adieu is the French word for **farewell**.

"Farewell" is not the word that you would like to hear from your mother as you are being led to the dungeon by two **oversize** mice in black hoods.

Words that you *would* like to hear are "Take me instead. I will go to the dungeon in my son's place." There is **a great deal of comfort** in those words.

But, reader, there is no comfort in the word "farewell," even if you say it in French. "Farewell" is a word that, in any language, is full of **sorrow**. It is a word that promises **absolute**ly nothing.

★ adieu [프랑스어] 안녕, 잘 가요, 잘 있어요.

Chapter Thirteen
perfidy unlimited

TOGETHER, THE THREE MICE traveled down, down, down.

The **thread** around Despereaux's neck was tight. He felt as if it was **choking** him. He **tugg**ed at it with one paw.

"Don't touch the thread," **bark**ed the second **hood**.

"Yeah," **echo**ed the first hood, "don't touch the thread."

They moved quickly. And whenever Despereaux slowed, one of the two hoods **poke**d him in the shoulder and told him to keep moving. They went through holes in the wall and down golden stairs. They went past rooms with doors that were closed and doors that were flung wide. The three mice traveled across **marble** floors and under heavy velvet **drapes**. They moved through warm **patches** of sunlight and dark **pools** of **shade**.

This, thought Despereaux, was the world he was leaving behind, the world that he knew and loved. And somewhere in it, the Princess Pea was laughing and smiling and **clapping** her hands to music, **unaware** of Despereaux's **fate**. That he would not be able to let the princess know what had become of him seemed suddenly **unbearable** to the mouse.

"Would it be possible for me to have a last word with the princess?" Despereaux asked.

"A word?" said the second hood. "You want a word with a human?"

"I want to tell her what has happened to me."

"Geez," said the first hood. He stopped and **stamped** a paw on the floor in **frustration**. "Cripes. You can't learn, can you."

The voice was terribly familiar to Despereaux.

"Furlough?" he said.

"What?" said the first hood **irritably**.

Despereaux **shuddered**. His own brother was delivering him to the dungeon. His heart stopped beating and **shrunk** to a small, cold, disbelieving **pebble**. But then, just as quickly, it **leapt** alive again, beating with hope.

"Furlough," Despereaux said, and he took one of his brother's paws in his own. "Please, let me go. Please. I'm your brother."

Furlough rolled his eyes. He took his paw out of Despereaux's. "No," he said. "No way."

"Please," said Despereaux.

"No," said Furlough. "Rules are rules."

Reader, do you **recall** the word "**perfidy**"? As our story **progress**es, "perfidy" becomes an ever more **appropriate** word, doesn't it?

"Perfidy" was certainly the word that was in Despereaux's mind as the mice finally approached the **narrow, steep** stairs that led to the black hole of the dungeon.

They stood, the three mice, two with hoods and one without, and **contemplate**d the **abyss** before them.

And then Furlough stood up on his **hind** legs and placed his right paw over his heart. "For the good of the castle mice," he **announce**d to the darkness, "we deliver this day to the dungeon, a mouse in need of **punish**ment. He is, **according to** the laws we have **establish**ed, wearing the red thread of death."

"The red thread of death?" repeated Despereaux in a small voice. "Wearing the red thread of death" was a terrible **phrase**, but the mouse didn't have long to **consider** its **implications**, because he was suddenly pushed from

Despereaux shuddered. His own brother was
delivering him to the dungeon.

behind by the hooded mice.

The push was a strong one, and it sent Despereaux flying down the stairs into the dungeon. As he **tumbled**, **whisker** over tail, through the darkness, there were only two words in his mind. One was "perfidy." And the other word that he **clung** to was "Pea."

Perfidy. Pea. Perfidy. Pea. These were the words that **pinwheel**ed through Despereaux's mind as his body **descend**ed into the darkness.

Chapter Fourteen
darkness

DESPEREAUX LAY ON HIS BACK at the bottom of the steps and touched the bones in his body one by one. They were all there. And, amazingly, they were unbroken. He **got to his feet** and became **aware** of a terrible, **foul, extremely insult**ing smell.

The **dungeon**, reader, **stank**. It stank of **despair** and suffering and hopelessness. Which is to say that the dungeon smelled of rats.

And it was so dark. Despereaux had never before **encounter**ed darkness so **awful**, so all-**encompass**ing. The darkness had a **physical** presence as if it were a being all its own. The mouse held one small **paw** up in front of his whiskers. He could not see it, and he had the truly alarming thought that perhaps he, Despereaux Tilling, did not even exist.

"Oh my!" he said out loud.

His voice echoed in the smelly darkness.

"Perfidy," said Despereaux, just to hear his voice again, just to assure himself that he did exist.

"Pea," said Despereaux, and the name of his beloved was immediately swallowed up by the darkness.

He shivered. He shook. He sneezed. His teeth chattered. He longed for his handkerchief. He grabbed hold of his tail (it took him a long, frightening moment to even locate his tail, so absolute was the darkness) to have something, anything, to hold onto. He considered fainting. He deemed it the only reasonable response to the situation in which he found himself, but then he remembered the words of the threadmaster: honor, courtesy, devotion, and bravery.

"I will be brave," thought Despereaux. "I will try to be brave like a knight in shining armor. I will be brave for the Princess Pea."

How best for him to be brave?

He cleared his throat. He let go of his tail. He stood up straighter. "Once upon a time," he said out loud to the darkness. He said these words because they were the best, the most powerful words that he knew and just the saying of them **comfort**ed him.

"Once upon a time," he said again, feeling a tiny bit braver. "There was a knight and he wore, always, an armor of shining silver."

"Once upon a time?" **boom**ed a voice from the darkness. "A knight in shining armor? What does a mouse know of such things?"

That voice, the loudest voice that Despereaux had ever heard, could only, he **assume**d, belong to the world's largest rat.

Despereaux's small, **overwork**ed heart stopped beating.

And for the second time that day, the mouse fainted.

Chapter Fifteen
light

WHEN DESPEREAUX AWOKE, he was cupped in the large, calloused hand of a human and he was staring into the fire of one match, and beyond the match there was a large, dark eye looking directly at him.

"A mouse with red thread," boomed the voice. "Oh, yes, Gregory knows the way of mice and rats. Gregory knows. And Gregory has his own thread, marking him. See here, mouse." And the match was held to a candle and the candle sputtered to life and Despereaux saw that there was a rope tied around the man's ankle. "Here is the difference between us: Gregory's rope saves him. And your thread will be the death of you." The man blew the candle out and the darkness descended and the man's hand closed more tightly around Despereaux and Despereaux felt his **beleaguer**ed heart start up a crazy **rhythm** of fear.

"Who are you?" he **whisper**ed.

"The answer to that question, mouse, is Gregory. You are talking to Gregory the **jailer**, who has been **buried** here, keeping watch over this dungeon for **decades**, for **centuries**, for **eons**. For **eternities**. You are talking to Gregory the jailer, who, in the richest of **ironies**, is nothing but a prisoner here himself."

"Oh," said Despereaux. "Um, may I get down, Gregory?"

"The mouse wants to know if Gregory the jailer will let him go. Listen to Gregory, mouse. You do not *want* to be let go. Here, in this dungeon, you are in the **treacherous** dark heart of the world. And if Gregory were to **release** you, the **twist**ings and turnings and dead ends and **false doorway**s of this place would **swallow** you for all eternity.

"Only Gregory and the rats can find their way through this **maze**. The rats because they know, because the way of it mirrors their own dark hearts. And Gregory because the rope is forever tied to his ankle to guide him back to the beginning. Gregory would let you go, but you would only **beg** him to take you up again. The rats are coming for you, you see."

"They are?"

"Listen," said Gregory. "You can hear their tails dragging through the muck and filth. You can hear them filing their nails and teeth. They are coming for you. They are coming to take you apart piece by piece."

Despereaux listened and he was quite certain that he heard the nails and teeth of the rats, the sound of sharp things being made sharper still.

"They will strip all the fur from your flesh and all the flesh from your bones. When they are done with you, there will be nothing left except red thread. Red thread and bones. Gregory has seen it many times, the tragic end of a mouse."

"But I need to live," said Despereaux. "I can't die."

"You cannot die. Ah, that is lovely. He says he cannot die!" Gregory closed his hand more tightly around Despereaux. "And why would that be, mouse? Why is it that you cannot die?"

"Because I'm in love. I love somebody and it is my duty to serve her."

"Love," said Gregory. "Love. Hark you, I will show you the twisted results of love." Another match was struck; the candle was lit again, and Gregory held it up so that its flame illuminated a massive, towering, teetering **pile** of spoons and **kettles** and soup bowls.

"Look on that, mouse," said Gregory. "That is a **monument** to the foolishness of love."

"What is it?" asked Despereaux. He stared at the great tower that reached up, up, up into the blackness.

"What it looks like. Spoons. Bowls. Kettles. All of them gathered here as hard **evidence** of the pain of loving a living thing. The king loved the queen and the queen died; this **monstrosity**, this **junk heap** is the result of love."

"I don't understand," said Despereaux.

"And you will not understand until you lose what you love. But enough about love," said Gregory. He blew out the candle. "We will talk instead about your life. And how Gregory will save it, if you so desire."

"Why would you save me?" Despereaux asked. "Have you saved any of the other mice?"

"Never," said Gregory, "not one."

"Why would you save me, then?"

"Because you, mouse, can tell Gregory a story. Stories are light. Light is **precious** in a world so dark. Begin at the beginning. Tell Gregory a story. Make some light."

And because Despereaux wanted very much to live, he said, "Once upon a time . . ."

"Yes," said Gregory happily. He raised his hand

"Go on, mouse," said Gregory. "Tell Gregory a story."

higher and then higher still until Despereaux's whiskers brushed against his **leathery, timeworn** ear. "Go on, mouse," said Gregory. "Tell Gregory a story."

And it was in this way that Despereaux became the only mouse sent to the dungeon whom the rats did not **reduce** to a pile of bones and a piece of red thread.

It was in this way that Despereaux was saved.

Reader, if you don't mind, that is where we will leave our small mouse for now: in the dark of the dungeon, in the hand of an old jailer, telling a story to save himself.

It is time for us to turn our attention elsewhere, time for us, reader, to speak of rats, and of one rat in **particular.**

End of the First Book

Book
THE SECOND

Chiaroscuro

Chapter Sixteen
blinded by the light

AS OUR STORY CONTINUES, reader, we must go backward in time to the birth of a rat, a rat named Chiaroscuro and called Roscuro, a rat born into the **filth** and darkness of the dungeon, several years before the mouse Despereaux was born upstairs, in the light.

Reader, do you know the **definition** of the word "chiaroscuro"★? If you look in your dictionary, you will find that it means the **arrange**ment of light and dark, darkness and light together. Rats do not care for light. Roscuro's parents were having a bit of fun when they named their son. Rats have a sense of **humor**. Rats, in

---

★ chiaroscuro 명암법. 밝기와 어둠을 표현하는 화법.

fact, think that life is very funny. And they are right, reader. They are right.

In the case of Chiaroscuro, however, the joke had a hint of **prophecy** to it, for it happened that when Roscuro was a very young rat, he **came upon** a great **length** of rope on the dungeon floor.

"Ah, what have we here?" said Roscuro.

Being a rat, he immediately began to **nibble** at the rope.

"Stop that," **boom**ed a voice, and a great hand came out of the darkness and picked the rat up by his tail and held him **suspended upside down.**

"Were you nibbling on Gregory's rope, rat?"

"Who wants to know?" said Roscuro, for even upside down he was still a rat.

"You **smart-alecky** rat, you smart-alecky rat nib-nib-nibbling on Gregory's rope. Gregory will teach you to **mess** with his rope."

And keeping Roscuro upside down, Gregory lit a **match** with the nail of his **thumb**, *ssssstttttt*, and then held the **brilliant flame** right in Roscuro's face.

"Ahhh," said Roscuro. He pulled his head back, away from the light. But, **alas**, he did not close his eyes, and the flame **explod**ed around him and danced inside him.

"Has no one told you the rules?" said Gregory.

"What rules?"

"Gregory's rope, rat, is off-limits."

"So?"

"Apologize for chewing on Gregory's rope."

"I will not," said Roscuro.

"Apologize."

"No."

"Filthy rat," said Gregory. "You black-souled thing. Gregory has had it with you rats." He held the match closer to Roscuro's face, and a terrible smell of burnt whiskers rose up around the jailer and the rat. And then the match went out and Gregory released Roscuro's tail. He flung him back into the darkness.

"Do not ever touch Gregory's rope again, or you will be sorry."

Roscuro sat on the dungeon floor. The whiskers on the left side of his face were gone. His heart was beating hard, and though the light from the match had disappeared, it danced, still, before the rat's eyes, even when he closed them.

"Light," he said aloud. And then he whispered the word again. "Light."

From that moment forward, Roscuro showed an abnormal, inordinate interest in illumination of all sorts. He was always, in the darkness of the dungeon, on the lookout for light, the smallest **glimmer**, the tiniest **shimmer**. His rat soul **long**ed **inexplicably** for it; he began to think that light was the only thing that gave life meaning, and he **despair**ed that there was so little of it to be had.

He finally voiced this **sentiment** to his friend, a very old one-eared rat named Botticelli Remorso.

"I think," said Roscuro, "that the meaning of life is light."

"Light," said Botticelli. "Ha-ha-ha—you kill me. Light **has nothing to do with** it."

"What does it all mean, then?" asked Roscuro.

"The meaning of life," said Botticelli, "is suffering, **specifically** the suffering of others. Prisoners, for instance. **Reducing** a prisoner to **weeping** and **wailing** and **begg**ing is a **delightful** way to **invest** your existence with meaning."

As he spoke, Botticelli **swung**, from the one **extraordinarily** long nail of his right front paw, a heart-shaped **locket**. He had taken the locket from a prisoner and hung it on a thin **braid**ed rope. Whenever Botticelli spoke, the locket moved. Back and forth, back and forth it swung. "Are you listening?" Botticelli said to Roscuro.

"I am listening."

"Good," said Botticelli. "Do as I say and your life will be full of meaning. This is how to **torture** a prisoner: first, you must **convince** him that you are a friend. Listen to him. **Encourage** him to **confess** his **sins**. And when the time is right, talk to him. Tell him what he wants to hear. Tell him, for instance, that you will forgive him. This is a wonderful joke to play upon a prisoner, to promise forgiveness."

"Why?" said Roscuro. His eyes went back and forth, back and forth, following the locket.

"Because," said Botticelli, "you will promise it— ha—but you will not **grant** it. You gain his trust. And then you **deny** him. You refuse to offer the very thing he wants. Forgiveness, freedom, friendship, whatever it is that his heart most desires, you **withhold**." At this point in his **lecture**, Botticelli laughed so hard that he had to sit down and catch his **breath**. The locket **swayed** slowly back and forth and then stopped altogether.

"Ha," said Botticelli, "ha-ha-ha! You gain his trust, you refuse him and—ha-ha—you become what he knew you were all along, what *you* knew you were all along, not a friend, not a confessor, not a forgiver, but—ha-ha!— a *rat*!" Botticelli **wiped** his eyes and shook his head and **sigh**ed a sigh of great **content**ment. He set the locket in **motion** again. "At that point, it is most effective to run back and forth over the prisoner's feet, **inducing physical terror** along with the emotional sort. Oh," he said, "it is such a lovely game, such a lovely game! And it is just absolutely **chock-full** of meaning."

"I would like very much to torture a prisoner," said Roscuro. "I would like to make someone suffer."

"Your time will come," said Botticelli. "**Current**ly, all the prisoners are spoken for. But another prisoner will arrive **sooner or later**. How do I know this to be true? Because, Roscuro, thankfully there is evil in the world. And the presence of evil **guarantee**s the existence of prisoners."

"So, soon, there will be a prisoner for me?"

"Yes," said Botticelli Remorso. "Yes."

"I'm **looking forward to** it."

"Ha-ha-ha! Of course you are looking forward to it. You are looking forward to it because you are a rat, a real rat."

"Yes," said Roscuro. "I am a real rat."

"**Concern**ed not at all with the light," said Botticelli.

"Concerned not at all with the light," repeated Roscuro.

Botticelli laughed again and shook his head. The locket, suspended from the long nail on his paw, swung back and forth, back and forth.

"You, my young friend, are a rat. Exactly. Yes. Evil. Prisoners. Rats. Suffering. It all **fits** together so **neat**ly, so sweetly. Oh, it is a lovely world, a lovely, dark world."

Chapter Seventeen
small comforts

NOT LONG AFTER this conversation between Botticelli and Roscuro, a prisoner did arrive. The **dungeon** door slammed and the two rats watched a man being led by a king's soldier down the stairs into the dungeon.

"Excellent," whispered Botticelli. "This one is yours."

Roscuro looked at the man closely. "I will make him suffer," he said.

But as he stared up at the man, the door to the dungeon was suddenly flung open and a thick and brilliant **shaft** of afternoon light cut into the dark of the dungeon.

"Ugh," said Botticelli. He covered his eyes with one

paw.

Roscuro, however, stared directly into the light.

Reader, this is important: The rat called Chiaroscuro did not look away. He let the light from the upstairs world enter him and fill him. He **gasp**ed aloud with the **wonder** of it.

"Give him his small **comfort**s," shouted a voice at the top of the stairs, and a red cloth was thrown into the light. The cloth hung **suspend**ed for a moment, bright red and **glow**ing, and then the door was slammed shut again and the light disappeared and the cloth fell to the floor. It was Gregory the jailer who **bent** to pick it up.

"Go on," said the old man as he held out the cloth to the prisoner, "take it. You'll need every last bit of warmth down here."

And so the prisoner took the cloth and **draped** it around his shoulders as if it were a **cloak**, and the soldier of the king said, "Right then, Gregory, he's all yours." And the soldier turned and went back up the steps and opened the door to the outside world and some small light **leak**ed in before he closed the door behind him.

"Did you see that?" Roscuro said to Botticelli.

"**Hideous**ly ugly," said Botticelli. "**Ridiculous.** What can they possibly mean by letting all that light in at once. Don't they know that this is a dungeon?"

82

Roscuro, however, stared directly into the light.

"It was beautiful," said Roscuro.

"No," said Botticelli. "No." He looked at Roscuro intently. "Not beautiful. No."

"I must see more light. I must see all of it," said Roscuro. "I must go upstairs."

Botticelli sighed. "Who cares about the light? Your obsession with it is tiresome. Listen. We are rats. Rats. We do not like light. We are about darkness. We are about suffering."

"But," said Roscuro, "upstairs."

"No 'buts,'" said Botticelli. "No 'buts.' None. Rats do not go upstairs. Upstairs is the domain of mice." He took the locket from around his neck.

"What," he said, swinging it back and forth, "is this rope made of?"

"Whiskers."

"The whiskers of whom?"

"Mice."

"Exactly. And who lives upstairs?"

"Mice."

"Exactly. Mice." Botticelli turned his head and spat on the floor. "Mice are nothing but little packages of blood and bones, afraid of everything. They are despicable, laughable, the opposite of everything we strive to be. Do you want to live in their world?"

Roscuro looked up, past Botticelli to the delicious sliver of light that shone out from underneath the door. He said nothing.

"Listen," said Botticelli, "this is what you should do: Go and torture the prisoner. Go and take the red cloth from him. The cloth will satisfy your craving for something from that world. But do not go up into the light. You will regret it." As he spoke, the locket swung back and forth, back and forth. "You do not belong in that world. You are a rat. A rat. Say it with me."

"A rat," said Roscuro.

"Ah, but you are cheating. You must say, '*I am* a rat,'" said Botticelli, smiling his slow smile at Roscuro.

"I am a rat," said Roscuro.

"Again," said Botticelli, swinging his locket.

"I am a rat."

"Exactly," said Botticelli. "A rat is a rat is a rat. End of story. World without end. Amen."

"Yes," said Roscuro. "Amen, I am a rat." He closed his eyes. He saw, again, the red cloth spinning against the backdrop of gold.

And he told himself, reader, that it was the cloth that he desired and not the light.

Chapter Eighteen
confessions

ROSCURO WENT, as Botticelli told him he must, to **torment** the new prisoner and to take the red cloth from him.

The man was sitting with his legs **stretch**ed out straight in front of him, **chain**ed to the floor. The red cloth was still **draped** over his shoulders.

Roscuro **squeezed** through the bars and **crept** slowly over the **damp, weeping** stones of the **cell** floor.

When he was close to the man, he said, "Ah, welcome, welcome. We are **delighted** to have you."

The man lit a **match** and looked at Roscuro.

Roscuro **stared longingly** into the light.

"Go on," said the prisoner. He waved a hand in the

direction of Roscuro and the match went out. "Yer★ nothing but a rat."

"I am," said Roscuro, "exactly that. A rat. Allow me to **congratulate** you on your very **astute** powers of **observation**."

"What do ye✳ want, rat?"

"What do I want? Nothing. Nothing **for my sake**, that is. I have come for you. I have come to keep you **company** here in the dark." He **crawl**ed closer to the man.

"I don't need the company of a rat."

"What about the **solace** a **sympathetic** ear can provide? Do you need that?"

"Huh?"

"Would you like to **confess** your **sins**?"

"To a rat? You're **kid**ding, you are."

"Come now," said Roscuro. "Close your eyes. **Pretend** that I am not a rat. Pretend that I am nothing but a voice in the darkness. A voice that cares."

The prisoner closed his eyes. "All right," he said. "I'll tell you. But I'm telling you because there ain't✳ no point in *not* telling you, no point in keeping secrets from a

---

★ yer 'you are'의 구어체.

✳ ye 'you'의 구어체.

✳ ain't am[are, is] not의 구어체, 단축형.

dirty little rat. I ain't in such a **desperate** way that I need to lie to a rat."

The man cleared his **throat**. "I'm here for **steal**ing six cows, two Jerseys★ and four Guernseys.✳ Cow **theft**, that's my **crime**." He opened his eyes and stared into the darkness. He laughed. He closed his eyes again. "But there's something else I done, many years ago, another crime, and they don't even know of it."

"Go on," said Roscuro softly. He crept closer. He allowed one paw to touch the magical red cloth.

"I **trade**d my girl, my own daughter, for this red **tablecloth** and for a **hen** and for a **handful** of **cigarette**s."

"Tsk,✲" said Roscuro. He was not **alarm**ed to hear of such a **hideous** thing. His parents, after all, had not much cared for him, and certainly, if there had been any **profit** in it, they would have sold him. And then, too, Botticelli Remorso, one lazy Sunday afternoon, had **recite**d from memory all the **confession**s he had heard from prisoners. What humans were capable of came as no surprise to Roscuro.

"And then . . . ," said the man.

"And then," **encourage**d Roscuro.

★ Jersey 영국 Jersey섬 원산의 젖소로, 고품질 우유를 생산한다.
✳ Guernsey 영국 Guernsey섬 원산의 젖소로, 우유 생산량이 아주 많다.
✲ tsk 쯧쯧. 혀를 차는 소리.

"And then I done the worst thing of all: I walked away from her and she was crying and calling out for me and I did not even look back. I did not. Oh, Lord,★ I kept walking." The prisoner cleared his throat. He **sniffed.**

"Ah," said Roscuro. "Yes. I see." By now he was standing so that all four of his paws were touching the red cloth.

"Do you find comfort in this cloth that you sold your child for?"

"It's warm," said the man.

"Was it **worth** your child?"

"I like the color of it."

"Does the cloth **remind** you of what you have done wrong?"

"It does," the prisoner said. He sniffed. "It does."

"Allow me to **ease** your **burden,**" said Roscuro. He stood on his **hind** legs and **bow**ed at the waist. "I will take this **reminder** of your sin from you," he said. The rat took hold of the tablecloth in his strong teeth and pulled it off the shoulders of the man.

"Hey, see here. I want that back."

But Roscuro, reader, was quick. He pulled the tablecloth through the bars of the cell, *whoosh,*✶ like a

---

★ Oh, Lord [감탄사] 어이쿠, 이런.
✶ whoosh 휙, 쉭. 빠르게 움직이는 소리.

magic trick in **reverse**.

"Hey!" shouted the prisoner. "Bring that back. It's all I got."

"Yes," said Roscuro, "and that is exactly why I must have it."

"You dirty rat!" shouted the prisoner.

"Yes," said Roscuro. "That is right. That is most **accurate**."

And he left the man and **dragg**ed the tablecloth back to his nest and **consider**ed it.

What a disappointment it was! Looking at it, Roscuro knew that Botticelli was wrong. What Roscuro wanted, what he needed, was not the cloth, but the light that had shone behind it.

He wanted to be filled, **flood**ed, **blind**ed again with light.

And for that, reader, the rat knew that he must go upstairs.

Chapter Nineteen
light, light everywhere

IMAGINE, IF YOU WILL, having spent the whole of your life in a dungeon. Imagine that late one spring day you step out of the dark and into a world of bright windows and **polished** floors, **winking copper** pots, shining suits of **armor** and **tapestries sewn** in gold.

Imagine. And while you are imagining things, imagine this, too. Imagine that at the same time as the rat steps from the dungeon and into the castle, a mouse is being born upstairs, a mouse, reader, who is **destined** to meet the light-**bedazzled** rat.

But that meeting will **occur** much later, and for now, the rat is nothing but happy, **delighted**, amazed to find himself standing in so much light.

"I," said Roscuro, **spin**ning **dizzily** from one bright thing to the next, "will never leave. No, never. I will never go back to the dungeon. Why would I? I will never **torture** another prisoner. It is here that I belong."

The rat **waltz**ed happily from room to room until he found himself at the door to the **banquet** hall. He looked inside and saw gathered there King Phillip, Queen Rosemary, the Princess Pea, twenty **noble** people, a **juggle**r, four **minstrel**s and all the king's men. This party, reader, was a sight for a rat's eyes. Roscuro had never seen happy people. He had known only the **miserable** ones. Gregory the **jailer** and those who were **consign**ed to his **domain** did not laugh or smile or **clink** glasses with the person sitting next to them.

Roscuro was **enchant**ed. Everything **glitter**ed. Everything. The gold spoons on the table and the **jingle** bells on the juggler's cap, the **string**s on the minstrels' guitars and the crowns on the king's and the queen's heads.

And the little princess! How lovely she was! How much like light itself. Her **gown** was covered in **sequin**s that winked and **glimmer**ed at the rat. And when she laughed, and she laughed often, everything around her seemed to **glow** brighter.

"Oh, really," said Roscuro, "this is too **extraordinary**. This is too wonderful. I must tell Botticelli that he was wrong. Suffering is not the answer. *Light* is the answer."

And he made his way into the banquet hall. He lifted his tail off the ground and held it at an **angle** and **marched in time** to the music the minstrels were playing on their guitars.

The rat, reader, invited himself to the party.

Chapter Twenty
a view from a chandelier

THERE WAS, in the **banquet** hall, a most beautiful and **ornate chandelier**. The crystals that hung from it caught the light of the candles on the table and the light from the face of the laughing princess. They danced to the **rhythm** of the **minstrels'** music, **swaying** back and forth, **twinkling** and **beckon**ing. What better place to view all this **glory**, all this beauty?

There was so much laughing and singing and **juggling** that no one noticed as Roscuro crawled up a table leg and onto the table, and from there **flung** himself onto the lowest **branch** of the chandelier.

Hanging by one **paw** he **swung** back and forth, **admiring** the **spectacle** below him: the smells of the food, the sound of the music, and the light, the light, the light. Amazing. **Unbelievable.** Roscuro smiled and shook his head.

Unfortunately, a rat can hang from a chandelier for only so long before he is discovered. This would be true at even the loudest party.

Reader, do you know who it was that **spot**ted him?

You're right.

The sharp-eyed Princess Pea.

"A rat!" she shouted. "A rat is hanging from the chandelier!"

The party, as I have **noted,** was loud. The minstrels were **strum**ming and singing. The people were laughing and eating. The man with the **jingle** cap was juggling and jingling.

No one, in the **midst** of all this **merriment,** heard the Pea. No one except for Roscuro.

Rat.

He had never before been **aware** of what an ugly word it was.

Rat.

In the middle of all that beauty it **immediately** became clear that it was an **extremely distasteful syllable.**

Rat.

A **curse,** an **insult,** a word totally without light. And

"A rat!" she shouted.
"A rat is hanging from the chandelier!"

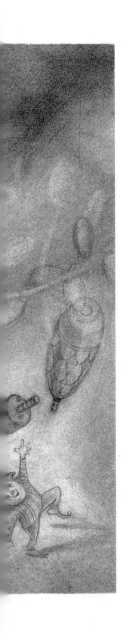

not until he heard it from the mouth of the princess did Roscuro realize that he did not like being a rat, that he did not want to be a rat. This **revelation** hit Roscuro with such force that it made him lose his **grip** on the chandelier.

The rat, reader, fell.

And, alas, he fell, directly into the queen's bowl of soup.

Chapter Twenty-one
the queen's last words

THE QUEEN LOVED SOUP. She loved soup more than anything in the world except for the Princess Pea and the king. And because the queen loved it, soup was **served** in the castle for every banquet, every lunch and every dinner.

And what soup it was! Cook's love and **admiration** for the queen and her **palate** moved the broth* that she **concoct**ed from the level of **mere** food to a high art.

On this **particular** day, for this particular banquet, Cook had **outdo**ne herself. The soup was a **masterwork**, a **delicate mingling** of chicken, watercress* and garlic.

★ broth 걸쭉한 수프.

✳ watercress [식물] 물냉이. 샐러드, 수프 등에 넣는다.

Roscuro, as he surfaced from the bottom of the queen's capacious bowl, could not help taking a few appreciative sips.

"Lovely," he said, distracted for a moment from the misery of his existence. "Delightful."

"See?" shouted the Pea. "See!" She stood. She pointed her finger right at Roscuro. "It is a rat. I told you that it was a rat. He was hanging from the chandelier, and now he is in Mama's soup!"

The musicians stopped playing their guitars. The juggler stopped juggling. The noble people stopped eating.

The queen looked at Roscuro.

Roscuro looked at the queen.

Reader, in the spirit of honesty I must utter a difficult and unsavory truth: Rats are not beautiful creatures. They are not even cute. They are, really, rather nasty beasts, particularly if one happens to appear in your bowl of soup with pieces of watercress clinging to his whiskers.

There was a long moment of silence, and then Roscuro said to the queen, "I beg your pardon."

In response, the queen flung her spoon in the air and made an incredible noise, a noise that was in no way worthy of a queen, a noise somewhere between the neigh of a horse and the squeal of a pig, a noise that sounded something like this: *neiggghhhhiiiinnnnkkkkkk*.

And then she said, "There is a rat in my soup."

The queen was really a simple soul and always, her whole life, had done nothing except state the **overly obvious.**

She died as she lived.

"There is a rat in my soup" were the last words she uttered. She **clutch**ed her chest and fell over backward. Her **royal** chair hit the floor with a **thump,** and the banquet hall **exploded.** Spoons were dropped. Chairs were flung back.

"Save her!" **thunder**ed the king. "You must save her!"

All the king's men ran to try and **rescue** the queen.

Roscuro climbed out of the bowl of soup. He felt that, under the **circumstances,** it would be best if he left. As he **crawl**ed across the **tablecloth** he remembered the words of the prisoner in the **dungeon,** his regret that he did not look back at his daughter as he left her. And so, Roscuro turned.

He looked back.

And he saw that the princess was **glaring** at him. Her eyes were filled with **disgust** and anger.

"Go back to the dungeon" was what the look she gave him said. "Go back into the darkness where you belong."

This look, reader, broke Roscuro's heart.

Did you think that rats do not have hearts? Wrong.

All living things have a heart. And the heart of any living thing can be broken.

If the rat had not looked over his shoulder, perhaps his heart would not have broken. And it is possible, then, that I would not have a story to tell.

But, reader, he did look.

Chapter Twenty-two
he puts his heart together again

ROSCURO HURRIED from the banquet hall.

"A rat," he said. He put a paw over his heart. "I am a rat. And there is no light for rats. There will be no light for me."

The king's men were still **bent** over the queen. The king was still shouting, "Save her! Save her!" And the queen was still dead, of course, when Roscuro **encounter**ed the queen's **royal** soup spoon lying on the floor.

"I will have something beautiful," he said aloud. "I am a rat, but I will have something beautiful. I will have a crown of my own." He picked up the spoon. He put it on his head.

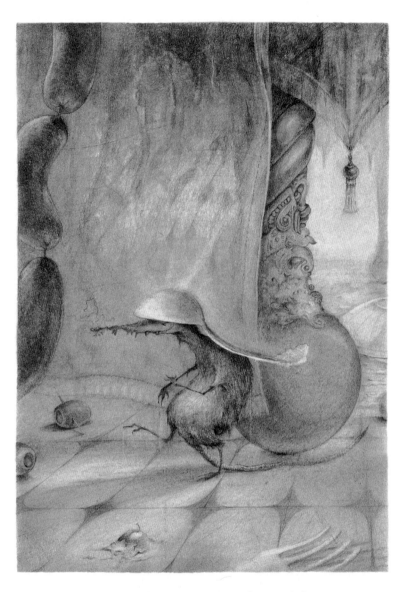

"I will have something beautiful.
And I will have revenge."

"Yes," said Roscuro. "I will have something beautiful. And I will have **revenge**. Both things. **Somehow**."

There are those hearts, reader, that never **mend** again once they are broken. Or if they do mend, they **heal** themselves in a **crooked** and **lopsided** way, as if **sewn** together by a **careless craftsman**. Such was the **fate** of Chiaroscuro. His heart was broken. Picking up the spoon and placing it on his head, speaking of revenge, these things helped him to put his heart together again. But it was, **alas**, put together wrong.

"Where is the rat?" shouted the king. "Find that rat!"

"If you want me," **mutter**ed Roscuro as he left the banquet hall, "I will be in the dungeon, in the darkness."

Chapter Twenty-three

consequences

THERE WERE, OF COURSE, **dire consequences** of Roscuro's behavior. Every action, reader, no matter how small, has a consequence. For instance, the young Roscuro **gnaw**ed on Gregory the **jailer's** rope, and because he gnawed on the rope, a **match** was lit in his face, and because a match was lit in his face, his soul was set **afire.**

The rat's soul was set afire, and because of this he **journey**ed upstairs, **seeking** the light. Upstairs, in the **banquet** hall, the Princess Pea spotted him and called out the word "rat," and because of this Roscuro fell into the queen's soup. And because the rat fell into the queen's soup, the queen died. You can see, can't you, how everything is related to everything else? You can see, quite clearly, how every action has a consequence.

For instance (if, reader, you will **indulge** me, and **allow** me to continue this **meditation** on consequences), because the queen died while eating soup, the heartbroken king **outlaw**ed soup; and because soup was outlawed, so were all the **instrument**s involved in the making and eating of soup: spoons and bowls and **kettles**. These things were collected from all the people of the Kingdom of Dor, and they were **pile**d in the dungeon.

And because Roscuro was **dazzle**d by the light of one match and journeyed upstairs and fell into the queen's soup and the queen died, the king ordered the death of every rat in the land.

The king's men went bravely into the dungeon to kill the rats. But the thing about killing a rat is that you must first *find* a rat. And if a rat does not want to be found, reader, he will not be found.

The king's men succeeded only in getting lost in the dungeon's **tortuous mazes**. Some of them, in fact, did not ever find their way out again and died there in the dark heart of the castle. And so, the killing of all rats was not successful. And in **desperation**, King Phillip **declare**d that rats were **illegal**. He declared them outlaws.

This, of course, was a **ridiculous** law, as rats are

outlaws to begin with. How can you outlaw an outlaw? It is a waste of time and energy. But still, the king **officially** **decree**d that all rats in the Kingdom of Dor were outlaws and should be treated as such. When you are a king, you may make as many ridiculous laws as you like. That is what being a king is all about.

But, reader, we must not forget that King Phillip loved the queen and that without her he was lost. This is the danger of loving: No matter how powerful you are, no matter how many kingdoms you rule, you cannot stop those you love from dying. Making soup illegal, outlawing rats, these things **soothe**d the poor king's heart. And so we must forgive him.

And what of the outlawed rats? What of one outlawed rat in **particular**?

What of Chiaroscuro?

In the darkness of the dungeon, he sat in his nest with the spoon **atop** his head. He set to work **fashion**ing for himself a **kingly cape** made out of a **scrap** of the red tablecloth. And as he worked, old one-eared Botticelli Remorso sat next to him **swing**ing his **locket** back and forth, back and forth, saying, "You see what comes from a rat going upstairs? I hope that you have learned your lesson. Your job in this world is to make others suffer."

"Yes," muttered Roscuro. "Yes. That is exactly what I

intend to do. I will make the princess suffer for how she looked at me."

And as Roscuro worked and planned, the jailer Gregory held tight to his rope and made his own way through the darkness, and in a **dank cell**, the prisoner who had once had a red tablecloth and now had nothing spent his days and nights **weeping** quietly.

High above the dungeon, upstairs, in the castle, a small mouse stood alone one evening as his brothers and sisters **sniffed** for **crumbs**. He stood with his head **cocked** to one side, listening to a sweet sound he did not yet have a name for. There would be consequences of the mouse's love for music. You, reader, know already some of those consequences. Because of the music, the mouse would find his way to a princess. He would fall in love.

And speaking of consequences, the same evening that Despereaux stood inside the castle hearing music for the first time, outside the castle, in the **gloom** of **dusk**, more consequences **drew near**. A **wagon** driven by a king's soldier and piled high with spoons and bowls and kettles, was making its way to the castle. And beside the soldier there sat a young girl with ears that looked like nothing so much as pieces of cauliflower* **stuck** on either side of her head.

The girl's name, reader, was Miggery Sow. And though

she did not yet know it, she would be **instrumental** in helping the rat work his **revenge.**

End of the Second Book

★ cauliflower [식물] 콜리플라워, 꽃양배추.

Book

THE THIRD

Gor!
The Tale of Miggery Sow

Chapter Twenty-four
a handful of cigarettes,
a red tablecloth and a hen

AGAIN, READER, we must go backward before we can go forward. With that said, here begins a short history of the life and times of Miggery Sow, a girl born into this world many years before the mouse Despereaux and the rat Chiaroscuro, a girl born far from the castle, a girl named for her father's favorite prize-winning pig.

Miggery Sow was six years old when her mother, holding onto Mig's hand and **staring** directly into Mig's eyes, died.

"Ma?" said Mig. "Ma, couldn't you stay here with me?"

"Oh," said her mother. "Who is that? Who is that holding my hand?"

"It's me, Ma, Miggery Sow."

"Ah, child, let me go."

"But I want you to stay here," said Mig, wiping first at her runny nose and then at her runny eyes.

"You want," said her mother.

"Yes," said Mig, "I want."

"Ah, child, and what does it matter what you are wanting?" said her mother. She squeezed Mig's hand once, twice, and then she died, leaving Mig alone with her father, who, on a market day* in spring soon after his wife's death, sold his daughter into service for a handful of cigarettes, a red tablecloth, and a hen.

"Papa?" said Mig, when her father was walking away from her with the hen in his arms, a cigarette in his mouth, and the red tablecloth draped across his shoulders like a cape.

"Go on, Mig," he said. "You belong to that man now."

"But I don't want to, Papa," she said. "I want to go with you." She took hold of the red tablecloth and tugged on it.

"Lord, child," her father said, "and who is asking you what you want? Go on now." He untangled her fingers

---

★ market day 장날, 장이 서는 날.

from the cloth and turned her in the direction of the man who had bought her.

Mig watched her father walk away, the red tablecloth **billow**ing out behind him. He left his daughter. And, reader, as you already know, he did not look back. Not even once.

Can you imagine it? Can you imagine your father selling you for a tablecloth, a hen, and a handful of cigarettes? Close your eyes, please, and **consider** it for just a moment.

Done?

I hope that the hair on the back of your neck stood up as you thought of Mig's fate and how it would be if it were your own.

Poor Mig. What will become of her? You must, **frighten**ed though you may be, read on and see for yourself.

Reader, it is your **duty**.

Chapter Twenty-five
a vicious circle

MIGGERY SOW called the man who **purchased** her Uncle, as he said she must. And also, as he said she must, Mig **tend**ed Uncle's sheep and cooked Uncle's food and **scrub**bed Uncle's kettle. She did all of this without a word of thanks or **praise** from the man himself.

Another **unfortunate** fact of life with Uncle was that he very much liked giving Mig what he **refer**red to as "a good **clout** to the ear." In **fairness** to Uncle, it must be reported that he did always **inquire** whether or not Mig was interested in receiving the clout.

Their daily exchanges went something like this:

Uncle: "I thought I told you to clean the kettle."

Mig: "I cleaned it, Uncle. I cleaned it good."

Uncle: "Ah, it's **filthy**. You'll have to be **punish**ed, won't ye?"

Mig: "Gor,★ Uncle, I cleaned the kettle."

Uncle: "Are ye saying that I'm a liar, girl?"

Mig: "No, Uncle."

Uncle: "Do ye want a good clout to the ear, then?"

Mig: "No, thank you, Uncle, I don't."

Alas, Uncle seemed to be as **entirely unconcerned** with what Mig wanted as her mother and father had been. The discussed clout to the ear was always delivered . . . delivered, I am afraid, with **a great deal of enthusiasm** on Uncle's part, and received with **absolute**ly no enthusiasm at all on the part of Mig.

These clouts were **alarm**ingly **frequent**. And Uncle was **scrupulous**ly fair in paying attention to both the right and left side of Miggery Sow. So it was that after a time the young Mig's ears came to **resemble** not so much ears as pieces of cauliflower stuck to either side of her head.

And they became about as useful to her as pieces of cauliflower. That is to say that they all but **ceased** their **function**ing as ears. Words, for Mig, lost their sharp **edge**s. And then they lost their edges altogether and

---

★ gor [감탄사] 설마, 저런!

became **blurry**, blankety★ things that she had a great deal of trouble **making** any **sense** out of at all.

The less Mig heard, the less she understood. The less she understood, the more things she did wrong; and the more things she did wrong, the more clouts to the ear she received, and the less she heard. This is what is known as a **vicious** circle. And Miggery Sow was right in the center of it.

Which is not, reader, where anybody would want to be.

But then, as you know, what Miggery Sow wanted had never been of much concern to anyone.

★ blankety 괘씸한, 빌어먹을.

Chapter Twenty-six
royalty

WHEN MIG TURNED SEVEN years old there was no cake, no **celebration**, no singing, no present, no **acknowledge**ment of her birthday at all other than Mig saying, "Uncle, today I am seven years old."

And Uncle saying in return, "Did I ask ye how old you were today? Get out of my face before I give ye a good **clout** to the ear."

A few hours after receiving her birthday clout to the ear, Mig was out in the field with Uncle's sheep when she saw something **glittering** and **glowing** on the **horizon**.

She thought for a moment that it was the sun. But she turned and saw that the sun was in the west, where it should be, **sink**ing to join the earth. This thing that

shone so brightly was something else. Mig stood in the field and **shaded** her eyes with her left hand and watched the **brilliant** light **draw closer** and closer and closer until it **reveal**ed itself to be King Phillip and his Queen Rosemary and their daughter, the young Princess Pea.

The **royal** family was **surround**ed by **knight**s in shining **armor** and horses in shining armor. And **atop** each member of the royal family's head there was a golden crown, and they were all, the king and the queen and the princess, dressed in **robes decorate**d with jewels and **sequin**s that glittered and glowed and captured the light of the setting sun and **reflect**ed it back.

"Gor," **breathe**d Mig.

The Princess Pea was riding on a white horse that picked up its legs very high and set them down very **daintily**. The Pea saw Mig standing and **staring**, and she raised a hand to her.

"Hello," the Princess Pea called out **merrily**, "hello." And she waved her hand again.

Mig did not wave back; instead, she stood and watched, open-mouthed, as the perfect, beautiful family passed her by.

"Papa," called the princess to the king, "what is wrong with the girl? She will not wave to me."

"Never mind," said the king. "It is of no **consequence**,

"Gor," breathed Mig.

my dear."

"But I am a princess. And I waved to her. She should wave back."

Mig, for her part, continued to stare. Looking at the royal family had **awaken**ed some deep and **slumbering** need in her; it was as if a small candle had been lit in her **interior, spark**ed to life by the **brilliance** of the king and the queen and the princess.

For the first time in her life, reader, Mig hoped.

And hope is like love . . . a **ridiculous**, wonderful, powerful thing.

Mig tried to name this strange emotion; she put a hand up to touch one of her **aching** ears, and she realized that the feeling she was experiencing, the hope **bloom**ing inside of her, felt exactly the **opposite** of a good clout.

She smiled and took her hand away from her ear. She waved to the princess. "Today is my birthday!" Mig called out.

But the king and the queen and the princess were by now too far away to hear her.

"Today," shouted Mig, "I am seven years old!"

Chapter Twenty-seven
a wish

THAT NIGHT, in the small, dark **hut** that she shared with Uncle and the sheep, Mig tried to speak of what she had seen.

"Uncle?" she said.

"Eh?"

"I saw some human stars today."

"How's that?"

"I saw them all glittering and glowing, and there was a little princess wearing her own crown and riding on a little white, **tippy-toe**d horse."

"What are ye going on about?" said Uncle.

"I saw a king and a queen and a itty-bitty* princess," shouted Mig.

"So?" shouted Uncle back.

"I would like . . . ," said Mig shyly. "I wish to be one of them princesses."

"Har," laughed Uncle. "Har. An ugly, **dumb** thing like you? You ain't even **worth** the **enormous** lot I paid for you. Don't I wish every night that I had back that good **hen** and that red **tablecloth** in place of you?"

He did not wait for Mig to guess the answer to this question. "I do," he said. "I wish it every night. That tablecloth was the color of blood. That hen could **lay** eggs **like nobody's business**."

"I want to be a princess," said Mig. "I want to wear a crown."

"A crown." Uncle laughed. "She wants to wear a crown." He laughed harder. He took the empty **kettle** and put it atop his head. "Look at me," he said. "I'm a king. See my crown? I'm a king just like I've always wanted to be. I'm a king because I *want* to be one."

He danced around the hut with the kettle on his head. He laughed until he cried. And then he stopped dancing and took the kettle from his head and looked at Mig and said, "Do ye want a good clout to the ear for such **nonsense**?"

★ itty-bitty (= itsy-bitsy) 아주 작은.

"No, thank you, Uncle," said Mig.

But she got one anyway.

"Look here," said Uncle after the clout had been delivered. "We will hear no more talk of princesses. Besides, who ever asked you what you wanted in this world, girl?"

The answer to that question, reader, as you well know, was absolutely no one.

Chapter Twenty-eight
to the castle

YEARS PASSED. Mig spent them **scrub**bing the kettle and **tend**ing the sheep and cleaning the **hut** and collecting **innumerable, uncountable, extreme**ly painful clouts to the ear. In the evening, spring or winter, summer or fall, Mig stood in the field as the sun set, hoping that the royal family would pass before her again.

"Gor, I would like to see that little princess another time, wouldn't I? And her little **pony,** too, with his **tippytoe**d feet." This hope, this wish, that she would see the princess again, was **lodge**d deep in Mig's heart; lodged **firm**ly right next to it was the hope that she, Miggery Sow, could someday become a princess herself.

The first of Mig's wishes was **grant**ed, in a **roundabout** way, when King Phillip **outlaw**ed soup. The king's men were sent out to deliver the **grim** news and to collect from the people of the Kingdom of Dor their kettles, their spoons, and their bowls.

Reader, you know exactly how and why this law came to pass, so you would not be as surprised as Uncle was when, one Sunday, a soldier of the king knocked on the door of the hut that Mig and Uncle and the sheep shared and **announce**d that soup was against the law.

"How's that?" said Uncle.

"By royal order of King Phillip," repeated the soldier, "I am sent here to tell you that soup has been outlawed in the Kingdom of Dor. You will, by order of the king, never again **consume** soup. Nor will you think of it or talk about it. And I, as one of the king's **loyal servant**s, am here to take from you your spoons, your kettle and your bowls."

"But that can't be," said Uncle.

"**Nevertheless**, it is."

"What'll we eat? And what'll we eat it with?"

"Cake," suggested the soldier, "with a fork."

"And wouldn't that be lovely," said Uncle, "if we could **afford** to eat cake."

The soldier **shrugged**. "I am only doing my **duty**. Please **hand over** your spoons, your bowls, and your kettle."

Uncle **grab**bed hold of his **beard**. He **let go of** his beard and grabbed the hair on his head. "**Unbelievable!**" he shouted. "I suppose next the king will be wanting my sheep and my girl, seeing as those are the only **possessions** I have left."

"Do you own a girl?" said the soldier.

"I do," said Uncle. "A worthless one, but still, she is mine."

"Ah," said the soldier, "that, I am afraid, is against the law too; no human may own another in the Kingdom of Dor."

"But I paid for her **fair and square** with a good laying **hen** and a **handful** of **cigarettes** and a blood-red tablecloth."

"No matter," said the soldier. "It is against the law to own another. Now, you will hand over to me, if you please, your spoons, your bowls, your kettle, *and* your girl. Or if you choose not to hand over these things then you will come with me to be **imprison**ed in the castle **dungeon**. Which will it be?"

And that is how Miggery Sow came to be sitting in a **wagon** full of soup-related items, next to a soldier of the king.

"Do you have parents?" said the soldier. "I will return

you to them."

"Eh?"

"A ma?" shouted the soldier.

"Dead!" said Mig.

"Your pa?" shouted the soldier.

"I ain't seen him since he sold me."

"Right. I'll take you to the castle then."

"Gor," said Mig, looking around the wagon in **confusion**. "You want me to **paddle**?"

"To the castle!" shouted the soldier. "I'll take you to the castle."

"The castle? Where the itty-bitty princess lives?"

"That's right."

"Gor," said Mig, "I aim to be a princess, too, someday."

"That's a fine dream," said the solider. He **cluck**ed to the horse and **tap**ped the **rein**s and they took off.

"I'm happy to be going," said Mig, putting a hand up and gently touching one of her cauliflower ears.

"Might just as well be happy, seeing as it doesn't make a difference to anyone but you if you are or not," said the soldier. "We will take you to the castle and they will set you up fine. You will no longer be a **slave**. You will be a paid servant."

"Eh?" said Mig.

"You will be a servant!" shouted the soldier. "Not a

slave!"

"Gor!" said Mig, satisfied. "A servant I will be, not a slave."

She was twelve years old. Her mother was dead. Her father had sold her. Her Uncle, who wasn't her uncle at all, had clouted her until she was almost **deaf**. And she wanted, more than anything in the world, to be a little princess wearing a golden crown and riding a high-stepping white horse.

Reader, do you think that it is a terrible thing to hope when there is really no reason to hope at all? Or is it (as the soldier said about happiness) something that you might just as well do, since, in the end, it really makes no difference to anyone but you?

Chapter Twenty-nine
start with the cursy and finish with the thread

MIGGERY SOW'S LUCK CONTINUED. On her first day on the job as a castle **servant** she was sent to deliver a **spool** of red **thread** to the princess.

"Mind," said the head of the **serving** staff, a **dour** woman named Louise, "she is **royalty**, so you must make sure you **curtsy**."

"How's that?" shouted Mig.

"You must curtsy!" shouted Louise.

"Gor," said Mig, "yes'm."

She took the spool of thread from Louise and made her way up the golden stairs to the princess's room, talking to herself as she went.

"Here I am, off to see the princess. Me, Miggery Sow,

seeing the princess up close and **personal**-like. And first off, I must cursy because she is the royalty."

At the door to the princess's room, Mig had a sudden **crisis** of **confidence**. She stood a moment, **clutch**ing the spool of thread and **muttering** to herself.

"Now, how did that go?" she said. "Give the princess the thread and then give her a cursy? No, no, first the cursy and then the thread. That's it. Gor, that's right, that's the order. Start with the cursy and finish with the thread."

She knocked at the princess's door.

"Enter," said the Pea.

Mig, hearing nothing, knocked again.

"Enter," said the Pea.

And Mig, still hearing nothing, knocked yet again. "Maybe," she said to herself, "the princess ain't home."

But then the door was **flung** wide and there was the princess herself, **staring** right at Miggery Sow.

"Gor," said Mig, her mouth hanging open.

"Hello," said the Pea. "Are you the new serving maid? Have you brought me my thread?"

"Cursy I must!" shouted Mig.

She gathered her skirts, dropped the spool of thread, **stuck** a foot out and stepped on the spool, **rocked** back and forth for what seemed like quite a long time (both to the watching princess and the rocking Mig), and finally fell to the floor with a Miggish★ **thud.**

"Whoopsie," said Miggery Sow.

The Pea could not help it—she laughed. "That's all right," she said to Mig, shaking her head. "It's the **spirit** of the thing that counts."

"How's that?" shouted Mig.

"It's the spirit of the thing that counts!" shouted Pea.

"Thank you, miss," said Mig. She **got** slowly **to her feet.** She looked at the princess. She looked down at the floor. "First the cursy and then the thread," Mig muttered.

"Pardon?" said the Pea.

"Gor!" said Mig. "The thread!" She dropped to her hands and knees to **locate** the spool of thread; when she found it, she stood back up and offered it to Pea. "I brought you yer thread, didn't I?"

"Lovely," said the princess as she took the thread from Mig.

"Thank you so much. I cannot seem to hold onto a spool of red thread. Every one I have disappears **somehow.**"

"Are you making a thing?" asked Mig, **squint**ing at the cloth in the Pea's hand.

★ **Miggish** 'Miggery Sow와 같은'이라는 의미로 이름을 형용사처럼 만들었다.

"Whoopsie," said Miggery Sow.

"I am making a history of the world, my world," said the Pea, "in **tapestry**. See? Here is my father, the king. And he is playing the guitar because that is something he loves to do and does quite well. And here is my mother, the queen, and she is eating soup because she loved soup."

"Soup! Gor! That's against the law."

"Yes," said the princess, "my father **outlaw**ed it because my mother died while she was eating it."

"Your ma's dead?"

"Yes," said the Pea. "She died just last month." She bit her bottom lip to stop it from **trembling**.

"Ain't that the thing?" said Mig. "My ma is dead too."

"How old were you when she died?"

"**Bold** was I?" said Mig, taking a step back, away from the princess. "I'm sorry, then."

"No, no, how *old*. How *old* were you?" shouted the Pea.

"Not but six," said Mig.

"I'm sorry," said the princess. She gave Mig a quick, deep look of **sympathy**. "How old are you now?"

"Twelve years."

"So am I," said the princess. "We're the same age. What is your name?" she shouted.

"Miggery. Miggery Sow, but most just calls me Mig.

And I saw you once before, Princess. You passed me by on a little white horse. On my birthday, it was, and I was in the field with Uncle's sheep and it was sunset time."

"Did I wave to you?" asked the princess.

"Eh?"

"Did I wave?" shouted the Pea.

"Yes," nodded Mig.

"But you didn't wave back," said the princess.

"I did," said Mig. "Only you didn't see. Someday, I will sit on a little white horse and wear a crown and wave. Someday," said Mig, and she put up a hand to touch her left ear, "I will be a princess too."

"Really?" said the Pea. And she gave Mig another quick, deep look, but said nothing else.

When Mig finally made her way back down the golden stairs, Louise was waiting for her.

"How long," she roared, "did it take you to deliver a spool of thread to the princess?"

"Too long?" guessed Mig.

"That's right," said Louise. And she gave Mig a good clout to the ear. "You are not destined to be one of our star servants. That is already abundantly clear."

"No, ma'am," said Mig. "That's all right, though, because I aim to be a princess."

"You? A princess? Don't make me laugh."

This, reader, was a little joke on Louise's part, as she was not a person who laughed. Ever. Not even at a **notion** as **ridiculous** as Miggery Sow becoming a princess.

Chapter Thirty
to the dungeon

AT THE CASTLE, for the first time in her young life, Mig had enough to eat. And eat she did. She quickly became **plump** and then plumper still. She grew rounder and rounder and bigger and bigger. Only her head stayed small.

Reader, as the teller of this tale it is my duty from time to time to **utter** some hard and rather **disagreeable** truths. In the **spirit** of honesty, then, I must inform you that Mig was the tiniest bit lazy. And, too, she was not the sharpest knife in the **drawer.**★ That is, she was a bit **slow-witted.**

★ not the sharpest knife in the drawer '서랍 속에 있는 가장 날카로운 칼이 아니다'는 뜻에서 '똑똑하지 못한, 머리가 둔한'이라는 의미가 파생되었다.

Because of these **shortcomings**, Louise was **hard-pressed** to find a job that Miggery Sow could effectively perform. In quick **succession**, Mig failed as a lady-in-waiting★ (she was caught trying on the **gown** of a visiting **duchess**), a **seamstress** (she sewed the **cloak** of the riding **master** to her own **frock** and **ruin**ed both), and a **chambermaid** (sent to clean a room, she stood, open-mouthed and **delighted**, **admiring** the gold walls and floors and tapestries, **exclaim**ing over and over again, "Gor, ain't it pretty? Gor, ain't it something, then?" and did no cleaning at all).

And while Mig was trying and failing at these many **domestic chore**s, other important things were happening in the castle: The rat, in the dungeon below, was **pacing** and **mutter**ing in the darkness, waiting to take his **revenge** on the princess. And upstairs in the castle, the princess had met a mouse. And the mouse had fallen in love with her.

Will there be **consequences**? You **bet**.

Just as Mig's **inability** to perform any job well had its consequences. For, finally, as a **last resort**, Louise sent Mig to the kitchen, where Cook had a **reputation** for dealing effectively with difficult help. In Cook's kitchen

---

★ lady-in-waiting 여왕이나 공주의 시녀.

Mig dropped **eggshells** in the pound-cake★ **batter**; she **scrub**bed the kitchen floor with cooking oil instead of cleaner; she **sneezed** directly on the king's pork **chop**,✻ moments before it was to be served to him.

"Of all the **good-for-nothing**s I have **encounter**ed," shouted Cook, "surely you are the worst, the most cauliflower-eared, the good-for-nothing-est. There's only one place left for you. The dungeon."

"Eh?" said Mig, **cupping** a hand around her ear.

"You are being sent to the dungeon. You are to take the **jailer** his **noonday** meal. That will be your duty from now on."

Reader, you know that the mice of the castle feared the dungeon. Must I tell you that the humans feared it too? Certainly it was never far from their thoughts. In the warm months, a **foul odor** rose out of its dark depths and **permeated** the whole of the castle. And in the still, cold nights of winter, terrible **howls issued** from the dark place, as if the castle itself were **weep**ing and **moan**ing.

"It's only the wind," the people of the castle **assured** each other, "nothing but the wind."

Many a serving girl had been sent to the dungeon

★ pound-cake 파운드 케이크. 밀가루, 달걀, 설탕, 버터를 각각 1파운드씩 넣어 만들었다 해서 붙여진 이름이다.

✻ pork chop 돼지 고기를 뼈째로 잘라 소스를 발라 구운 요리.

"There's only one place left for you. The dungeon."

bearing the jailer's meal only to return **white-faced** and weeping, hands trembling, teeth **chattering**, **insisting** that they would never go back. And worse, there were **whispered** stories of those **servant** girls who had been given the job of feeding the jailer, who had gone down the stairs and into the dungeon and who had never been seen or heard from again.

Do you believe that this will be Mig's **fate**?

Gor! I hope not. What kind of a story would this be without Mig?

"Listen, you cauliflower-eared fool!" shouted Cook. "This is what you do. You take the tray of food down to the dungeon and you wait for the old man to eat the food and then you bring the tray back up. Do you think that you can manage that?"

"Aye, I **reckon** so," said Mig. "I take the old man the tray and he eats what's on it and then I bring the tray back up. Empty it would be then. I bring the empty tray back up from the deep downs."

"That's right," said Cook. "Seems simple, don't it? But I'm sure you'll find a way to **bungle** it."

"Eh?" said Mig.

"Nothing," said Cook. "Good luck to you. You'll be needing it."

She watched as Mig **descend**ed the dungeon stairs.

They were the very same stairs, reader, that the mouse Despereaux had been pushed down the day before. Unlike the mouse, however, Mig had a light: on the tray with the food there was a single, **flickering** candle to show her the way. She turned on the stairs and looked back at Cook and smiled.

"That cauliflower-eared, good-for-nothing fool," said Cook, shaking her head. "What's to become of someone who goes into the dungeon smiling, I ask you?"

Reader, for the answer to Cook's question you must read on.

Chapter Thirty-one
a song in the dark

THE TERRIBLE FOUL **ODOR** of the dungeon did not bother Mig. Perhaps that is because, sometimes, when Uncle was giving her a good **clout** to the ear, he had missed his **mark** and delivered a good clout to Mig's nose instead. This happened often enough that it **interrupt**ed the proper workings of Mig's **olfactory** senses. And so it was that the **overwhelm**ing **stench** of **despair** and hopelessness and evil was not at all **discernible** to her, and she went happily down the **twist**ing and turning stairs.

"Gor!" she shouted. "It's dark, ain't it?"

"Yes, it is Mig," she answered herself, "but if I was a princess, I would be so **glitter**y lightlike, there wouldn't be a place in the world that was dark to me."

At this point, Miggery Sow broke into a little song that went something like this:

"I ain't the Princess Pea
But someday I will be,
The Pea, ha-hee.
Someday, I will be."

Mig, as you can imagine, wasn't much of a singer, more of a **bellow**er, really. But in her little song there was, to the rightly tuned ear, a certain kind of music. And as Mig went singing down the stairs of the dungeon there appeared from the shadows a rat **wrap**ped in a cloak of red and wearing a spoon on his head.

"Yes, yes," whispered the rat, "a lovely song. Just the song I have been waiting to hear."

And Roscuro quietly fell in step beside Miggery Sow.

At the bottom of the stairs, Mig shouted out into the darkness, "Gor, it's me, Miggery Sow, most calls me Mig, delivering your food! Come and get it, Mr. Deep Downs!"

There was no response.

The dungeon was quiet, but it was not quiet in a good way. It was quiet in an **ominous** way; it was quiet in the way of small, **frighten**ing sounds. There was the **snail**-like **slither** of water **oozing** down the walls and from around a darkened corner there came the low **moan** of someone in pain. And then, too, there was the noise of the rats going about their business, their sharp nails hitting the stones of the dungeon and their long tails **drag**ging behind them, through the blood and **muck**.

Reader, if you were standing in the dungeon you would certainly hear all of these **disturb**ing and ominous sounds.

If I were standing in the dungeon, *I* would hear these sounds.

If we were standing together in the dungeon, we would hear these sounds and we would be very frightened; we would **cling** to each other in our fear.

But what did Miggery Sow hear?

That's right.

Absolutely nothing.

And so she was not afraid at all, not in the least.

She held the tray up higher, and the candle **shed** its weak light on the **towering pile** of spoons and bowls and **kettle**s. "Gor," said Mig, "look at them things. I ain't never imagined there could be so many spoons in the whole wide world."

"There is more to this world than anyone could imagine," said a **boom**ing voice from the darkness.

"True, true," whispered Roscuro. "The old jailer

speaks true."

"Gor," said Mig. "Who said that?" And she turned in the direction of the jailer's voice.

Chapter Thirty-two
beware of the rats

THE CANDLELIGHT on Mig's tray revealed Gregory limping toward her, the thick rope tied around his ankle, his hands outstretched.

"You, Gregory presumes, have brought food for the jailer."

"Gor," said Mig. She took a step backward.

"Give it here," said Gregory, and he took the tray from Mig and sat down on an overturned kettle that had rolled free from the tower. He balanced the tray on his knees and stared at the covered plate.

"Gregory assumes that today, again, there is no soup."

"Eh?" said Mig.

"Soup!" shouted Gregory.

"**Illegal!**" shouted Mig back.

"Most foolish," **mutter**ed Gregory as he lifted the cover off the plate, "too foolish to be borne, a world without soup." He picked up a drumstick and put the whole of it in his mouth and **chew**ed and **swallow**ed.

"Here," said Mig, staring hard at him, "you forgot the bones."

"Not forgotten. Chewed."

"Gor," said Mig, staring at Gregory with respect. "You eats the bones. You are most **ferocious.**"

Gregory ate another piece of chicken, a wing, bones and all. And then another. Mig watched him **admiringly.**

"Someday," she said, moved suddenly to tell this man her deepest wish, "I will be a princess."

At this **pronounce**ment, Chiaroscuro, who was still at Mig's side, did a small, **deliberate jig** of joy; in the light of the one candle his dancing shadow was large and **fearsome indeed.**

"Gregory sees you," Gregory said to the rat's shadow.

Roscuro **cease**d his dance. He moved to hide beneath Mig's skirts.

"Eh?" shouted Mig. "What's that?"

"Nothing," said Gregory. "So you aim to be a princess. Well, everyone has a foolish dream. Gregory, for instance, dreams of a world where soup is legal. And that rat, Gregory is sure, has some foolish dream too."

"If only you knew," whispered Roscuro.

"What?" shouted Mig.

Gregory said nothing more. Instead, he reached into his pocket and then held his napkin up to his face and **sneezed** into it, once, twice, three times.

"Bless you!" shouted Mig. "Bless you, bless you."

"Back to the world of light," Gregory whispered. And then he balled the napkin up and placed it on the tray.

"Gregory is done," he said. And he held the tray out to Mig.

"Done are you? Then the tray goes back upstairs. Cook says it must. You take the tray to the deep downs, you wait for the old man to eat and then you bring the tray back. Them's my **instructions**."

"Did they instruct you, too, to **beware** of the rats?"

"The what?"

"The rats."

"What about 'em?"

"Beware of them!" shouted Gregory.

"Right," said Mig. "Beware the rats."

Roscuro, hidden beneath Mig's skirts, rubbed his front paws together. "Warn her all you like, old man," he whispered. "My hour has arrived. The time is now, and your rope must break. No nib-nib-**nibbling** this time, rather a serious chew that will break it in two. Yes, it is all coming clear. **Revenge** is **at hand**."

Chapter Thirty-three
a rat who knows her name

MIG HAD CLIMBED the dungeon stairs and was preparing to open the door to the kitchen, when the rat spoke to her.

"May I **detain** you for a moment?"

Mig looked to her left and then to her right.

"Down here," said Roscuro.

Mig looked at the floor.

"Gor," she said, "but you're a rat, ain't you? And didn't the old man just warn me of such? 'Beware the rats,' he said." She held the tray up higher so that the light from the candle shone directly on Roscuro and the golden spoon on his head and the blood-red **cloak** around his neck.

"There is no need to **panic**, none at all," said Roscuro. As he talked, he reached behind his back and, using the handle, he raised the soup spoon off his head, much in the manner of a man lifting his hat to a lady.

"Gor," said Mig, "a rat with manners."

"Yes," said Roscuro. "How do you do?"

"My papa had him some cloth much like yours, Mr. Rat," said Mig. "Red like that. He **trade**d me for it."

"Ah," said Roscuro, and he smiled a large, knowing smile. "Ah, did he really? That is a terrible story, a **tragic** story."

Reader, if you will **pardon** me, we must pause for a moment to **consider** a great and unusual thing, a **portentous** thing. That great, unusual, portentous thing is this: Roscuro's voice was **pitch**ed perfectly to make its way through the **tortuous** path of Mig's broken-down, cauliflower ears. That is to say, dear reader, Miggery Sow heard, perfect and true, every single word the rat Roscuro **uttered**.

"You have known your share of **tragedy**," said Roscuro to Mig. "Perhaps it is time for you to make the **acquaintance** of **triumph** and **glory**."

"Triumph?" said Mig. "Glory?"

"Allow me to introduce myself," said Roscuro. "I am Chiaroscuro. Friends call me Roscuro. And your name

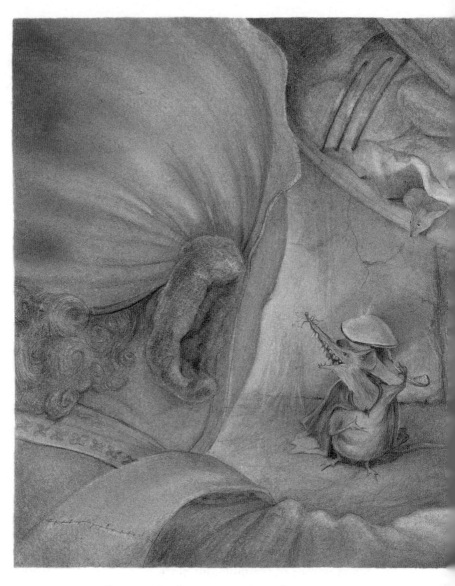

"A rat who knows my name!"

is Miggery Sow. And it is true, is it not, that most people call you simply Mig?"

"Ain't that the thing?" shouted Mig. "A rat who knows my name!"

"Miss Miggery, my dear, I do not want to appear too forward so early in our acquaintance, but, may I **inquire**, am I right in **ascertain**ing that you have **aspiration**s?"

"What do ye mean 'aspirations'?" shouted Mig.

"Miss Miggery, there is no need to shout. None at all. As you can hear me, so I can hear you. We two are perfectly **suited**, each to the other." Roscuro smiled again, displaying a **mouthful** of sharp yellow teeth. "'Aspirations,' my dear, are those things that would make a **serving** girl wish to be a princess."

"Gor," agreed Mig, "a princess is exactly what I want to be."

"There is, my dear, a way to make that happen. I believe that there is a way to make that dream come true."

"You mean that I could be the Princess Pea?"

"Yes, Your **Highness**," said Roscuro. And

he swept the spoon off his head and **bow**ed deeply at the waist. "Yes, your most **royal** Princess Pea."

"Gor!" said Mig.

"May I tell you my plan? May I **illustrate** for you how we can make your dream of becoming a princess a reality?"

"Yes," said Mig, "yes."

"It begins," said Roscuro, "with yours truly, and the chewing of a rope."

Mig held the tray with the one small candle burning bright, and she listened as the rat went on, speaking directly to the wish in her heart. So **passionate**ly did Roscuro speak and so **intent**ly did the serving girl listen that neither noticed as the napkin on the tray moved.

Nor did they hear the small mouselike noises of **disbelief** and **outrage** that **issued** from the napkin as Roscuro went on **unfold**ing, step by step, his **diabolical** plan to bring the princess to darkness.

End of the Third Book

Book

THE FOURTH

Recalled
to the Light

Chapter Thirty-four
kill 'em, even if they's already dead

READER, you did not forget about our small mouse, did you?

"Back to the light," that was what Gregory **whispered** to him when he **wrapped** Despereaux in his napkin and placed him on the tray. And then Mig, after her conversation with Roscuro, carried the tray into the kitchen, and when she saw Cook she shouted, "It's me, Miggery Sow, back from the deep downs."

"Ah, lovely," said Cook. "And ain't we all **relieved**?"

Mig put the tray on the counter.

"Here, here," said Cook, "your **duties** ain't done. You must clear it."

"How's that?" shouted Mig.

"You must clear the tray!" shouted Cook. She reached over and took hold of the napkin and gave it a good shake, and Despereaux tumbled out of the napkin and landed right directly, *plop*, in a measuring cup full of oil.

"Acccck," said Cook, "a mouse in my kitchen, in my cooking oil, in my measuring cup. You, Mig, kill him directly."

Mig bent her head and looked at the mouse slowly sinking to the bottom of the glass cup.

"Poor little meecy," she said. And she stuck her hand into the oil and pulled him out by his tail.

Despereaux, gasping and coughing and blinking at the bright light, could have wept with joy at his rescue. But he was not given time to cry.

"Kill him!" shouted Cook.

"Gor!" said Mig. "All right." Holding Despereaux by the tail, she went to get the kitchen knife. But the mouse tail, covered as it was in oil, was slick and difficult to hold onto and Mig, in reaching for the knife, loosened her grip, and Despereaux fell to the floor.

Mig looked down at the little bundle of brown fur.

"Gor," she said, "that killed him for sure."

"Kill him even if he's already dead," shouted Cook. "That's my philosophy with mice. If they're alive, kill them. If they're dead, kill them. That way you can be certain of having yourself a dead mouse, which is the only kind of mouse to have."

"That's some good sophosy, that is, kill 'em, even if they's already dead."

"Hurry, you cauliflower-eared fool!" shouted Cook. "Hurry!"

Despereaux lifted his head from the floor. The afternoon sun was shining through the large kitchen window. He just had time to think how **miraculous** the light was and then it disappeared and Mig's face **loom**ed into view. She studied him, breathing through her mouth.

"Little meecy," she said, "ain't you going to **skedaddle**?"

Despereaux looked for a long moment into Mig's small, **concern**ed eyes and then there came a **blind**ing flash and the sound of metal moving through air as Mig brought the kitchen knife down, down, down.

Despereaux felt a very **intense** pain in his **hindquarters**. He **leapt** up and into action. Reader, he **scurried**. He scurried like a professional mouse. He **zigg**ed to the left. He **zagg**ed to the right.

"Gor!" shouted Mig. "Missed him."

"Ain't that a surprise?" said Cook just as Despereaux scurried under a **crack** in the **pantry** door.

"I got the little meecy's tail, though," said Mig. She

"Gor!" shouted Mig. "Missed him."

bent over and picked up Despereaux's tail and held it up, proudly displaying it to Cook.

"So?" shouted Cook. "What good will that do us when the rest of him has disappeared into the pantry?"

"I don't know," said Mig. And she **braced** herself as Cook **advanced** upon her, **intend**ing to give her a good **clout** to the ear. "I don't know."

Chapter Thirty-five
the knight in shining armor

DESPEREAUX WAS **PONDERING** the **reverse** of
that question. He was wondering not what he would do
with his tail, but what he would do without it. He was
sitting on a bag of **flour** high **atop** a shelf in the **pantry**,
crying for what he had lost.

The pain in his **hindquarters** was **intense** and he wept
because of it. But he also cried because he was happy.
He was out of the **dungeon**; he had been **recall**ed to life.
His rescue had happened just **in time** for him to save
the Princess Pea from the terrible **fate** that the rat had
planned for her.

So Despereaux wept with joy and with pain and
with **gratitude**. He wept with **exhaustion** and **despair**

and hope. He wept with all the emotions a young, small mouse who has been sent to his death and then been delivered from it in time to save his **beloved** can feel.

Reader, the mouse wept.

And then he lay down on the **sack** of flour and slept. Outside the castle the sun set and the stars came out one by one, and then they disappeared and gave way to the rising sun and still Despereaux slept. And while he slept, he dreamt.

He dreamt of the **stained**-glass windows and the dark of the dungeon. In Despereaux's dream, the light came to life, **brilliant** and **glorious**, in the shape of a **knight swing**ing a sword. The knight fought the dark.

And the dark took many shapes. First the dark was his mother, uttering **phrases** in French. And then the dark became his father **beat**ing the drum. The dark was Furlough wearing a black **hood** and shaking his head no. And the dark became a huge rat smiling a smile that was evil and sharp.

"The dark," Despereaux cried, turning his head to the left.

"The light," he **murmur**ed, turning his head to the right.

He called out to the knight. He shouted, "Who are you? Will you save me?"

But the knight did not answer him.

"Tell me who you are!" Despereaux shouted.

The knight stopped swinging his sword. He looked at Despereaux. "You know me," he said.

"No," said Despereaux, "I don't."

"You do," said the knight. He slowly took the armor off his head and revealed . . . nothing, no one. The suit of armor was empty.

"No, oh no," said Despereaux. "There is no knight in shining armor; it's all just make-believe, like happily ever after."

And in his sleep, reader, the small mouse began to cry.

Chapter Thirty-six
what Mig carried

AND WHILE THE MOUSE SLEPT, Roscuro put his terrible plan into effect. Would you like to hear, reader, how it all **unfold**ed? The story is not a pretty one. There is violence in it. And **cruelty**. But stories that are not pretty have a certain value, too, I suppose. Everything, as you well know (having lived in this world long enough to have figured out a thing or two for yourself), cannot always be sweetness and light.

Listen. This is how it happened. First, the rat finished, **once and for all**, the job he had started long ago: He **chew**ed through Gregory's rope, all the way through it, so that the **jailer** became lost in the **maze** of the dungeon. Late at night, when the castle was dark, the **serving** girl Miggery Sow climbed the stairs to the princess's room.

In her hand she carried a candle. And in the pockets of her **apron** were two very **ominous** things. In the right pocket, hidden in case they should **encounter** anyone on the stairs, was a rat with a spoon on his head and a **cloak** of red around his shoulders. In the left pocket was a kitchen knife, the same knife that Miggery Sow had used to cut off the tail of a certain mouse. These were the things, a rat and a knife and a candle, that Mig carried with her as she climbed up, up, up the stairs.

"Gor!" she shouted to the rat. "It's dark, ain't it?"

"Yes, yes," whispered Roscuro from her pocket. "It is quite dark, my dear."

"When I'm princess . . . ," began Mig.

"Shhhh," said Roscuro, "may I suggest that you keep your **glorious** plans for the future to yourself? And may I further suggest that you keep your voice down to a whisper? We are, after all, on a **covert** mission. Do you know how to whisper, my dear?"

"I do!" shouted Mig.

"Then, please," said Roscuro, "please **institute** this knowledge **immediately**."

"Gor," whispered Mig, "all right."

"Thank you," said Roscuro. "Do I need to review

with you again our plan of action?"

"I got it all straight right here in my head," whispered Mig. And she tapped the side of her head with one finger.

"How comforting," said Roscuro. "Perhaps, my dear, we should go over it again. One more time, just to be sure."

"Well," said Mig, "we go into the princess's room and she will be sleeping and snoozing and snoring, and I will wake her up and show her the knife and say, 'If you does not want to get hurt, Princess, you must come with me.'"

"And you will not hurt her," said Roscuro.

"No, I won't. Because I want her to live so that she can be my lady in waiting when I become the princess."

"Exactly," said Roscuro. "That will be her divine comeuppance."

"Gor," whispered Mig. "Yes. Her divine comeuppance."

Mig had, of course, no idea what the phrase "divine comeuppance" meant, but she very much liked the sound of it, and she repeated it over and over to herself until Roscuro said, "And then?"

"And then," continued Mig, "I tells her to get out of her princess bed and come with me on a little journey."

"Ha," said Roscuro, "a little journey. That is right. Ha. I love the understatement of that phrase. A little journey. Oh, it will be a little journey. **Indeed**, it will."

"And then," said Mig, who was now coming to her favorite part of the plan, "we take her to the deep downs and we gives her some long lessons in how to be a serving girl and we gives me some short lessons in how to be a princess and when we is all done studying up, we **switch** places. I gets to be the princess and she gets to be the maid. Gor!"

Reader, this is the very plan that Roscuro presented to Mig when he first met her. It was, of course, a **ridiculous** plan.

No one would ever, **not for one blind minute**, mistake Mig for the princess or the princess for Mig. But Miggery Sow, as I pointed out to you before, was not the sharpest knife in the **drawer**. And, reader, too, she wanted so **desperate**ly to become a princess. She wanted, oh, how she wanted. And it was because of this terrible wanting that she was able to believe in Roscuro's plan with every **ounce** of her heart.★

The rat's real plan was, in a way, more simple and more terrible. He **intend**ed to take the princess to the deepest, darkest part of the dungeon. He intended to have Mig put chains on the princess's hands and her feet,

★ every ounce of one's heart 온 마음을 다해. 마음의 모든 온스(무게 단위)를 다한다는 의미
이다.

and he intended to keep the **glittering, glow**ing, laughing princess there in the dark.

Forever.

Chapter Thirty-seven
a small taste

SHE WAS ASLEEP and dreaming of her mother, the queen, who was holding out a spoon to her and saying, "Taste this, my sweet Pea, taste this, my darling, and tell me what you think."

The princess leaned forward and sipped some soup from the spoon her mother held out to her.

"Oh, Mama," she said, "it's wonderful. It's the best soup I have ever eaten."

"Yes," said the queen. "It is wonderful, isn't it?"

"May I have some more?" said the Pea.

"I gave you a small taste so that you would not forget," said her mother. "I gave you a small taste so that you would remember."

"I want more."

But as soon as the princess said this, her mother was gone. She disappeared and the bowl and the soup spoon disappeared along with her.

"Lost things," said the Pea, "more lost things." And then she heard her name. She turned, happy, thinking that her mother had come back. But the voice was not her mother's. The voice belonged to somebody else and it was coming from some place far away and it was telling her to wake up, wake up.

The Pea opened her eyes and saw Miggery Sow standing over her bed, a knife in one hand and a candle in the other.

"Mig?" she said.

"Gor," said Mig softly.

"Say it," **command**ed Roscuro.

Mig closed her eyes and shouted her piece. "If you does not want to get hurt, Princess, you must come with me."

"Whatever for?" said the princess in an **annoy**ed tone. As I have **note**d before, the princess was not a person who was used to being told what to do. "What are you talking about?"

Mig opened her eyes and shouted, "You got to come with me so after we take some lessons, you some long lessons and me some short ones, together way down in the deep downs, I can be you and you can be me."

"No!" shouted Roscuro from Mig's pocket. "No! No! You are doing it wrong."

"Who said that?"

"Your **Highness**," said Roscuro. And he **crawl**ed out of Mig's pocket and made his way up to her shoulder and **situated** himself there, **laying** his tail across her neck to **balance** himself. "Your Highness," he said again. And he raised the spoon slowly off his head and smiled, displaying his **mouthful** of truly **hideous** teeth. "I think it would be best if you do as Miggery Sow suggests. She is, as you can quite clearly see, in **possession** of a knife, a large knife. And she will, if pushed, use it."

"This is ridiculous," the princess said. "You can't **threaten** me. I'm a princess."

"We," said Roscuro, "are all too aware of the fact of what you are. A knife, however, cares nothing for the fact that you are **royalty**. And you will **bleed**, I **assume**, just like any other human."

The Pea looked at Mig. Mig smiled. The knife **glint**ed in the light of the candle. "Mig?" she said, her voice shaking the tiniest bit.

"I really do not think," said Roscuro, "that Mig would need much **persuasion** to use that knife, Princess.

She is a dangerous **individual**, easily led."

"But we are friends," said the Pea, "aren't we, Mig?"

"Eh?" said Mig.

"Trust me," said Roscuro. "You are not friends. And I think it would be best if you **address**ed all your communications to me, Princess. I am the one **in charge** here. Look at me."

The Pea looked right directly at the rat and at the spoon on his head. Her heart **skip**ped one beat and then two.

"Do you know me, Princess?"

"No," she said, lowering her head, "I don't know you."

But, reader, she did know him. He was the rat who had fallen in her mother's soup. And he was wearing her dead mother's spoon on his head! The princess kept her head down. She **concentrate**d on **contain**ing the **rage** that was **leap**ing up inside of her.

"Look again, Princess. Or can you not **bear** to look? Does it pain your **royal sensibilities** to let your eyes rest on a *rat?*"

"I don't know you," she said, "and I'm not afraid to look at you." The Pea raised her head slowly. Her eyes were **defiant**. She **stare**d at the rat.

"Very well," said Roscuro, "have it your way. You do

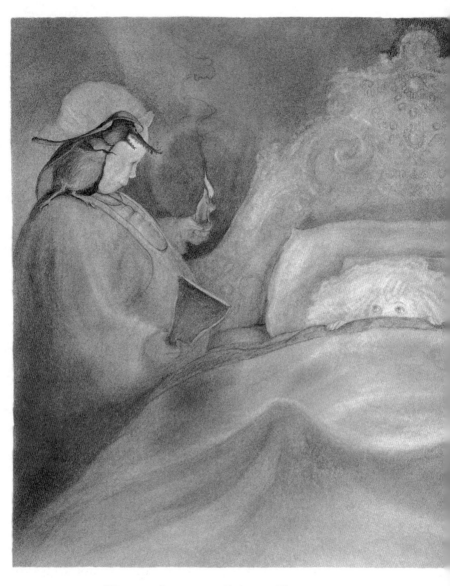

"Do you know me, Princess?"

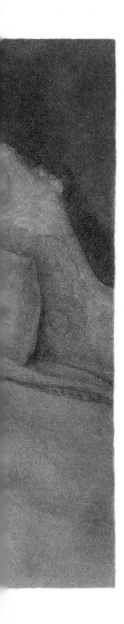

not know me. **Nonetheless**, you must do as I say, as my friend here has a knife. So get out of bed, Princess. We are going on a little **journey**. I would like it if you dressed in your loveliest **gown**, the one that you were wearing at a **banquet** not so long ago."

"And put on your crown," said Mig. "Put that on your princess head."

"Yes," said Roscuro. "Please, Princess, do not forget your crown."

The Pea, still staring at Roscuro, pushed the covers back and got out of bed.

"Move quickly," said Roscuro. "We must take our little journey while it is still dark and while the rest of the castle sleeps on— **ignorant**, oh so ignorant, I am afraid, of your **fate**."

The princess took a gown from her closet.

"Yes," said Roscuro to himself, "that is the one. The very one. Look at how it **sparkle**s in the light. Lovely."

"I will need someone to do my buttons," said the princess as she stepped into the dress. "Mig, you must help me."

"Little princess," said Roscuro, "do you

think that you can **outsmart** a rat? Our dear Miggery Sow will not lay down her knife. Not even for a moment. Will you, Miggery Sow? Because that might **ruin** your chances of becoming a princess, isn't that right?"

"Gor," said Mig, "that's right."

And so while Mig held the knife pointed in the direction of the princess, the Pea sat and let the rat crawl over her back, doing her buttons up for her, one by one.

The princess held very **still**. The only movement she allowed herself was this: she **lick**ed her lips, over and over again, because she thought that she could taste there the sweet **saltiness** of the soup that her mother had fed her in her dream.

"I have not forgotten, Mama," she whispered. "I have not forgotten you. I have not forgotten soup."

Chapter Thirty-eight
to the dungeon

THE STRANGE **THREESOME** made their way down
the golden stairs of the castle. The princess and Mig
walked side by side and Roscuro hid himself again in
the pocket of Mig's **apron**, and Mig pointed the sharp
tip of the knife at the princess's back and together they
went down, down, down.

The princess was led to her fate as, around her,
everyone slept. The king slept in his giant bed with his
crown on his head and his hands crossed on his chest,
dreaming that his wife, the queen, was a bird with green
and gold **feather**s who called his name, *Phillip, Phillip,
Phillip*, without **ceasing**.

Cook slept in a too-small bed off the kitchen,

dreaming of a **recipe** for soup that she could not find. "Where did I put that?" she **mumbled** in her sleep. "Where did that recipe go? It was for the queen's favorite soup. I must find it."

And not far from Cook, in the **pantry**, **atop** a bag of **flour**, slept the mouse Despereaux, dreaming, as you know, reader, of knights in shining **armor**, of darkness, and of light.

And in the whole of the darkened, sleeping castle, there was only the light of the candle in the hand of Miggery Sow. The candle **shone** on the princess's dress and made it **sparkle**, and the princess walked tall in the light and tried not to be afraid.

In this story, reader, we have talked about the heart of the mouse and the heart of the rat and the heart of the serving girl Miggery Sow, but we have not talked about the heart of the princess. Like most hearts, it was **complicated**, **shaded** with dark and **dappled** with light. The dark things in the princess's heart were these: a very small, very hot, burning **coal** of **hatred** for the rat who was responsible for her mother's death. And the other darkness was a **tremendous sorrow**, a deep sadness that her mother was dead and that the princess could, now, only talk to her in her dreams.

And what of the light in the princess's heart? Reader, I

am pleased to tell you that the Pea was a kind person, and perhaps more important, she was **empathetic**. Do you know what it means to be empathetic?

I will tell you: It means that when you are being **forcibly** taken to a **dungeon**, when you have a large knife pointed at your back, when you are trying to be brave, you are able, still, to think for a moment of the person who is holding that knife.

You are able to think: "Oh, poor Mig, she wants to be a princess so badly and she thinks that this is the way. Poor, poor Mig. What must it be like to want something that **desperately**?"

That, reader, is **empathy**.

And now you have a small map of the princess's heart (hatred, sorrow, kindness, empathy), the heart that she carried inside her as she went down the golden stairs and through the kitchen and, finally, just as the sky outside the castle began to lighten, down into the dark of the dungeon with the rat and the serving girl.

Chapter Thirty-nine
missing!

THE SUN ROSE AND **SHED** LIGHT on what Roscuro and Miggery Sow had done.

And finally Despereaux awoke. But, **alas**, he awoke too late.

"I haven't see her," Louise was shouting, "and I tell you, I wash my hands of her. If she's missing, I say **good riddance**! Good riddance to bad **rubbish**."

Despereaux sat up. He looked behind him. Oh, his tail! Gone! Given over to the knife, and where the tail should be . . . nothing but a **bloody stub**.

"And more **foul** play. Gregory dead!" shouted Cook. "Poor old man, that rope of his broken by who knows what and him lost in the dark and **frighten**ed to death because of it. It's too much."

"Oh no," whispered Despereaux. "Oh no, Gregory is dead." The mouse **got to his feet** and began the long climb down from the shelf. Once he was on the floor, he **stuck** his head around the door of the **pantry** and saw Cook standing in the center of the kitchen, **wring**ing her fat hands. Beside her stood a tall woman **jangling** a ring of keys.

"That's right," said Louise. "All the king's men was down there searching for her in the dungeon and when they come back up, who do they have with them? They have the old man. Dead! And now you tell me that Mig is missing and I say who cares?"

Despereaux made a small noise of **despair**. He had slept too long. The rat had already acted. The princess was gone.

"What kind of world is it, Miss Louise, where princesses are taken from right under our noses and queens drop dead and we cannot even take **comfort** in soup?" And with this, Cook started to cry.

"Shhhh," said Louise, "I **beg** you. Do not say that word."

"Soup!" shouted Cook. "I will say it. No one can stop me. Soup, soup, *soup!*" And then she began to cry **in earnest**, **wailing** and **sobbing**.

"There," said Louise. She put a hand out to touch Cook, and Cook slapped it away.

"It will be all right," said Louise. Cook brought the hem of her apron up to wipe at her tears. "It won't," she said. "It won't be all right ever again. They've taken our little darling away. There ain't nothing left to live for without the princess."

Despereaux was amazed to have exactly what was in his heart spoken aloud by such a ferocious, mouse-hating woman as Cook.

Louise again reached out to touch Cook, and this time Cook allowed her to put an arm around her shoulder. "What will we do? What will we do?" wailed Cook.

And Louise said, "Shhh. There, there."

Alas, there was no one to comfort Despereaux. And there was no time, anyway, for him to cry. He knew what he had to do. He had to find the king.

For, having heard Roscuro's plan, reader, Despereaux knew that the princess was hidden in the dungeon. And being somewhat smarter than Miggery Sow, he sensed the terrible unspoken truth behind Roscuro's words. He knew that Mig could never be a princess. And he knew that the rat, once he captured the Pea, would never let her go.

184

And so, the small mouse who had been **dipp**ed in oil, covered in flour and **relieved** of his tail **slipp**ed out of the pantry and past the **weep**ing ladies.

He went to find the king.

Chapter Forty
forgiveness

HE WENT FIRST to the **throne** room, but the king was not there. And so Despereaux **slipped** through a hole in the **molding**, and was making his way to the princess's room when he **came upon** the Mouse **Council**, thirteen mice and one Most Very **Honor**ed Head Mouse, sitting around their piece of wood **debating** important mouse **matters**.

Despereaux stopped and stood very **still**.

"**Fellow** honored mice," said the Most Very Honored Head Mouse, and then he looked up from the **makeshift** table and saw Despereaux. "Despereaux," he **whispered**.

The other mice of the council **lean**ed forward, **straini**ng to **make** some **sense** of the word that the Head

Mouse had just uttered.

"Pardon?" one said.

"Excuse me?" said another.

"I didn't hear right," said a third. "I thought you said 'Despereaux.'"

The Head Mouse gathered himself. He tried speaking again. "Fellow members," he said, "a ghost. A ghost!" And he raised a shaking paw and pointed it at Despereaux.

The other mice turned and looked.

And there was Despereaux Tilling, covered in flour, looking back at them, the telltale red thread still around his neck like a thin trail of blood.

"Despereaux," said Lester. "Son. You have come back!"

Despereaux looked at his father and saw an old mouse whose fur was shot through with gray. How could that be? Despereaux had been gone only a few days, but his father seemed to have aged many years in his absence.

"Son, ghost of my son," said Lester, his whiskers trembling, "I dream about you every night. I dream about beating the drum that sent you to your death. I was wrong. What I did was wrong."

"No!" called the Most Very Honored Head Mouse. "No!"

"I've destroyed it," said Lester. "I've destroyed the

"Son. You have come back!"

drum. Will you forgive me?" He clasped his front paws together and looked at his son.

"No!" shouted the Head Mouse again. "No. Do not ask the ghost to forgive you, Lester. You did as you should. You did what was best for the mouse community."

Lester ignored the Head Mouse. "Son," he said, "please."

Despereaux looked at his father, at his gray-streaked fur and trembling whiskers and his front paws clasped together in front of his heart, and he felt suddenly as if his own heart would break in two. His father looked so small, so sad.

"Forgive me," said Lester again.

Forgiveness, reader, is, I think, something very much like hope and love, a powerful, wonderful thing.

And a ridiculous thing, too.

Isn't it ridiculous, after all, to think that a son could forgive his father for beating the drum that sent him to his death? Isn't it ridiculous to think that a mouse could ever forgive anyone for such perfidy?

But still, here are the words Despereaux Tilling spoke to his father. He said, "I forgive you, Pa."

And he said those words because he sensed that it was the only way to save his own heart, to stop it from breaking in two. Despereaux, reader, spoke those words to save himself.

And then he turned from his father and spoke to the whole Mouse Council. "You were wrong," he said. "All of you. You asked me to **renounce** my **sins**; I ask you to renounce yours. You wronged me. **Repent.**"

"Never," said the Head Mouse.

Despereaux stood before the Mouse Council, and he realized that he was a different mouse than he had been the last time he had **faced** them. He had been to the dungeon and back up out of it. He knew things that they would never know; what they thought of him, he realized, did not matter, not at all.

And so, without saying another word, Despereaux turned and left the room.

After he was gone, the Head Mouse **slap**ped his trembling paw on the table. "Mice of the Council," he said, "we have been paid a visit by a ghost who has told us to repent. We will now take a **vote**. All in favor of saying that this visit did *not* occur, vote 'aye.'"

And from the members of the Mouse Council there came a tiny but **emphatic chorus** of "ayes."

Only one mouse said nothing. That mouse was Despereaux's father. Lester Tilling had turned his head away from the other members of the Mouse Council; he was trying to hide his tears.

He was crying, reader, because he had been forgiven.

Chapter Forty-one
the tears of a king

DESPEREAUX FOUND THE KING in the Pea's room, sitting on his daughter's bed, clutching the tapestry of her life to his chest. He was weeping. Although "weeping," really, is too small a word for the activity that the king had undertaken. Tears were cascading from his eyes. A small puddle had formed at his feet. I am not exaggerating. The king, it seemed, was intent on crying himself a river.

Reader, have you ever seen a king cry? When the powerful are made weak, when they are revealed to be human, to have hearts, their diminishment is nothing short of terrifying.

You can be sure that Despereaux was terrified.

Absolutely. But he spoke up anyway.

"Sir?" the mouse said to the king.

But the king did not hear him, and as Despereaux watched, King Phillip dropped the tapestry and took his great golden crown from his **lap** and used it to beat himself on the chest over and over again. The king, as I have already **mention**ed, had several faults. He was **nearsighted**. He made ridiculous, **unreasonable**, difficult-to-**enforce** laws. And, much in the way of Miggery Sow, he was not exactly the sharpest knife in the **drawer**.

But there was one **extraordinary**, wonderful, **admirable** thing about the king. He was a man who was able and willing to love with the whole of his heart. And just as he had loved the queen with the whole of his heart, so, too, he loved his daughter with the whole of it, even more than the whole. He loved the Princess Pea with every **particle** of his being, and she had been taken from him.

But what Despereaux had come to say to the king had to be said, and so he tried again. "Excuse me," he said. He wasn't certain, really, how a mouse should **address** a king. "Sir" did not seem like a big enough word. Despereaux thought about it for a long moment.

He cleared his **throat**. He spoke as loudly as he was capable of speaking. "Excuse me, Most Very Honored Head Person."

King Phillip stopped beating his crown against his chest. He looked around the room.

"Down here, Most Very Honored Head Person," said Despereaux.

The king, tears still falling from his eyes, looked at the floor. He **squint**ed.

"Is that a bug speaking to me?" he asked.

"No," said Despereaux, "I am a mouse. We met before."

"A mouse!" **bellow**ed the king. "A mouse is but one step removed from a rat."

"Sir," said Despereaux, "Most Very Honored Head Person, please, you have to listen to me. This is important. I know where your daughter is."

"You do?" said the king. He **sniff**ed. He blew his nose on his **royal cloak**. "Where?" he said, and as he **bent** over to look more closely at Despereaux, one tear, two tears, three **enormous**, king-sized tears fell with an **audible** *plop* onto Despereaux's head and rolled down his back, washing away the white of the flour and revealing his own brown **fur**.

"Sir, Most Very Honoured Head Person, sir," said Despereaux as he wiped the king's tears out of his own eyes, "she's in the **dungeon**."

"Liar," said the king. He sat back up. "I knew it. All

rodents are liars and thieves. She is not in the dungeon. My men have searched the dungeon."

"But no one really knows the dungeon except the rats, sir. There are thousands of places where she could be hidden, and only the rats would know. Your men would never be able to find her if the rats did not want her found."

"Accccck," said the king, and he clapped his hands over his ears. "Do not speak to me of rats and what they know!" he shouted. "Rats are illegal. Rats are against the law. There are no rats in my kingdom. They do not exist."

"Sir, Most Very Honored Head Person, that is not true. Hundreds of rats live in the dungeon of this castle. One of them has taken your daughter, and if you will send—"

The king started humming. "I can't hear you!" he stopped to shout. "I cannot hear you! And anyway, what you say is wrong because you are a rodent and therefore a liar." He started to hum again. And then he stopped and said, "I have hired fortunetellers. And a magician. They are coming from a distant land. They will tell me where my beautiful daughter is. They will speak the truth. A mouse cannot speak the truth."

"I am telling you the truth," said Despereaux. "I promise."

But the king would not listen. He sat with his hands over his ears. He hummed loudly. Big fat tears rolled down his face and fell to the floor.

Despereaux sat and stared at him in dismay. What should he do now? He put a nervous paw up to his neck and pulled at the red thread, and suddenly his dream came flooding back to him . . . the dark and the light and the knight swinging his sword and the terrible moment when he had realized that the suit of armor was empty.

And then, reader, as he stood before the king, a wonderful, amazing thought occurred to the mouse. What if the suit of armor had been empty for a reason? What if it had been empty because it was waiting?

For him.

"You know me," that was what the knight in his dream had said.

"Yes," said Despereaux out loud in wonder. "I do know you."

"I can't hear you," sang the king.

"I'll have to do it myself," said the mouse. "I will be the knight in shining armor. There is no other way. It has to be me."

Despereaux turned. He left the weeping king. He went to find the threadmaster.

Chapter Forty-two *the rest of the thread*

THE THREADMASTER was sitting **atop** his **spool** of thread, swinging his tail back and forth and eating a piece of **celery**.

"Well, look here," he said when he saw Despereaux. "Would you just look at that. It's the mouse who loved a human princess, back from the dungeon in one piece. The old threadmaster would say that I didn't do my job well, that because you are still alive I must have tied the thread incorrectly. But it is not so. And how do I know it is not so? Because the thread is still around your neck." He nodded and took a bite of his celery.

"I need the rest of it," said Despereaux.

"The rest of what? Your neck?"

"The rest of the thread."

"Well, I can't just hand it over to any old mouse," said the threadmaster. "They say red thread is special, **sacred**; though I, myself, after having spent so much time with it, know it for what it is."

"What is it?" said Despereaux.

"Thread," said the threadmaster. He **shrugged** and took another loud bite of celery. "Nothing more. Nothing less. But I **pretend**, friend, I pretend. And what, may I ask, do you **intend** to do with the thread?"

"Save the princess."

"Ah, yes, the princess. The beautiful princess. That's how this whole story started, isn't it?"

"I have to save her. There is no one but me to do it."

"It seems to be that way with most things. No one to do the really **disagreeable** jobs except oneself. And how, exactly, will you use a spool of thread to save a princess?"

"A rat has taken her and hidden her in the dungeon, so I have to go back to the dungeon, and it is full of **twists** and turns and hidden **chambers**."

"Like a **maze**," said the threadmaster.

"Yes, like a maze. And I have to find my way to her, wherever she is hidden, and then I have to lead her back out again, and the only way to do that is with the thread. Gregory the **jailer** tied a rope around his **ankle** so that he

198

would not **get lost**." As the mouse said this he **shudder**ed, thinking of Gregory and his broken rope, dying, lost in the darkness. "I," said Despereaux, "I . . . I will use thread."

The threadmaster nodded. "I see, I see," he said. He took a **meditative** bite of celery. "You, friend, are on a **quest**."

"I don't know what that is," said Despereaux.

"You don't have to know. You just have to feel **compel**led to do the thing, the impossible, important task **at hand**."

"Impossible?" said Despereaux.

"Impossible," said the threadmaster. "Important." He sat **chew**ing his celery and staring somewhere past Despereaux, and then suddenly he **leapt** off his spool.

"Who am I to stand in the way of a quest?" he said. "Roll her away."

"I can have it?"

"Yes. For your quest."

Despereaux put his front paws up and touched the spool. He gave it an **experimental** push forward.

"Thank you," he said, looking into the eye of the threadmaster.

"I don't know your name."

"Hovis."

"Thank you, Hovis."

"There's something else. Something that belongs with the thread." Hovis went into a corner and came back with a needle. "You can use it for protection."

"Like a sword," said Despereaux. "Like a knight would have."

"Yes," said Hovis. He gnawed off a length of thread and used it to tie the needle around Despereaux's waist. "Like so."

"Thank you, Hovis," said Despereaux. He put his right shoulder against the spool of thread and pushed it forward again.

"Wait," said Hovis. He stood up on his hind legs, put his paws on Despereaux's shoulders, and leaned in close to him. Despereaux smelled the sharp, clean scent of celery as the threadmaster bent his head, took hold of the thread around Despereaux's neck in his sharp teeth, and pulled on it hard.

"There," said Hovis, when the piece of thread broke and dropped to the ground. "Now you're free. You see, you're not going into the dungeon because you have to. You're going because you choose to."

"Yes," said Despereaux, "because I am on a quest." The word felt good and right in his mouth.

Quest.

"You see, you're not going into the dungeon because you have to. You're going because you choose to."

Say it, reader. Say the word "quest" out loud. It is an extraordinary word, is it not? So small and yet so full of **wonder**, so full of hope.

"Goodbye," said Hovis as Despereaux pushed the spool of thread out of the threadmaster's hole. "I have never known a mouse who has made it out of the dungeon only to go back into it again. Goodbye, friend. Goodbye, mouse among mice."

Chapter Forty-three ⌒
what Cook was stirring

THAT NIGHT Despereaux rolled the **thread** from the threadmaster's **lair**, along **innumerable hallways** and down three **flights** of stairs.

Reader, **allow** me to put this in **perspective** for you: Your **average** house mouse (or castle mouse, if you will) **weigh**s somewhere in the neighbourhood of four **ounces**.

Despereaux, as you well know, was in no way average. In fact, he was so **incredibly** small that he weighed about half of what the average mouse weighs: two ounces. That is all. Think about it: He was nothing but two ounces of mouse pushing a spool of thread that weighed almost as much as he did.

Honestly, reader, what do you think the chances are of

such a small mouse succeeding in his **quest**?

Zip. Zero. **Nada**.

Goose eggs.★

But you must, when you are **calculating** the **odds** of the mouse's success, factor in his love for the princess. Love, as we have already discussed, is a powerful, wonderful, **ridiculous** thing, capable of moving mountains. And spools of thread.

Even with the love and purpose in his heart, Despereaux was very, very tired when he reached the door to the castle kitchen at midnight. His **paws** were shaking and his muscles were jumping and the place where his tail should be was **throb**bing. And he still had a very, very long way to go, into the kitchen and down the many stairs of the dungeon, and then, through, **somehow**, some way, *through* the rat-filled darkness of the dungeon itself, not knowing where he was going . . . and oh, reader, when he stopped to **consider** what lay ahead of him Despereaux was filled with a **nasty** feeling of **despair**.

He **lean**ed his head against the spool of thread, and he smelled **celery** there and he thought of Hovis and how Hovis seemed to believe in him and his quest. So

---

★ goose egg 무득점, 0. 야구 경기에서 양팀이 한 점도 득점을 하지 못해서 득점판에 기록되는 숫자 0의 행렬이 마치 거위알 같다해서 붙여진 말이다.

the mouse raised his head and **squared** his shoulders and pushed the spool of thread forward again, into the kitchen, where he saw, too late, that there was a light burning.

Despereaux froze.

Cook was in the kitchen. She was bent over the stove. She was **stir**ring something.

Was it a sauce? No.

Was it a stew? No.

What Cook was stirring was . . . soup. Soup, reader! In the king's own castle, against the king's law, right under the king's very nose, Cook was making soup!

As the mouse looked on, Cook put her face into the steam rising from the pot and took a deep breath. She smiled a **beatific** smile, and the steam rose around her and caught the light of the candle and made a **halo** over her head.

Despereaux knew how Cook felt about mice in her kitchen. He remembered quite clearly her **instruct**ions to Mig **regard**ing himself: Kill him. The only good mouse is a dead mouse.

But he had to go through Cook's kitchen to get to the dungeon door. And he had no time to waste. Soon daylight would **dawn** and the whole castle would be awake and a mouse would have no chance at all of pushing a spool of thread across the floor without attracting **a great deal of** attention. He would have to **sneak** past the mouse-hating Cook now.

And so, **screwing** his courage to the **stick**ing place, Despereaux leaned against the spool of thread and set it rolling across the floor.

Cook turned from the stove, a **drip**ping spoon in her hand and a **frighten**ed look on her face, and shouted, "Who's there?"

Chapter Forty-four
whose ears are those?

"WHO'S THERE?" shouted Cook again.

Despereaux, wisely, said nothing.

The kitchen was silent.

"Hmmmmph," said Cook. "Nothing. It's nothing at all. Just my nervous Nellie ears playing tricks on me. You're an old fool," she said to herself as she turned back to the stove. "You're just an old fool afraid of being caught making soup."

Despereaux **slump**ed against the spool of thread. And as he leaned there, his heart **pound**ing, his paws shaking, a small wonderful something occurred. A midnight breeze entered the kitchen and danced over to the stove and picked up the **scent** of the soup and then **swirled** across the floor and delivered the smell right directly to the mouse's nose.

Despereaux put his head up in the air. He sniffed. He sniffed some more. He had never in his life smelled anything so lovely, so **inspiring**. With each sniff he took, he felt himself growing stronger, braver.

Cook leaned in close to the **kettle** and put the spoon in and took the spoon out and blew upon the spoon and then brought it to her lips and **sipped** and **swallow**ed.

"Hmmmmm," she said. "Huh." She took another sip. "Missing something," she said. "More salt, maybe." She put the spoon down and took up an **enormous** salt shaker* and **sprinkle**d salt into the kettle.

And Despereaux, feeling **embolden**ed by the smell of soup, again set to work pushing the spool of thread.

"Quickly," he said to himself, rolling the spool across the floor, "do it quickly. Do not think. Just push."

Cook **whirl**ed, the salt shaker in her hand, and shouted, "Who goes there?"

Despereaux stopped pushing. He hid behind the spool of thread as Cook took the candle from the stove and held it up high.

"Hmmmmmph," she said.

★ salt shaker 소금을 담아 뿌리는 용기.

208

The candlelight came closer, closer.

"What's this?"

The light came to rest directly on Despereaux's big ears sticking up from behind the spool of thread.

"Ho," said Cook, "whose ears are those?"

And the light from the candle then **shone** full in Despereaux's face.

"A mouse," said Cook. "A mouse in my kitchen."

Despereaux closed his eyes. He prepared for his death.

He waited, reader. And waited. And then he heard the sound of laughter.

He opened his eyes and looked at Cook.

"Ho," said Cook. "Ho-hee. For the first time in my life, I am glad to see a mouse in my kitchen.

"Why," she asked, "why am I glad?

"Ho-hee. Because a mouse is not a king's man here to **punish** me for making soup. That is why. Because a mouse is not a king's man here to take me to the dungeon for owning a spoon. Ho-hee. A mouse. I, Cook, am glad to see a mouse."

Cook's face was red and her stomach was shaking. "Ho-hee," she said again. "And not just any mouse. A mouse with a needle tied around his waist, a mouse with no tail. Ain't it lovely? Ho-hee." She shook her head and wiped at her eyes. "Look, mouse, these are extraordinary times. And because of that, we must have some peace between us. I will not ask what you are doing in my kitchen. And you, in return, will tell no one what I am cooking."

She turned then and went back to the stove and set down the candle and picked up the spoon and again put it in the pot of soup and took it back out and tasted the soup, **smacking** her lips together.

"Not right," she said, "not quite right. Missing something, still."

Despereaux did not move. He could not move. He was **paralyzed** by fear. He sat on the kitchen floor. One small tear fell out of his left eye. He had expected Cook to kill him.

Instead, reader, she had laughed at him.

And he was surprised how much her laughter hurt.

Chapter Forty-five
some soup

COOK STIRRED THE SOUP and then put the spoon down and held up the candle and looked over at Despereaux.

"What are you waiting for?" she said. "Go, go, go. There will never be another **opportunity** for a mouse to escape from my kitchen unharmed."

The smell of soup again **wafted** in Despereaux's direction. He put his nose up in the air. His **whiskers trembled.**

"Yes," said Cook. "That is soup that you are smelling. The princess, not that you would know or care, is missing, bless her **goodhearted** self. And times are terrible. And when times are terrible, soup is the answer.

Don't it smell like the answer?"

"Yes," said Despereaux. He nodded.

Cook turned away from him. She put the candle down and picked up her spoon and started to stir. "Oh," she said, "these are dark days." She shook her head. "And I'm kidding myself. There ain't no point in making soup unless others eat it. Soup needs another mouth to taste it, another heart to be warmed by it."

She stopped stirring. She turned and looked at Despereaux.

"Mouse," said Cook, "would you like some soup?" And then, without waiting for an answer, she took a **saucer** and spooned some soup into it and set it on the kitchen floor.

"Come closer," she said. "I don't aim to hurt you. I promise."

Despereaux **sniff**ed. The soup smelled wonderful, **incredible**. Keeping one eye on Cook, he stepped out from behind the spool of thread and **crept** closer.

"Go on," said Cook, "taste it."

Despereaux stepped onto the saucer. Soup covered his paws. He **bent** his head to the hot **broth**. He **sipped**. Oh, it was lovely. Garlic and chicken and watercress, the same soup that Cook had made the day the queen died.

"How is it?" asked Cook anxiously.

"Wonderful," said Despereaux.

"Too much garlic?" said Cook, **wring**ing her fat hands.

"No," said Despereaux. "It's perfect."

Cook smiled. "See?" she said. "There ain't a body, be it mouse or man, that ain't made better by a little soup."

Despereaux bent his head and sipped again, and Cook stood over him and smiled, saying, "It don't need a thing, then? Is that what you're saying? It's just right?"

Despereaux nodded.

He drank the soup in big, noisy **gulp**s. And when he stepped out of the saucer, his paws were **damp** and his whiskers were **drip**ping and his stomach was full.

Cook said to him, "Not done already, are you? Surely you ain't done. You must want more."

"I can't," said Despereaux. "I don't have time. I'm on my way to the dungeon to save the princess."

"Ho-hee." Cook laughed. "You, a mouse, are going to save the princess?"

"Yes," said Despereaux, "I'm on a **quest**."

"Well, don't let me stand in your way."

And so it was that Cook held open the door to the dungeon while Despereaux rolled the spool of thread through it. "Good luck," she said to him. "Ho-hee, good luck saving the princess."

"It's perfect," he said.

She closed the door behind her and then **lean**ed against it and shook her head. "And if that ain't an **indicator** of what strange days these are," she said to herself, "then I don't know what is. Me. Cook. Feeding a mouse soup and then wishing him good luck in saving the princess. Oh my. Strange days, **indeed**."

Chapter Forty-six
mouse blood, yes

DESPEREAUX STOOD at the top of the dungeon stairs and peered into the darkness that waited for him below.

"Oh," he said, "oh my."

He had forgotten how dark the dark of the dungeon could be. And he had forgotten, too, its terrible smell, the stench of rats, the odor of suffering.

But his heart was full of love for the princess and his stomach was full of Cook's soup and Despereaux felt brave and strong. And so he began, immediately and without despair, the hard work of maneuvering the spool of thread down the narrow dungeon steps.

Down, down, down went Despereaux Tilling and the

spool of thread. Slowly, oh so slowly, they went. And the passage was dark, dark, dark.

"I will tell myself a story," said Despereaux. "I will make some light. Let's see. It will begin this way: Once upon a time. Yes. Once upon a time, there was a mouse who was very, very small. **Exceptionally** small. And there was a beautiful human princess whose name was Pea. And it so happened that this mouse was the one who was selected by **fate** to **serve** the princess, to **honor** her and to save her from the darkness of a terrible dungeon."

This story cheered up Despereaux **considerably**. His eyes became **accustomed** to the **gloom**, and he moved down the stairs more quickly, more surely, **whispering** to himself the tale of a **devious** rat and a fat serving girl and a beautiful princess and a brave mouse and some soup and a spool of red thread. It was a story, in fact, very similar to the one you are reading right now, and the telling of it gave Despereaux strength.

He pushed the spool of thread with **a great deal of gusto**. And the thread, eager, perhaps, to begin its **honorable** task of **aiding** in the **rescue** of a princess, **leapt** forward and away from the mouse and went down the dungeon stairs ahead of him, without him.

"No," cried Despereaux, "no, no, no!" He broke into a **trot, chasing** the thread through the darkness.

But the spool had a head start. And it was faster. It flew down the dungeon stairs, leaving Despereaux far behind. When it came to the end of the stairs, it rolled and rolled, until finally, lazily, it came to a stop right at the **gnarled** paw of a rat.

"What have we here?" said the one-eared rat to the spool of thread.

"I will tell you what we have," said Botticelli Remorso, answering his own question. "We have red thread. How **delightful**. Red thread means one thing to a rat."

He put his nose up in the air. He sniffed. He sniffed again. "I smell . . . could it be? Yes, most **definite**ly it is. Soup. How strange." He sniffed some more. "And I smell tears. Human tears. Delightful. And I also **detect** the smell"—he put his nose high into the air and took a big **whiff**—"of flour and oil. Oh my, what a **cornucopia** of **scents**. But below it all, what do I smell? The blood of a mouse. **Unmistakably**, mouse blood, yes. Ha-ha-ha! Exactly! Mouse."

Botticelli looked down at the spool of thread and smiled. He gave it a gentle push with one paw.

"Red thread. Yes. Exactly. Just when you think that life in the dungeon cannot get any better, a mouse arrives."

Chapter Forty-seven
no choice

DESPEREAUX STOOD **TREMBLING** on the steps. The thread was most **definite**ly gone. He could not hear it. He could not see it. He should have tied it to himself when he had the chance. But it was too late now.

Despereaux's **dire** situation suddenly became quite clear to him. He was a two-**ounce** mouse alone in a dark, twisting **dungeon** full of rats. He had nothing but a **sewing** needle with which to **defend** himself. He had to find a princess. And he had to save her once he found her.

"It's impossible," he said to the darkness. "I can't do it."

He stood very **still**. "I'll go back," he said. But

he didn't move. "I have to go back." He took a step backward. "But I can't go back. I don't have a choice. I have no choice."

He took one step forward. And then another.

"No choice," his heart **beat** out to him as he went down the stairs, "no choice, no choice, no choice."

At the bottom of the stairs, the rat Botticelli sat waiting, and when Despereaux stepped from the last stair onto the dungeon floor Botticelli called out to him as if he were a **long-lost** friend. "Ah," said Botticelli, "there you are. Exactly. I've been waiting for you."

Despereaux saw the dark shape of a rat, that thing that he had feared and **dread**ed for so long, finally step out of the **gloom** and come to greet him.

"Welcome, welcome," said Botticelli.

Despereaux put his **paw** on the needle.

"Ah," said Botticelli, "you are **armed**. How **charming**." He put his paws up in the air. "I **surrender**. Oh, yes, certainly, exactly, I surrender!"

"I . . . ," said Despereaux.

"Yes," said Botticelli. "You." He took the **locket** from around his neck. He began to **swing** it back and forth.

"Please, go on."

"I don't want to hurt you," said Despereaux. "I just

need to get by you. I . . . I am on a **quest**."

"Really?" said Botticelli. "How **extraordinary**. A mouse on a quest." Back and forth, back and forth went the locket. "A quest for what?"

"A quest to save the princess."

"The princess," said Botticelli, "the princess, the princess. Everything seems to be about the princess these days. The king's men were down here searching for her, you know. They didn't find her. That goes without saying. But now a mouse has arrived. And he is on a quest to save the princess."

"Yes," said Despereaux. He took a step to the left of Botticelli.

"How **inspiring**," said Botticelli. He lazily took a step to his right, blocking Despereaux's way. "Why the hurry, little friend?"

"Because," said Despereaux, "I have to—"

"Yes. Yes. You have to save the princess. Exactly. But before you save her, you must find her. Correct?"

"Yes," said Despereaux.

"What if," said Botticelli, "what if I told you that I know exactly where the princess is? What if I told you that I could take you right directly to her?"

"Ummm," said Despereaux. His voice shook. His paw on the needle trembled. "Why would you do that?"

"Why would I do that? Why would I help you? Why . . . to be of service. To do my part for **humanity**. To **aid** in the **rescue** of a princess."

"But you are a . . ."

"A rat," supplied Botticelli. "Yes. I am a rat. And I see by your trem-trem-trembling that the greatly **exaggerat**ed rumors of our evil nature have reached your **oversize** ears."

"Yes," said Despereaux.

"If," said Botticelli, swinging the locket back and forth, "if you allow me to be of **assist**ance, you will be doing me a **tremendous** favor. Not only can I do a good **deed** for you and for the princess, but my actions will help to **dispel** this terrible **myth** of evil that seems to **surround** rats everywhere. Will you let me assist you? Will you let me assist myself and my kind?"

Reader, was it a trick?

Of course it was!

Botticelli did not want to be of service. Far from it. You know what Botticelli wanted. He wanted others to suffer. **Specifi**cally, he wanted this small mouse to suffer. How best to do that?

Why, take him right directly to what he wanted. The princess. Let him see what his heart desired, and then, and only then, **faced** with what he loved, would

Despereaux die. And at the end of it all, how tasty the mouse would be . . . **season**ed with hope and tears and **flour** and oil and **thwart**ed love!

"My name, little friend, is Botticelli Remorso. And you may trust me. You must trust me. Will you tell me your name?"

"Despereaux. Despereaux Tilling."

"Despereaux Tilling, take your paw from your weapon. Come with me."

Despereaux **stare**d at him.

"Come, come," said Botticelli, "**let go of** your needle. Take hold of my tail. I will lead you to your princess. I promise."

What, reader, in your experience, is the promise of a rat worth?

That's right.

Zero. **Zip. Nada.** Goose eggs.

But I must ask you this question too. What else was there for Despereaux to hold onto?

You are right again.

Nothing.

And so the mouse reached out. He took hold of the rat's tail.

Chapter Forty-eight
on the tail of a rat

HAVE YOU EVER had hold of the tail of a rat? At best it is an unpleasant **sensation**, **scaly** and cold, similar to holding onto a small, narrow snake. At worst, when you are **dependent** upon a rat for your survival, and when a part of you is certain that you are being led nowhere except to your death, it is a **hideous** sensation, **indeed**, to have nothing but a rat's tail to **cling** to.

Nonetheless, Despereaux held onto Botticelli Remorso. And the rat led him deeper and deeper into the dungeon.

Despereaux's eyes had, by this point, **adjust**ed quite well to the darkness, though it would have been better if they had not, for the things he saw made him **shiver** and shake.

What did he see?

He saw that the floor of the dungeon was littered with tufts of fur, knots of red thread and the skeletons of mice. Everywhere there were tiny white bones glowing in the darkness. And he saw, in the dungeon tunnels through which Botticelli led him, the bones of human beings too, grinning skulls and delicate finger bones, rising up out of the darkness and pointing toward some truth best left unspoken.

Despereaux closed his eyes.

But it didn't help. He saw as if his eyes were still open wide the bones, the tufts of hair, the knots of thread, the despair.

"Ha-ha, exactly!" Botticelli laughed as he negotiated the twists and turns. "Oh, yes, exactly."

If what was in front of Despereaux was too horrible to contemplate, what followed behind him was, perhaps, even worse: rats, a happy, hungry, vengeful parade of rats, their noses up in the air, sniffing, sniffing.

"Mouse!" sang out one rat joyfully.

"Yes, oh yes, mouse," agreed another. "But something else, too."

"Soup!" called out another rat.

"Yes, soup," the others agreed.

Despereaux closed his eyes.

"Blood!" sang a rat.

"Blood," they all agreed together.

And then they sang: "Here, mousie, mousie, mousie! Here, little mousie!"

Botticelli called out to the other rats. "Mine," he said. "This little treasure is all mine, gentlemen and ladies. Please, I **beg** you. Do not **infringe** on my discovery."

"Mr. Remorso," said Despereaux. He turned and looked behind him and saw the rats, their red eyes and their smiling mouths. He closed his eyes again. He kept them closed. "Mr. Remorso!" he shouted.

"Yes?" said Botticelli.

"Mr. Remorso," said Despereaux. And he was crying now. He couldn't help it. "Please. The princess."

"Tears!" shouted the rats. "We smell tears, mousie, we do."

"Please!" shouted Despereaux.

"Little friend," said Botticelli. "Little Despereaux Tilling. I promised you. And I will keep that promise."

The rat stopped.

"Look ahead of you," he said. "What do you see?"

Despereaux opened his eyes.

"Light," he said.

"Exactly," said Botticelli. "Light."

Chapter Forty-nine
what do you want, Miggery Sow?!

AGAIN, READER, we must go forward, before we go backward. We must **consider**, for a moment, what had **occurred** with the rat and the **serving** girl and the princess down in the dungeon before Despereaux made his way to them.

What happened was this: Roscuro led the Pea and Mig deep into the dungeon to a hidden **chamber**, and there he directed Mig to put the princess in chains.

"Gor," said Mig, "she's going to have a hard time learning her lessons if she's all **chain**ed up-like."

"Do as I say," said Roscuro.

"Maybe," said Mig, "before I lock her up, her and me could **switch outfits**, so we could start in already with her being me and me being a princess."

"Oh, yes," said Roscuro. "Certainly. A wonderful idea, Miss Miggery. Princess, take off your crown and give it to the serving girl."

The Pea sighed and took off her crown and handed it to Mig, and Mig put it on and it slid immediately right down her small head and came to rest, quite painfully, on her poor, abused ears. "It's a biggish thing," she said, "and painful-like."

"Well, well," said Roscuro.

"How do I look?" Mig asked, smiling at him.

"Ridiculous," he said. "Laughable."

Mig stood, blinking back tears. "You mean I don't look like a princess?" she said to the rat.

"I mean," said Roscuro, "you will *never* look like a princess, no matter how big a crown you put on your tiny head. You look exactly like the fool you are and always will be. Now, make yourself useful and chain the princess up. Dress-up time is over."

Mig sniffed and wiped at her eyes and then bent to look at the pile of chains and locks on the floor.

"And now, Princess," he said, "I'm afraid that the time for *your* truth has arrived. I will now tell you what your future holds. As you consigned me to darkness, so I consign you, too, to a life spent in this dungeon."

Mig looked up. "Ain't she going upstairs to be a serving maid?"

"No," said Roscuro.

"Ain't I going to be a princess, then?"

"No," said Roscuro.

"But I want to be a princess."

"No one," said Roscuro, "cares what you want."

As you know, reader, Miggery Sow had heard this **sentiment** expressed many times in her short life. But now, in the dungeon, it hit her full force: The rat was right. No one cared what she wanted. No one had ever cared. And perhaps, worst of all, no one ever would care.

"I want!" cried Mig.

"Shhhh," said the princess.

"Shut up," said the rat.

"I want . . . ," **sob**bed Mig, "I want . . . I want . . ."

"What do you want, Mig?" the princess said softly.

"Eh?" shouted Mig.

"What do you want, Miggery Sow?!" the princess shouted.

"Don't ask her that," said Roscuro. "Shut up. Shut up."

But it was too late. The words had been said; the question, at last, had been asked. The world stopped **spin**ning and all of creation held its breath, waiting to

"What do you want, Miggery Sow?!"

hear what it was that Miggery Sow wanted.

"I want . . . ," said Mig.

"Yes?" shouted the Pea.

"I want my ma!" cried Mig, into the silent, waiting world. "*I want my ma!*"

"Oh," said the princess. She held out her hand to Mig. Mig took hold of it.

"I want my mother, too," said the princess softly. And she **squeezed** Mig's hand.

"Stop it!" shouted Roscuro. "Chain her up. Chain her up."

"Gor," said Mig, "I ain't going to do it. You can't make me do it. *I* got the knife, don't I?" She took the knife and held it up.

"If you have any sense at all," said Roscuro, "and I **heartily** doubt that you do, you will not use that **instrument** on me. Without me you will never find your way out of the dungeon, and you will **starve** to death here, or worse."

"Gor," said Mig, "then lead us out now, or I will **chop** you up into little rat bits."

"No," said Roscuro. "The princess will stay here in the darkness. And you, Mig, will stay with her."

"But I want to go upstairs," said Mig.

"I'm afraid that we are **stuck** here, Mig," said the

princess, "unless the rat has a change of heart and decides to lead us out."

"There will be no changes of heart," said Roscuro. "None."

"Gor," said Mig. She lowered the knife.

And so the rat and the princess and the serving girl sat together in the dungeon as, outside the castle, the sun rose and moved through the sky and **sank** to the earth again, and night fell. They sat together until the candle had burned out and another one had to be lit. They sat together in the dungeon. They sat. And sat.

And, reader, **truthful**ly, they might be sitting there still if a mouse had not arrived.

Chapter Fifty
in which the princess says his name

"PRINCESS!" Despereaux shouted. "Princess, I have come to save you."

The Princess Pea heard her name. She looked up.

"Despereaux," she **whisper**ed.

And then she shouted it, "Despereaux!"

Reader, nothing is sweeter in this sad world than the sound of someone you love calling your name.

Nothing.

For Despereaux, the sound was worth everything: his lost tail, his trip to the **dungeon** and back out of it and back into it again.

He ran toward the princess.

But Roscuro, **baring** his teeth, blocked the mouse's

way.

The princess cried, "Oh no, rat, please. Don't hurt him. He is my friend."

Mig said, "Don't worry, Princess. I will save the meecy."

She took the kitchen knife. She aimed to cut off the rat's head, but she missed her **mark**.

"Whoopsie," said Miggery Sow.

Chapter Fifty-one
what is that smell?

"OWWWWWWWW!" screamed Roscuro.

He turned to look at where his tail had been, and as he did, Despereaux drew his needle and placed the sharp **tip** of it right where the rat's heart should be.

"Don't move," said Despereaux. "I will kill you."

"Ha-ha-ha!" Botticelli laughed from the **sidelines**. "Exactly." He **slapped** his tail on the floor in **approval**. "**Absolutely delightful**. A mouse is going to kill a rat. Oh, all of this is much better than I **anticipated**. I love it when mice come to the dungeon."

"Let me see!" said the other rats, pushing and **shoving**.

"Stand back," Botticelli told them, still laughing. "Let

"Don't move," said Despereaux. *"I will kill you."*

the mouse do his work."

Despereaux held the **trembling** needle against Roscuro's heart. The mouse knew that as a **knight** it was his duty to protect the princess. But would killing the rat really make the darkness go away?

Despereaux **bowed** his head ever so slightly. And as he did so, his **whiskers** brushed against the rat's nose.

Roscuro **sniffed**.

"What . . . is that smell?" he asked.

"Mousie blood!" shouted one rat.

"Blood and bones!" shouted another.

"You're smelling tears," said Botticelli. "Tears and **thwart**ed love."

"Exactly," said Roscuro. "And yet . . . there's something else."

He sniffed again.

And the smell of soup **crash**ed through his soul like a great wave, bringing with it the memory of light, the **chandelier**, the music, the laughter, everything, all the things that were not, would never, could never be available to him as a rat.

"Soup," **moan**ed Roscuro.

And he began to cry.

"Booooooo!" shouted Botticelli.

"Sssssssss," **hiss**ed the other rats.

"Kill me," said Roscuro. He fell down before Despereaux. "It will never work. All I wanted was some light. That is why I brought the princess here, really, just for some beauty . . . some light of my own."

"Please," shouted Botticelli, "do kill him! He is a **miserable** excuse for a rat."

"No, Despereaux," said the princess. "Don't kill him."

Despereaux lowered his needle. He turned and looked at the Pea.

"Boooo!" shouted Botticelli again. "Kill him! Kill him. All this goodness is making me sick. I've lost my **appetite.**"

"Gor!" shouted Mig, waving her knife. "I'll kill him."

"No, wait," said the princess. "Roscuro," she said to the rat.

"What?" he said. Tears were falling out of his eyes and **creep**ing down his whiskers and **drip**ping onto the dungeon floor.

And then the princess took a deep breath and put a hand on her heart.

I think, reader, that she was feeling the same thing that Despereaux had felt when he was **faced** with his father begging him for forgiveness. That is, Pea was **aware** suddenly of how **fragile** her heart was, how much darkness was inside it, fighting, always, with the light.

She did not like the rat. She would never like the rat, but she knew what she must do to save her own heart.

And so, here are the words that the princess spoke to her enemy.

She said, "Roscuro, would you like some soup?"

The rat sniffed. "Don't **torment** me," he said.

"I promise you," said the princess, "that if you lead us out of here, I will get Cook to make you some soup. And you can eat it in the **banquet** hall."

"Speaking of eating," shouted one of the rats, "give us the mousie!"

"Yeah," shouted another, "**hand over** the mouse!"

"Who would want him now?" said Botticelli. "The **flavor** of him will be **ruin**ed. All that forgiveness and goodness. Blech. I, for one, am leaving."

"Soup in the banquet hall?" Roscuro asked the princess.

"Yes," said the Pea.

"Really?"

"Truly. I promise."

"Gor!" shouted Mig. "Soup is **illegal**."

"But soup is good," said Despereaux.

"Yes," said the Pea. "Isn't it?"

The princess **bent** down before the mouse. "You are my knight," she said to him, "with a shining needle. And

I am so glad that you found me. Let's go upstairs. Let's eat some soup."

And, reader, they did.

Chapter Fifty-two
happily ever after

BUT THE QUESTION you want answered, I know, is did they live happily ever after?

Yes . . . and no.

What of Roscuro? Did he live happily ever after? Well . . . the Princess Pea gave him free **access** to the upstairs of the castle. And he was allowed to go back and forth from the darkness of the **dungeon** to the light of the upstairs. But, **alas,** he never really belonged in either place, the sad **fate,** I am afraid, of those whose hearts break and then **mend** in **crooked** ways. But the rat, in **seeking** forgiveness, did manage to **shed** some small light, some happiness, into another life.

How?

Roscuro, reader, told the princess about the prisoner who had once owned a red tablecloth, and the princess saw to it that the prisoner was **released**. And Roscuro led the man up out of the dungeon and to his daughter, Miggery Sow. Mig, as you might have guessed, did not get to be a princess. But her father, to **atone** for what he had done, treated her like one for the rest of his days.

And what of Despereaux? Did he live happily ever after? Well, he did not marry the princess, if that is what you mean by happily ever after. Even in a world as strange as this one, a mouse and a princess cannot marry.

But, reader, they can be friends.

And they were. Together, they had many adventures. Those adventures, however, are another story, and this story, I'm afraid, must now draw to a close.

But before you leave, reader, imagine this: Imagine an **adoring** king and a **glow**ing princess, a **serving** girl with a crown on her head and a rat with a spoon on his, all gathered around a table in a **banquet** hall. In the middle of the table, there is a great **kettle** of soup. Sitting in the place of **honor**, right next to the princess, is a very small mouse with big ears.

And **peek**ing out from behind a **dusty** velvet curtain, looking in amazement at the **scene** before them, are four

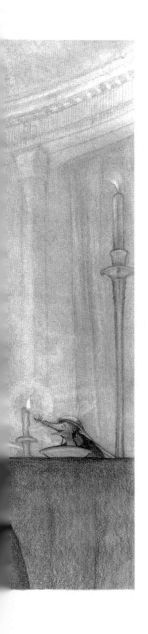

other mice.

"*Mon Dieu*, look, look," says Antoinette. "He lives. He lives! And he seems such the happy mouse."

"Forgiven," **whispers** Lester.

"**Cripes**," says Furlough, "**unbelievable**."

"Just so," says the **threadmaster** Hovis, smiling, "just so."

And, reader, it is just so.

Isn't it?

THE END

Coda

Do you remember when Despereaux was in the dungeon, cupped in Gregory the jailer's hand, whispering a story in the old man's ear?

I would like it very much if you thought of me as a mouse telling you a story, this story, with the whole of my heart, whispering it in your ear in order to save myself from the darkness, and to save you from the darkness, too.

"Stories are light," Gregory the jailer told Despereaux.

Reader, I hope you have found some light here.

THE TALE OF
Despereaux

The Tale of Despereaux

1판 1쇄   2013년 3월 4일
2판 2쇄   2024년 7월 15일

지은이   Kate DiCamillo
기획   이수영
책임편집   김보경 차소향
콘텐츠제작및감수   롱테일 교육 연구소
저작권   명채린
마케팅   두잉글 사업 본부

펴낸이   이수영
펴낸곳   롱테일북스
출판등록   제2015-000191호
주소   04033 서울특별시 마포구 양화로 113, 3층(서교동, 순흥빌딩)
전자메일   help@ltinc.net

ISBN 979-11-91343-95-3 14740

THE TALE OF

Despereaux

Kate DiCamillo

WORKBOOK

Contents

'아동 도서계의 노벨상!' 미국 최고 권위의 아동 문학상

뉴베리 상(Newbery Award)은 미국 도서관 협회에서 해마다 미국 아동 문학 발전에 가장 크게 이바지한 작가에게 수여하는 아동 문학상입니다. 1922년에 시작된 이 상은 미국에서 가장 오랜 역사를 지닌 아동 문학상이자, '아동 도서계의 노벨상'이라 불릴 만큼 높은 권위를 자랑하는 상입니다.

뉴베리 상은 그 역사와 권위만큼이나 심사 기준이 까다롭기로 유명한데, 심사단은 책의 주제 의식은 물론 정보의 깊이와 스토리의 정교함, 캐릭터와 문체의 적정성 등을 꼼꼼히 평가하여 수상작을 결정합니다.

그해 최고의 작품으로 선정된 도서에게는 '뉴베리 메달(Newbery Medal)'이라고 부르는 금색 메달을 수여하며, 최종 후보에 올랐던 주목할 만한 작품들에게는 '뉴베리 아너(Newbery Honor)'라는 이름의 은색 마크를 수여합니다.

뉴베리 상을 받은 도서는 미국의 모든 도서관에 비치되어 더 많은 독자들을 만나게 되며, 대부분 수십에서 수백만 부가 판매되는 베스트셀러가 됩니다. 뉴베리 상을 수상한 작가는 그만큼 필력과 작품성을 인정받게 되어, 수상 작가의 다른 작품들 또한 수상작 못지않게 커다란 주목과 사랑을 받습니다.

왜 뉴베리 수상작인가?
쉬운 어휘로 쓰인 '검증된' 영어원서!

뉴베리 수상작들은 '검증된 원서'로 국내 영어 학습자들에게 큰 사랑을 받고 있습니다. 뉴베리 수상작이 원서 읽기에 좋은 교재인 이유는 무엇일까요?

1. 아동 문학인 만큼 어휘가 어렵지 않습니다.
2. 어렵지 않은 어휘를 사용하면서도 '문학상'을 수상한 만큼 문장의 깊이가 상당합니다.
3. 적당한 난이도의 어휘와 깊이 있는 문장으로 구성되어 있기 때문에 초등 고학년부터 성인까지, 영어 초보자부터 실력자까지 모든 영어 학습자들이 읽기에 좋습니다.

실제로 뉴베리 수상작은 국제중·특목고에서는 입시 필독서로, 대학교에서는 영어 강독 교재로 다양하고 폭넓게 활용되고 있습니다. 이런 이유로 뉴베리 수상작은 한국어 번역서보다 오히려 원서가 훨씬 많이 판매되는 기현상을 보이고 있습니다.

'베스트 오브 베스트'만을 엄선한 「뉴베리 컬렉션」

「뉴베리 컬렉션」은 뉴베리 메달 및 아너 수상작, 그리고 뉴베리 수상 작가의 유명 작품들을 엄선하여 한국 영어 학습자들을 위한 최적의 교재로 재탄생시킨 영어 원서 시리즈입니다.

1. 어휘 수준과 문장의 난이도, 분량 등 국내 영어 학습자들에게 적합한 정도를 종합적으로 검토하여 선정하였습니다.
2. 기존 원서 독자층 사이의 인기도까지 감안하여 최적의 작품들을 선별하였습니다.
3. 판형이 좁고 글씨가 작아 읽기 힘들었던 원서 디자인을 대폭 수정하여, 판형을 시원하게 키우고 읽기에 최적화된 영문 서체를 사용하여 가독성을 극대화하였습니다.
4. 함께 제공되는 워크북은 어려운 어휘를 완벽하게 정리하고 이해력을 점검하는 퀴즈를 덧붙여 독자들이 원서를 보다 쉽고 재미있게 읽을 수 있도록 구성하였습니다.
5. 기존에 높은 가격에 판매되어 구입이 부담스러웠던 오디오북을 부록으로 제공하여 리스닝과 소리 내어 읽기에까지 원서를 두루 활용할 수 있도록 했습니다.

케이트 디카밀로(Kate DiCamillo)는 화려한 수상 경력을 가지고 있는, 미국의 대표적인 아동 문학 작가입니다. 그녀는 『Because of Winn-Dixie』로 뉴베리 아너를 수상하여 이름을 알리기 시작했고, 『The Tiger Rising』으로 전미도서상(National Book Award)의 최종 후보에 올랐습니다. 그리고 판타지 문학 작품인 『The Tale of Despereaux』는 "미국 아동 문학에 가장 크게 기여한" 작품이라는 평과 함께 뉴베리 메달을 수상하여 큰 인기몰이를 하였습니다. 또한 『The Miraculous Journey of Edward Tulane』으로 우수한 아동 문학에 수여하는 보스턴 글로브-혼 도서상(Boston Globe-Horn Book Award)을 받는 등 문학성을 여러 차례 검증 받고 있습니다.

『The Tale of Despereaux』는 절대 영웅처럼 보이지 않는 영웅, 생쥐 데스페로(Despereaux)의 이야기를 담고 있습니다. 데스페로는 작고 병약한데다 큰 귀를 가지고 태어나, 다른 생쥐들에게 놀림을 받습니다. 사람의 노래를 들으며 감동받고 책을 갉아먹는 대신 이야기를 읽는 데스페로는 심지어 성에 사는 피(Pea) 공주에게 사랑에 빠집니다. 데스페로의 이런 유별난 행동은 생쥐 공동체에서 도저히 용서받을 수 없었고, 생쥐 의회는 그를 지하 감옥에 보내기로 결정합니다. 어두운 지하 감옥에는 시궁쥐 로스쿠로(Roscuro)가 살고 있습니다. 빛을 동경했지만 결국 어둠 속에서 살게 된 로스쿠로는 공주의 시녀가 된 미거리 소우(Miggery Sow)를 꾀어 음모를 꾸미려고 합니다. 사랑하는 피 공주가 위험에 빠졌다는 사실을 알게 된 데스페로는 공주를 지키기 위해 칼 대신 바늘을 차고 감옥을 탈출합니다.
작가 케이트 디카밀로는 작고 보잘것없는 생쥐 데스페로를 통해 독자들에게 절망에서 희망이 피어나는 모습을 생생히 전달합니다. 그리고 모든 고난을 겪어낼 수 있는 것은 바로 사랑이라는 사실을 알려줍니다. 이 작품은 2004년 뉴베리 메달을 수상하였고, 2008년 애니메이션으로도 만들어져 많은 사람들에게 사랑 받았습니다.

원서 본문

내용이 담긴 원서 본문입니다.
원어민이 읽는 일반 원서와 같은 텍스트지만, 암기해야 할 중요 어휘들은 볼드체로 표시되어 있습니다. 이 어휘들은 지금 들고 계신 워크북에 챕터별로 정리되어 있습니다.

학습 심리학 연구 결과에 따르면, 한 단어씩 따로 외우는 단어 암기는 거의 효과가 없다고 합니다. 단어를 제대로 외우기 위해서는 문맥(context) 속에서 단어를 암기해야 하며, 한 단어당 문맥 속에서 15번 이상 마주칠 때 완벽하게 암기할 수 있다고 합니다.

이 책의 본문에서는 중요 어휘를 볼드체로 강조하여, 문맥 속의 단어들을 더 확실히 인지(word cognition in context)하도록 돕고 있습니다. 또한 대부분의 중요 단어들은 다른 챕터에서도 반복해서 등장하기 때문에 이 책을 읽는 것만으로도 자연스럽게 어휘력을 향상시킬 수 있습니다.

또한 본문 하단에는 내용 이해를 돕기 위한 '각주'가 첨가되어 있습니다. 각주는 굳이 암기할 필요는 없지만, 알아 두면 도움이 될 만한 정보를 설명하고 있습니다. 각주를 참고하면 스토리를 더 깊이 있게 이해할 수 있어 원서를 읽는 재미가 배가됩니다.

워크북(Workbook)

Check Your Reading Speed

해당 챕터의 단어 수가 기록되어 있어, 리딩 속도를 측정할 수 있습니다. 특히 리딩 속도를 중시하는 독자들이 유용하게 사용할 수 있습니다.

Build Your Vocabulary

본문에 볼드 표시되어 있던 단어들이 정리되어 있습니다. 리딩 전, 후에 반복해서 보면 원서를 더욱 쉽게 읽을 수 있고, 어휘력도 빠르게 향상될 것입니다.

단어는 〈스펠링 – 빈도 – 발음기호 – 품사 – 한글 뜻 – 영문 뜻〉 순서로 표기되어 있으며 빈도 표시(★)가 많을수록 필수 어휘입니다. 반복해서 등장하는 단어는 빈도 대신 '복습'으로 표기되어 있습니다. 품사는 아래와 같이 표기했습니다.

n. 명사 | **a.** 형용사 | **ad.** 부사 | **vi.** 자동사 | **vt.** 타동사 | **v.** 자·타동사 모두 쓰이는 동사

conj. 접속사 | **prep.** 전치사 | **int.** 감탄사 | **phrasal v.** 구동사 | **idiom** 숙어 및 관용구

Comprehension Quiz

간단한 퀴즈를 통해 읽은 내용에 대한 이해력을 점검해 볼 수 있습니다.

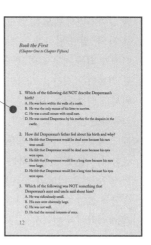

「뉴베리 컬렉션」 이렇게 읽어 보세요!

아래와 같이 프리뷰(Preview) → 리딩(Reading) → 리뷰(Review) 세 단계를 거치면서 읽으면, 더욱 효과적으로 영어실력을 향상할 수 있습니다!

1. 프리뷰(Preview) : 오늘 읽을 내용을 먼저 점검하자!

• 워크북을 통해 오늘 읽을 챕터에 나와 있는 단어들을 쭉 훑어봅니다. 어떤 단어들이 나오는지, 내가 아는 단어와 모르는 단어가 어떤 것들이 있는지 가벼운 마음으로 살펴봅니다.

• 평소처럼 하나하나 쓰면서 암기하려고 하지는 마세요! 익숙하지 않은 단어들을 주의 깊게 보되, 어차피 리딩을 하면서 점차 익숙해질 단어라는 것을 기억하며 빠르게 훑어봅니다.

• 뒤 챕터로 갈수록 '복습'이라고 표시된 단어들이 늘어나는 것을 알 수 있습니다. '복습' 단어인데도 여전히 익숙하지 않다면 더욱 신경을 써서 봐야겠죠? 매일매일 꾸준히 읽는다면, 익숙한 단어들이 점점 많아진다는 것을 몸으로 느낄 수 있습니다.

2. 리딩(Reading) : 내용에 집중하며 빠르게 읽어 나가자!

• 프리뷰를 마친 후 바로 리딩을 시작합니다. 방금 살펴봤던 어휘들을 문장 속에서 다시 만나게 되는데 이 과정에서 단어의 쓰임새와 어감을 자연스럽게 익히게 됩니다.

• 모르는 단어나 이해되지 않는 문장이 나오더라도 멈추지 말고 전체적인 맥락을 잡아가면서 속도감 있게 읽어 나가세요. 이해되지 않는 문장들은 따로 표시를 하되, 일단 넘어가고 계속 읽는 것이 좋습니다. 뒷부분을 읽다 보면 자연히 이해가 되는 경우도 있고, 정 이해가 되지 않는 부분은 리딩을 마친 이후에 따로 리뷰하는 시간을 가지면 됩니다. 문제집을 풀듯이 모든 문장을 분석하면서 원서를 읽는 것이 아니라, 리딩을 할 때는 리딩에만, 리뷰를 할 때는 리뷰에만 집중하는 것이 필요합니다.

• 볼드 처리된 단어의 의미가 궁금하더라도 워크북을 바로 펼치지 마세요. 정 궁금하다면 한 번씩 참고하는 것도 나쁘진 않지만, 워크북과 원서를 번갈아 보면서 읽는 것은 리딩의 흐름을 끊고 단어 하나하나에 집착하는 좋지 않은 리딩 습관을 심어 줄 수 있습니다.

• 같은 맥락에서 번역서를 구해 원서와 동시에 번갈아 보는 것도 좋은 방법이 아닙니다. 한글 번역을 가지고 있다고 해도 일단 영어로 읽을 때는 영어에만 집중하고 어느 정도 분량을 읽은 후에 번역서와 비교하도록 하세요. 모든 문장을

일일이 번역해서 완벽하게 이해하려는 것은 오히려 좋지 않은 리딩 습관을 심어 주어 장기적으로는 바람직하지 않은 결과를 얻을 수 있습니다. 처음부터 완벽하게 이해하려고 하는 것보다는 빠른 속도로 2~3회 반복해서 읽는 방식이 실력 향상에 더 도움이 됩니다. 만일 반복해서 읽어도 내용이 전혀 이해되지 않아 곤란하다면 책 선정에 문제가 있다고 할 수 있습니다. 그럴 때는 좀 더 쉬운 책을 골라 실력을 다진 뒤 다시 도전하는 것이 좋습니다.

• 초보자라면 분당 150단어의 리딩 속도를 목표로 잡고 리딩을 합니다. 분당 150단어는 원어민이 말하는 속도로, 영어 학습자들이 리스닝과 스피킹으로 넘어가기 위해 가장 기초적으로 달성해야 하는 단계입니다. 분당 50~80단어 정도의 낮은 리딩 속도를 가지고 있는 경우는 대부분 영어 실력이 부족해서라기보다 '잘못된 리딩 습관'을 가지고 있어서 그렇습니다. 이해력이 조금 떨어진다고 하더라도 분당 150단어까지는 속도에 대한 긴장감을 놓치지 말고 속도감 있게 읽어 나가도록 하세요.

3. 리뷰(Review) : 이해력을 점검하고 꼼꼼하게 다시 살펴보자!

• 해당 챕터의 Comprehension Quiz를 통해 이해력을 점검해 봅니다.

• 오늘 만난 어휘들을 다시 한번 복습합니다. 이때는 읽으면서 중요하다고 생각했던 단어를 연습장에 써 보면서 꼼꼼하게 외우는 것도 좋습니다.

• 이해가 되지 않는다고 표시해 두었던 부분도 주의 깊게 분석해 봅니다. 다시 한번 문장을 꼼꼼히 읽고, 어떤 이유에서 이해가 되지 않았는지 생각해 봅니다. 따로 메모를 남기거나 노트를 작성하는 것도 좋은 방법입니다.

• 사실 꼼꼼히 리뷰하는 것은 매우 고된 과정입니다. 원서를 읽고 리뷰하는 시간을 가지는 것이 영어 실력 향상에 많은 도움이 되기는 하지만, 이 과정을 철저히 지키려다가 원서 읽기의 재미를 반감시키는 것은 바람직하지 않습니다. 그럴 때는 차라리 리뷰를 가볍게 하는 것이 좋을 수 있습니다. '내용에 빠져서 재미있게', 문제집에서는 상상도 못할 '많은 양'을 읽으면서, 매일매일 조금씩 꾸준히 실력을 키워가는 것이 원서를 활용하는 기본적인 방법이며, 영어 공부의 왕도입니다. 문제집 풀듯이 원서 읽기를 시도하고 접근해서는 실패할 수밖에 없습니다.

• 이런 방식으로 원서를 끝까지 다 읽었다면, 다시 반복해서 읽거나 오디오북을 활용하는 등 다양한 방식으로 원서 읽기를 확장해 나갈 수 있습니다. 이에 대한 자세한 안내가 워크북 말미에 실려 있습니다.

Book the First
(Chapter One to Chapter Fifteen)

1. Which of the following did NOT describe Despereaux's birth?
   A. He was born within the walls of a castle.
   B. He was the only mouse of his litter to survive.
   C. He was a small mouse with small ears.
   D. He was named Despereaux by his mother for the despairs in the castle.

2. How did Despereaux's father feel about his birth and why?
   A. He felt that Despereaux would be dead soon because his ears were small.
   B. He felt that Despereaux would be dead soon because his eyes were open.
   C. He felt that Despereaux would live a long time because his ears were large.
   D. He felt that Despereaux would live a long time because his eyes were open.

3. Which of the following was NOT something that Despereaux's aunt and uncle said about him?
   A. He was ridiculously small.
   B. His ears were obscenely large.
   C. He was not well.
   D. He had the normal interests of mice.

4. When Despereaux was taught to track down crumbs, what did he show interest in instead?
   A. He showed interest in eating cake instead of cake crumbs.
   B. He showed interest in the sounds of people eating.
   C. He showed interest in a sweet sound that no other mice seemed to hear.
   D. He showed interest in the sounds of crumbs hitting the floor.

5. What did Furlough try to teach Despereaux?
   A. Furlough tried to teach him the art of scratching.
   B. Furlough tried to teach him the art of digging.
   C. Furlough tried to teach him the art of searching for crumbs.
   D. Furlough tried to teach him the art of scurrying.

6. Why did Despereux tell Merlot that he could not nibble the pages of the book?
   A. It would spoil his appetite.
   B. It would ruin the story.
   C. It would cut his tongue.
   D. It would taste awful.

7. Why was Despereaux free to wander the castle?
   A. Despereaux's siblings stopped trying to teach him mouse ways.
   B. Despereaux's siblings thought he had learned everything well.
   C. Despereaux's parents wanted him to learn about the real world.
   D. Despereaux's parents thought he would be happy with humans.

8. Why did Despereaux reveal himself to the princess and king?
   A. He wanted to get closer to hear the music being played.
   B. He wanted to introduce himself to them.
   C. He wanted to warn them of a dangerous plan by rats.
   D. He wanted them to hear his song that he made for their music.

9. How did the princess react to Despereaux and how did he react to her?
   A. She was disgusted by him and he felt bad about himself.
   B. She smiled at him and touched his head and he smiled back and fell in love.
   C. She smiled at him, but Despereaux was too shy to smile back and went back home.
   D. She smiled at him but Despereaux was frightened and trembled before her.

10. What did Furlough do when he saw Despereaux at the foot of the king?
    A. He was happy that Despereaux finally found friends and did nothing.
    B. He went off to tell Lester what he had seen.
    C. He went to tell his siblings to help him save Despereaux.
    D. He rushed out and grabbed Despereaux in order to protect him.

11. Who decided to call the Mouse Council to meeting and how was it done?
    A. Lester used a drum to call the Mouse Council.
    B. Lester used a horn to call the Mouse Council.
    C. Furlough used a guitar to call the Mouse Council.
    D. Furlough used a drum to call the Mouse Council.

12. Which of the following was NOT something that Lester said about Despereaux?
    A. He could not be his son.
    B. The French blood from his mother made him crazy.
    C. He would be the end of all of them.
    D. He was destined to be a heroic mouse in the castle.

13. Why did the king react negatively toward Despereaux?
    A. He thought that mice were ruining the castle's food.
    B. He thought that Despereaux was a bug and hated bugs.
    C. He thought that mice were rodents and closely related to rats which he hated.
    D. He thought that mice spread diseases among humans.

14. What was the last ancient rule of mice that Despereaux broke?
    A. He spoke to a human.
    B. He touched a human.
    C. He stood on his back legs in front of a human.
    D. He read a human book.

15. What did the Mouse Council decide to do to punish Despereaux?
    A. They decided to send him outside of the castle to live in the wild.
    B. They decided to send him to the dungeon to go to the human prisoners.
    C. They decided to send him to the kitchen to do a dangerous job of stealing food.
    D. They decided to send him to the dungeon to go to the rats.

16. How did Lester react to the decision to punish Despereaux?
    A. He loudly opposed the decision to punish his own son.
    B. He did nothing to oppose the decision and only cried.
    C. He voted in favor of punishing his own son and did not react at all.
    D. He tried to have another vote taken to decide his son's fate.

17. Where was Despereaux when Furlough was sent to bring him to the council?
    A. He was in the library reading the story about the knight and the fair maiden.
    B. He was in the princess's bedroom still talking with the king and princess.
    C. He was in the kitchen eating cake crumbs.
    D. He was in his family's home thinking about the princess.

18. What topic did Despereaux try to discuss with Furlough?
    A. He tried to talk about justice.
    B. He tried to talk about fairy tales.
    C. He tried to talk about honor.
    D. He tried to talk about love.

19. For what reasons did Despereaux say he broke the rules?
    A. For food and love
    B. For music and friends
    C. For music and love
    D. For music and food

20. What did Despereaux do when given the chance to renounce his actions?
    A. He sincerely renounced his actions.
    B. He only renounced his actions in order to save his life.
    C. He refused to renounce his actions because he loved the princess.
    D. He refused to renounce his actions because he was angry with the mice.

21. After being punished, how did Despereaux's feel about the story about the knight and the fair maiden?
    A. He doubted whether the knight and maiden had really lived happily ever after.
    B. He felt confident that love was a good thing.
    C. He felt that stories were for children and only told lies.
    D. He felt certain that he could save himself and the princess just like the knight in the story.

22. What did the threadmaster urge Despereaux to do?
    A. He urged him to renounce his love for the princess.
    B. He urged him to be brave for the princess.
    C. He urged him to be afraid of the rats in the dungeon.
    D. He urged him to accept his punishment quietly.

23. How did Antoinette react to hearing about Despereaux's fate?
    A. She cried but let the hooded rats take him away.
    B. She quietly accepted his fate and watched them take him away.
    C. She dramatically fainted and said one last word to Despereaux.
    D. She had her heart broken and died immediately.

24. What was the meaning of the French word that Antoinette shouted to Despereaux and what emotion did it carry?
    A. It meant fight and carried strength.
    B. It meant fight and carried comfort.
    C. It meant farewell and carried comfort.
    D. It meant farewell and carried sorrow.

25. How did the hooded mice lead Despereaux to the dungeon?
   A. They led him walking by a thread tied around his neck.
   B. They pulled him in a cage on wheels.
   C. They carried him down a secret passageway.
   D. They pushed him from behind with sticks.

26. What surprised Despereaux about the hooded mice?
   A. They had no idea why Despereaux was being sent to the dungeon.
   B. One of the mice was his own brother, Furlough.
   C. They knew the way to the dungeon very well.
   D. They were actually rats and not mice.

27. What did Despereaux do to be brave in the darkness?
   A. He fainted and hoped that nobody would find him.
   B. He tried to find a match to bring some light.
   C. He began to tell the story about the knight to himself out loud.
   D. He closed his eyes and imagined being back with the princess.

28. What was Despereaux's first assumption about the voice booming in the darkness?
   A. It belonged to the world's largest rat.
   B. It belonged to a ghost haunting the dungeon.
   C. It belonged to the castle's jailer.
   D. It belonged to a human prisoner.

29. Why was Gregory in the dungeon?
   A. He was sent there to protect mice from the rats.
   B. He was lost and searching for a way back to the castle.
   C. He was a prisoner being punished from stealing from the king.
   D. He was the castle's jailer who kept watch over the dungeon and prisoners.

30. What did Gregory say about stories and why was this important for Despereaux?
    A. Stories were light and telling Gregory a story would save Despereaux's life.
    B. Stories were light and telling Gregory a story would give Despereaux comfort.
    C. Stories were light and telling Gregory a story would make Gregory upset.
    D. Stories were light and telling Gregory a story would protect him from rats.

Check Your Reading Speed

1분에 몇 단어를 읽는지 리딩 속도를 측정해보세요.

$$\frac{505 \text{ words}}{\text{reading time ( ) sec}} \times 60 = (\quad) \text{ WPM}$$

Build Your Vocabulary

litter*
[lítər]

n. 한 배에서 난 새끼들; 쓰레기, 어질러진 물건; vt. (새끼를) 낳다; 어질러 놓다
A litter is a group of animals born to the same mother at the same time.

exhaust*
[igzɔ́:st]

vt. 기진맥진하게 만들다; 다 써 버리다, 고갈시키다 (exhausted a. 기운이 빠진)
If something exhausts you, it makes you so tired, either physically or mentally, that you have no energy left.

ordeal*
[ɔ:rdíːəl]

n. 고생, 호된 시련
If you describe an experience or situation as an ordeal, you think it is difficult and unpleasant.

for nothing

idiom 헛되이; 까닭 없이, 아무 이유 없이
If you do something for nothing, you don't achieve what you wanted.

sigh*
[sai]

v. 한숨 쉬다; n. 한숨, 탄식
When you sigh, you let out a deep breath, as a way of expressing feelings such as disappointment, tiredness, or pleasure.

luggage**
[lʌ́gidʒ]

n. 여행용 가방, 수하물
Luggage is the suitcases and bags that you take with you when travel.

diplomat*
[dípləmæt]

n. 외교관; 외교[사교]에 능한 사람
A diplomat is a senior official who discusses affairs with another country on behalf of his or her own country.

tragedy*
[trǽdʒədi]

n. 비극, 비극적인 이야기
A tragedy is an extremely sad event or situation.

handkerchief**
[hǽŋkərtʃif]

n. 손수건
A handkerchief is a small square piece of fabric which you use for blowing your nose.

sniff*
[snif]

v. 코를 훌쩍이다; 냄새를 맡다, 코를 킁킁거리다; n. 냄새 맡음
When you sniff, you breathe in air through your nose hard enough to make a sound, for example when you are trying not to cry, or in order to show disapproval.

despair*
[dispέər]

n. 절망, 자포자기; vi. 절망하다
Despair is the feeling that everything is wrong and that nothing will improve.

20

shard
[ʃaːrd]

n. (유리·도자기 등의) 파편, 사금파리
Shards are pieces of broken glass, pottery, or metal.

reflect**
[riflékt]

v. 비추다, 반사하다; 반영하다, 나타내다 (reflection n. (거울·물 등에 비친) 영상)
When something is reflected in a mirror or in water, you can see its image in the mirror or in the water.

gasp*
[gæsp]

v. 숨이 턱 막히다, 헉 하고 숨을 쉬다; n. (숨이 막히는 듯) 헉 하는 소리를 냄
When you gasp, you take a short quick breath through your mouth, especially when you are surprised, shocked, or in pain.

makeup*
[méikʌp]

n. 화장, 분장; 조립, 구성
Makeup consists of things such as lipstick, eye shadow, and powder which some women put on their faces to make themselves look more attractive or which actors use to change or improve their appearance.

fright*
[frait]

n. 섬뜩한 것, 추악한 것; 놀람, 공포, 경악
A fright is an experience which makes you suddenly afraid.

scrap*
[skræp]

n. 조각, 파편; vt. 부스러기로 만들다, 해체하다
A scrap of something is a very small piece or amount of it.

determined*
[ditə́ːrmind]

a. 결연한, 굳게 결심한
If you are determined to do something, you have made a firm decision to do it and will not let anything stop you.

shine***
[ʃain]

v. (shone—shone) 빛나(게 하)다, 반짝이다; n. 빛, 빛남, 광채
Something that shines is very bright and clear because it is reflecting light.

squeeze*
[skwiːz]

v. (억지로) 비집고 들어가다; (꼭) 짜다, 쥐다; n. (꼭) 짜기
If you squeeze a person or thing somewhere or if they squeeze there, they manage to get through or into a small space.

stare*
[stɛər]

v. 응시하다, 뚫어지게 보다
If you stare at someone or something, you look at them for a long time.

ceiling**
[síːliŋ]

n. 천장
A ceiling is the horizontal surface that forms the top part or roof inside a room.

oval*
[óuvəl]

n. 타원체; a. 타원형의, 달걀 모양의
Oval is a shape like a circle, but wider in one direction than the other.

brilliance
[bríljəns]

n. 환한 빛, 광명, 광택
Brilliance is great brightness of light or color.

proclaim*
[proukléim]

vt. 선언하다, 공포하다
If you proclaim something, you state it in a forceful way.

ruin**
[ruːin]

v. 망치다, 못쓰게 만들다; 몰락하다; n. 폐허; 파멸
To ruin something means to severely harm, damage, or spoil it.

Check Your Reading Speed

1분에 몇 단어를 읽는지 리딩 속도를 측정해보세요.

$$\frac{441 \text{ words}}{\text{reading time ( ) sec}} \times 60 = (\quad) \text{ WPM}$$

Build Your Vocabulary

exist[***]
[igzíst]

v. 존재하다, 실재하다 (existence n. 존재, 생존)
If something exists, it is present in the world as a real thing.

speculate[*]
[spékjulèit]

v. 추측하다, 짐작하다; 사색하다, 심사숙고하다 (speculation n. 추론, 추측)
If you speculate about something, you make guesses about its nature or identity, or about what might happen.

community[**]
[kəmjú:nəti]

n. 공동[지역] 사회, 공동체; 일반 사회, 대중
The community is all the people who live in a particular area or place.

ridiculous[**]
[ridíkjuləs]

a. 터무니없는; 웃기는, 우스꽝스러운
If you say that something or someone is ridiculous, you mean that they are very foolish.

narrow[***]
[nǽrou]

v. 좁히다, 작아지다; a. 좁은, 편협한
If your eyes narrow or if you narrow your eyes, you almost close them, for example because you are angry or because you are trying to concentrate on something.

entire[*]
[intáiər]

a. 전체의; 완전한 (entirely ad. 전적으로, 완전히)
You use entire when you want to emphasize that you are referring to the whole of something, for example, the whole of a place, time, or population.

wrap[**]
[ræp]

v. 감싸다; 포장하다; n. 싸개, 덮개
If someone wraps their arms, fingers, or legs around something, they put them firmly around it.

stare[복습]
[stɛər]

v. 응시하다, 뚫어지게 보다
If you stare at someone or something, you look at them for a long time.

observe[***]
[əbzɔ́:rv]

v. 관찰하다, 목격하다; 알다, 알아채다
If you observe a person or thing, you watch them carefully, especially in order to learn something about them.

donkey[*]
[dáŋki]

n. 당나귀
A donkey is an animal which is like a horse but which is smaller and has longer ears.

obscene
[əbsí:n]

a. 터무니없는, 가당찮은; 음란한, 외설적인 (obscenely ad. 터무니없이)
If you describe something as obscene, you disapprove of it very strongly and consider it to be offensive or immoral.

wiggle
[wigl]

v. (좌우로) 움직이다; (몸을) 뒤흔들다; n. 뒤흔듦
If you wiggle something or if it wiggles, it moves up and down or from side to side in small quick movements.

gasp^{복습}
[gæsp]

v. 숨이 턱 막히다, 헉 하고 숨을 쉬다; n. (숨이 막히는 듯) 헉 하는 소리를 냄
When you gasp, you take a short quick breath through your mouth, especially when you are surprised, shocked, or in pain.

whisper*
[hwíspər]

v. 속삭이다; n. 속삭임; 속삭이는 소리
When you whisper, you say something very quietly.

sneeze*
[sni:z]

vi. 재채기하다; n. 재채기
When you sneeze, you suddenly take in your breath and then blow it down your nose noisily without being able to stop yourself, for example because you have a cold.

defend*
[difénd]

v. 방어하다, 지키다 (defense n. 방어, 보호)
If you defend someone or something, you take action in order to protect them.

sickly
[síkli]

a. 병약한, 자주 앓는; 혐오스러운, 불쾌한; ad. 병적으로
A sickly person or animal is weak, unhealthy, and often ill.

cough**
[kɔ:f]

v. 기침하다; n. 기침
When you cough, you force air out of your throat with a sudden, harsh noise. You often cough when you are ill, or when you are nervous or want to attract someone's attention.

handkerchief^{복습}
[hǽŋkərtʃif]

n. 손수건
A handkerchief is a small square piece of fabric which you use for blowing your nose.

paw*
[pɔ:]

n. (갈고리 발톱이 있는 동물의) 발; v. 앞발로 차다
The paws of an animal such as a cat, dog, or bear are its feet, which have claws for gripping things and soft pads for walking on.

temperature**
[témpərətʃər]

n. 체온; 온도, 기온 (run a temperature idiom 열이 나다)
The temperature of something is a measure of how hot or cold it is.

faint*
[feint]

vi. 기절하다; n. 기절, 졸도; a. 희미한, 어렴풋한
If you faint, you lose consciousness for a short time, especially because you are hungry, or because of pain, heat, or shock.

alarm*
[əlá:rm]

vt. 놀라게 하다; 위급을 알리다; n. 놀람, 불안; 경보 (alarming a. 놀랄 만한)
If something alarms you, it makes you afraid or anxious that something unpleasant or dangerous might happen.

constant*
[kánstənt]

a. 일정한, 불변의, 끊임없는 (constantly ad. 끊임없이, 거듭)
You use constant to describe something that happens all the time or is always there.

intent*
[intént]

① a. 몰두하는, 여념이 없는 ② n. 의지, 의향
If you are intent on doing something, you are eager and determined to do it.

track**
[træk]

v. 추적하다, ~의 뒤를 쫓다; 자국을 내다; n. 발자국, 지나간 자취; 통로, 궤도
If you track animals or people, you try to follow them by looking for the signs that they have left behind.

crumb
[krʌm]

n. 빵 부스러기, 빵가루
Crumbs are tiny pieces that fall from bread, biscuits, or cake when you cut it or eat it.

sibling
[síbliŋ]

n. (한 부모에서 난) 형제, 자매
Your siblings are your brothers and sisters.

cock*
[kak]

v. (귀·꽁지를) 쫑긋 세우다, 위로 치올리다; n. 수탉; 마개
If you cock a part of your body in a particular direction, you lift it or point it in that direction.

still***
[stil]

a. 정지한, 움직이지 않는; 조용한, 고요한; ad. 여전히, 아직도; 더욱, 한층
If you stay still, you stay in the same position and do not move.

attach*
[ətǽʃ]

vt. 붙이다, 달다
If you attach something to an object, you connect it or fasten it to the object.

bark*
[baːrk]

v. 고함치다; (개가) 짖다; n. 짖는 소리
If you bark at someone, you shout at them aggressively in a loud, rough voice.

snap to it

idiom (명령하듯이) 서둘러라, 더 빨리[열심히] 일해라
Snap to it is used, especially in orders, to tell someone to start working harder or more quickly.

skinny
[skíni]

a. 바싹 여윈, 말라 빠진
A skinny person is extremely thin, often in a way that you find unattractive.

sniff ^{복습}
[snif]

v. 냄새를 맡다, 코를 킁킁거리다; 코를 훌쩍이다; n. 냄새 맡음
If you sniff something or sniff at it, you smell it by sniffing.

1분에 몇 단어를 읽는지 리딩 속도를 측정해보세요.

$$\frac{600 \text{ words}}{\text{reading time (} \quad \text{) sec}} \times 60 = (\quad) \text{ WPM}$$

Build Your Vocabulary

sibling ^{복습}
[síbliŋ]

n. (한 부모에서 난) 형제, 자매
Your siblings are your brothers and sisters.

demonstrate*
[démənstreit]

vt. 실지로 해보이다; 논증하다, 설명하다
If you demonstrate a particular skill, quality, or feeling, you show by your actions that you have it.

scurry
[skə́:ri]

vi. 종종걸음으로 달리다, 급히 가다
When people or small animals scurry somewhere, they move there quickly and hurriedly, especially because they are frightened.

instruct*
[instrʌ́kt]

vt. 가르치다; 지시[명령]하다
Someone who instructs people in a subject or skill teaches it to them.

scrabble
[skrǽbl]

v. 뒤지며[허우적거리며] 찾다
If you scrabble for something, especially something that you cannot see, you move your hands or your feet about quickly and hurriedly in order to find it.

wax*
[wæks]

v. 초를 칠하다, 초로 닦다; n. 왁스
If you wax a surface, you put a thin layer of a solid, slightly shiny substance made of fat or oil onto it, especially in order to polish it.

stain*
[stein]

v. 착색[염색]하다; 더러워지다, 얼룩지게 하다; n. 얼룩, 오점
If a liquid stains something, the thing becomes colored or marked by the liquid.

hind*
[haind]

a. 뒤쪽의, 후방의
An animal's hind legs are at the back of its body.

brilliant*
[bríljənt]

a. 빛나는, 반짝이는; 훌륭한, 멋진
You describe light, or something that reflects light, as brilliant when it shines very brightly.

cripes
[kraips]

int. 저런, 이것 참
Cripes is an expression of surprise.

molding
[móuldiŋ]

n. 쇠시리(벽·문 등의 윗부분에 돌·목재 등을 띠처럼 댄 장식)
A molding is a strip of plaster or wood along the top of a wall or round a door.

stream**
[stri:m]

v. (빛이) 비치다; 흐르다, 흘러나오다; n. 흐름, 시내, 개울
When light streams into or out of a place, it shines strongly into or out of it.

patch*
[pæʧ]

n. (주변과는 다른 조그만) 부분; 헝겊 조각; 반창고; v. 헝겊을 대고 깁다
A patch on a surface is a part of it which is different in appearance from the area around it.

nibble
[nibl]

v. 조금씩 물어뜯다, 갉아먹다; n. 조금씩 물어뜯기, 한 입 분량
If you nibble food, you eat it by biting very small pieces of it.

hop*
[hap]

v. 깡충깡충 뛰다; 급히 가다[움직이다]; n. 깡충 뛰기
If you hop, you move along by jumping on one foot.

crawl**
[krɔ:l]

vi. 기어가다, 느릿느릿 가다; 우글거리다; 들끓다; n. 서행; 기어감
When you crawl, you move forward on your hands and knees.

glue*
[glu:]

n. 풀, 접착제; v. 풀[접착제]로 붙이다, 접착하다
Glue is a sticky substance used for joining things together, often for repairing broken things.

edge**
[edʒ]

n. 끝, 가장자리, 모서리; (칼 등의) 날; 예리함, 날카로움
The edge of something is the place or line where it stops, or the part of it that is furthest from the middle.

crunch
[krʌnʧ]

v. 아삭아삭 씹다; 바삭바삭 소리를 내다; n. 깨물어 부수기, 씹는 소리
(crunchy a. 아삭아삭 소리 내는)
If you crunch something hard, such as a sweet, you crush it noisily between your teeth.

squiggle
[skwigl]

n. 휘갈겨 쓴 것; v. 아무렇게나 쓰다
A squiggle is a line that bends and curls in an irregular way.

remarkable*
[rimá:rkəbl]

a. 놀랄 만한, 주목할 만한
Someone or something that is remarkable is unusual or special in a way that makes people notice them and be surprised or impressed.

mark***
[ma:rk]

n. 표시, 부호; 표적, 목표물; v. 표시하다, 나타내다
A mark is a written or printed symbol, for example a letter of the alphabet.

arrange**
[əréindʒ]

v. 가지런히 하다, 배열하다; 준비하다
If you arrange things somewhere, you place them in a particular position, usually in order to make them look attractive or tidy.

spell**
[spel]

① v. 철자를 모두 적다[말하다] ② n. 주문, 마법
When you spell a word, you write or speak each letter in the word in the correct order.

phrase**
[freiz]

n. 구절; 관용구
A phrase is a short group of words that people often use as a way of saying something.

ruin복습
[ru:in]

v. 망치다, 못쓰게 만들다; 몰락하다; n. 폐허; 파멸
To ruin something means to severely harm, damage, or spoil it.

tremble*
[trembl]

v. 떨(리)다, 진동하다, 흔들리다
If something trembles, it shakes slightly.

indignant*
[indígnənt]

a. 분개한, 성난
If you are indignant, you are shocked and angry, because you think that something is unjust or unfair.

26

whisker* [wískər]

n. (고양이·쥐 등의) 수염; 구레나룻
The whiskers of an animal such as a cat or a mouse are the long stiff hairs that grow near its mouth.

paw^{복습} [pɔ:]

n. (갈고리 발톱이 있는 동물의) 발; v. 앞발로 차다
The paws of an animal such as a cat, dog, or bear are its feet, which have claws for gripping things and soft pads for walking on.

shiver* [ʃívə:r]

v. (추위·두려움·흥분 등으로) (몸을) 떨다; n. 전율
When you shiver, your body shakes slightly because you are cold or frightened.

sneeze^{복습} [sni:z]

vi. 재채기하다; n. 재채기
When you sneeze, you suddenly take in your breath and then blow it down your nose noisily without being able to stop yourself, for example because you have a cold.

relish [réliʃ]

v. 즐기다; 기쁘게 생각하다; n. 흥미, 의욕; 맛, 풍미
If you relish something, you get a lot of enjoyment from it.

trace* [treis]

v. (선·도형 등을) 긋다, 그리다; 추적하다; n. 자취, 흔적; 극미량, 조금
If you trace something such as a pattern or a shape, for example with your finger or toe, you mark its outline on a surface.

knight* [nait]

n. (중세의) 기사
In medieval times, a knight was a man of noble birth, who served his king or lord in battle.

serve*** [sə:rv]

v. 섬기다, 복무하다; 제공하다, 시중 들다; n. 서브
If you serve your country, an organization, or a person, you do useful work for them.

honor*** [ánər]

vt. 존경하다, 공경하다; n. 명예, 영예
To honor someone means to treat them or regard them with special attention and respect.

mention*** [ménʃən]

vt. 말하다, 언급하다; n. 언급, 진술
If you mention something, you say something about it, usually briefly.

dungeon [dʌ́ndʒən]

n. 지하 감옥; vt. 지하 감옥에 가두다
A dungeon is a dark underground prison in a castle.

destine [déstin]

vt. ~할 운명에 있다
If something is destined to happen or if someone is destined to behave in a particular way, that thing seems certain to happen or be done.

fate* [feit]

n. 운명, 숙명
A person's or thing's fate is what happens to them.

await* [əwéit]

v. (어떤 일이 사람 앞에) 기다리다, (~을) 기다리다
If you await someone or something, you wait for them.

conform* [kənfɔ́:rm]

v. 집단의 다른 구성원들과 행동[생각]을 같이 하다; 따르다, 순응하다; 일치시키다
If you conform, you behave in the way that you are expected or supposed to behave.

Check Your Reading Speed

1분에 몇 단어를 읽는지 리딩 속도를 측정해보세요.

$$\frac{606 \text{ words}}{\text{reading time (\quad) sec}} \times 60 = (\qquad) \text{ WPM}$$

Build Your Vocabulary

abandon[*]
[əbǽndən]

vt. 단념하다, 그만두다; 버리다
If you abandon an activity or piece of work, you stop doing it before it is finished.

thankless
[θǽŋklis]

a. 힘들기만 하고 보상은 못 받는, 생색 안 나는
If you describe a job or task as thankless, you mean that it is hard work and brings very few rewards.

wander[*]
[wándər]

v. 돌아다니다, 방황하다; n. 유랑, 방랑
If you wander in a place, you walk around there in a casual way, often without intending to go in any particular direction.

stream[복습]
[stri:m]

v. (빛이) 비치다, 흐르다, 흘러나오다; n. 흐름, 시내, 개울
When light streams into or out of a place, it shines strongly into or out of it.

stain[복습]
[stein]

v. 착색[염색]하다; 더러워지다, 얼룩지게 하다; n. 얼룩, 오점
If a liquid stains something, the thing becomes colored or marked by the liquid.

fair[**]
[fɛər]

a. 아름다운, 매력적인; 공평한, 공정한; ad. 정확하게, 알맞게
If you describe someone as fair, you mean that they are attractive and pleasing in appearance.

maiden[*]
[meidn]

n. 소녀, 아가씨
A maiden is a young girl or woman.

knight[복습]
[nait]

n. (중세의) 기사
In medieval times, a knight was a man of noble birth, who served his king or lord in battle.

rescue[*]
[réskju:]

vt. 구조하다, 구출하다; n. 구출, 구원
If you rescue someone, you get them out of a dangerous or unpleasant situation.

stick[**]
[stik]

① v. (stuck-stuck) 내밀다; 찔러 넣다; 붙이다, 달라붙다; 고수하다
② n. 막대기, 지팡이
If something is sticking out from a surface or object, it extends up or away from it.

indulge[*]
[indʌ́ldʒ]

v. 맘껏 하다, 제멋대로 하게 하다; (욕망·정열 따위를) 만족시키다, 충족시키다
If you indulge in something or if you indulge yourself, you allow yourself to have or do something that you know you will enjoy.

28

adhere
[ædhíər]

vi. 고수하다, 집착하다; 들러붙다
If you adhere to a rule or agreement, you act in the way that it says you should.

elemental
[èləméntl]

a. 기본[근본]적인
Elemental feelings and types of behavior are simple, basic, and forceful.

circumstance**
[sɔ́:rkəmstæns]

n. 상황, 환경, 사정
The circumstances of a particular situation are the conditions which affect what happens.

reveal*
[rivíːl]

vt. 드러내다, 폭로하다, 밝히다
If you reveal something that has been out of sight, you uncover it so that people can see it.

instinct*
[ínstiŋkt]

n. 본능; 직관
Instinct is the natural tendency that a person or animal has to behave or react in a particular way.

possess**
[pəzés]

vt. 소유하다, 가지고 있다; 지배하다 (possession n. 소유)
If you possess something, you have it or own it.

in no time

idiom 즉시, 당장에
In no time means so quickly or so soon.

spy*
[spai]

v. 발견하다, 알아차리다; 염탐하다, 몰래 조사하다; n. 스파이
If you spy someone or something, you notice them.

squint
[skwint]

v. 눈을 가늘게 뜨고[찡그리고] 보다; n. 사시, 사팔뜨기
If you squint at something, you look at it with your eyes partly closed.

near-sighted
[níər-sàitid]

a. 근시의; 근시안적인, 선견지명이 없는
Someone who is near-sighted cannot see distant things clearly.

grave**
[greiv]

① a. 중대한, 심상치 않은; 근엄한 ② n. 무덤, 묘
A grave event or situation is very serious, important, and worrying.

tremble^{복습}
[trembl]

v. 떨(리)다, 진동하다, 흔들리다
If you tremble, you shake slightly because you are frightened or cold.

consider***
[kənsídər]

v. 고려하다, 숙고하다
If you consider something, you think about it carefully.

faint^{복습}
[feint]

vi. 기절하다; n. 기절, 졸도; a. 희미한, 어렴풋한
If you faint, you lose consciousness for a short time, especially because you are hungry, or because of pain, heat, or shock.

frighten**
[fraitn]

v. 놀라게 하다, 섬뜩하게 하다; 기겁하다 (frightened a. 겁먹은, 무서워하는)
If something or someone frightens you, they cause you to suddenly feel afraid, anxious, or nervous.

wrinkle*
[riŋkl]

v. 주름이 지다, 구겨지다; n. 주름, 잔주름
When you wrinkle your nose or forehead, or when it wrinkles, you tighten the muscles in your face so that the skin folds.

forehead*
[fɔ́:rhèd]

n. 이마
Your forehead is the area at the front of your head between your eyebrows and your hair.

topsy-turvy
[tápsi-tɔ́:rvi]

a. 온통 뒤죽박죽인
Something that is topsy-turvy is in a confused or disorganized state.

adjust**
[ədʒʌ́st]

v. (옷매무새 등을) 바로 하다, 조절하다; 적응하다; 조정하다
If you adjust something such as your clothing or a machine, you correct or alter its position or setting.

throat**
[θrout]

n. 목구멍, 목 (clear one's throat idiom 목을 가다듬다, 헛기침하다)
Your throat is the back of your mouth and the top part of the tubes that go down into your stomach and your lungs.

strum
[strʌm]

v. (현악기를) 가볍게 퉁기다, 연주하다; n. 가볍게 타기
If you strum a stringed instrument such as a guitar, you play it by moving your fingers backward and forward across the strings.

captivate
[kǽptəvèit]

vt. ~의 마음을 사로잡다, 매혹하다
Someone or something that is captivating fascinates or attracts you.

creep*
[kri:p]

vi. (crept–crept) 살금살금 걷다, 기다; n. 포복
When people or animals creep somewhere, they move quietly and slowly.

1분에 몇 단어를 읽는지 리딩 속도를 측정해보세요.

$$\frac{284 \text{ words}}{\text{reading time (} \quad \text{) sec}} \times 60 = (\qquad) \text{ WPM}$$

Build Your Vocabulary

stare 복습
[stɛər]

v. 응시하다, 뚫어지게 보다
If you stare at someone or something, you look at them for a long time.

wonder***
[wʌ́ndə:r]

n. 경탄할 만한 것, 경이; v. 호기심을 가지다, 이상하게 여기다
If you say that it is a wonder that something happened, you mean that it is very surprising and unexpected.

fair 복습
[fɛər]

a. 아름다운, 매력적인; 공평한, 공정한; ad. 정확하게, 알맞게
If you describe someone as fair, you mean that they are attractive and pleasing in appearance.

maiden 복습
[meidn]

n. 소녀, 아가씨
A maiden is a young girl or woman.

incredible*
[inkrédəbl]

a. 놀라운, 믿어지지 않는
If you describe something or someone as incredible, you like them very much or are impressed by them, because they are extremely or unusually good.

ridiculous 복습
[ridíkjuləs]

a. 터무니없는; 웃기는, 우스꽝스러운
If you say that something or someone is ridiculous, you mean that they are very foolish.

sickly 복습
[síkli]

a. 병약한, 자주 앓는; 혐오스러운, 불쾌한; ad. 병적으로
A sickly person or animal is weak, unhealthy, and often ill.

in time

idiom 이윽고, 장차; 박자를 맞추어; 늦지 않게, 제시간에
In time means eventually, or after quite a long time.

adoring
[ədɔ́:riŋ]

a. 흠모하는 (adoringly ad. 흠모하여)
An adoring person is someone who loves and admires another person very much.

scurry 복습
[skə́:ri]

vi. 종종걸음으로 달리다, 급히 가다
When people or small animals scurry somewhere, they move there quickly and hurriedly, especially because they are frightened.

cripes 복습
[kraips]

int. 저런, 이것 참
Cripes is an expression of surprise.

whisker 복습
[wískər]

n. (고양이·쥐 등의) 수염; 구레나룻
The whiskers of an animal such as a cat or a mouse are the long stiff hairs that grow near its mouth.

bowstring
[bóustriŋ]

n. 활의 시위; 악기 활의 현
A bowstring is the string of an archer's bow.

nuts
[nʌts]

a. 미친, 제정신이 아닌
Nuts is a slang word for insane.

goner
[gɔ́:nər]

n. 가망이 없는 사람
If you say that someone is a goner, you mean that they are about to die, or are in such danger that nobody can save them.

execute[*]
[éksikjùːt]

vt. 실행하다, 집행하다; 처형하다
If you execute a difficult action or movement, you successfully perform it.

unbelievable
[ʌ̀nbilíːvəbl]

a. 믿을 수 없는, 놀라운
You can use unbelievable to emphasize that you think something is very bad or shocking.

1분에 몇 단어를 읽는지 리딩 속도를 측정해보세요.

$$\frac{443 \text{ words}}{\text{reading time ( ) sec}} \times 60 = (\qquad) \text{ WPM}$$

Build Your Vocabulary

clutch*
[klʌʧ]

v. 부여잡다, 꽉 잡다, 붙들다; n. 붙잡음, 움켜쥠
If you clutch at something or clutch something, you hold it tightly, usually because you are afraid or anxious.

despair복습
[dispέər]

n. 절망, 자포자기; vi. 절망하다
Despair is the feeling that everything is wrong and that nothing will improve.

blame**
[bleim]

n. 비난, 책망; 책임; vt. 비난하다, 나무라다, ~의 탓으로 돌리다
The blame for something bad that has happened is the responsibility for causing it or letting it happen.

unbelievable복습
[ʌnbilíːvəbl]

a. 믿을 수 없는, 놀라운
You can use unbelievable to emphasize that you think something is very bad or shocking.

dramatic*
[drəmǽtik]

a. 극적인, 놀라운; 과장된, 호들갑스러운
A dramatic change or event happens suddenly and is very noticeable and surprising.

be bound to

idiom 반드시 ~하다
If you say that something is bound to happen, you mean that you are sure it will happen, because it is a natural consequence of something that is already known or exists.

council**
[káunsəl]

n. 의회, 위원회; 회의
A council is a group of people who are elected to govern a local area such as a city or, a county.

punish***
[pʌ́niʃ]

v. 처벌하다, 벌주다
To punish someone means to make them suffer in some way because they have done something wrong.

bring up

phrasal v. ~을 법원에 호출하다, 고발하다
To bring someone up means to make them appear for trial in court.

tribunal
[traibjúːnl]

n. 재판소, 법원
A tribunal is a special court or committee that is appointed to deal with particular problems.

dig**
[dig]

v. (dug-dug) (구멍 등을) 파다; 뒤지다; n. 파기
If people or animals dig, they make a hole in the ground or in a pile of earth, stones, or rubbish.

furious**
[fjúəriəs]

a. 맹렬한, 사나운; 격노한, 몹시 화가 난 (furiously ad. 미친 듯이, 맹렬하게)
Furious is used to describe something that is done with great energy, effort, speed, or violence.

pile**
[pail]

n. 쌓아 올린 더미; 다수; v. 쌓아 올리다, 쌓(이)다
A pile of things is a mass of them that is high in the middle and has sloping sides.

scrap^복습
[skræp]

n. 조각, 파편; vt. 부스러기로 만들다, 해체하다
A scrap of something is a very small piece or amount of it.

uncover*
[ʌnkʌvər]

v. 덮개를 벗기다, 뚜껑을 열다; 폭로하다
When people who are digging somewhere uncover something, they find a thing or a place that has been under the ground for a long time.

thimble
[θimbl]

n. 골무
A thimble is a small metal or plastic object which you use to protect your finger when you are sewing.

leather**
[léðər]

n. 가죽
Leather is treated animal skin which is used for making shoes, clothes, bags, and furniture.

stretch**
[streʧ]

v. 뻗어 있다; 늘이다; 쭉 펴다, 뻗다; n. 뻗침
Something that stretches over an area or distance covers or exists in the whole of that area or distance.

breath**
[breθ]

n. 숨, 호흡
Your breath is the air that you let out through your mouth when you breathe.

beat**
[biːt]

v. 치다, 두드리다; 패배시키다, 이기다; n. [음악] 박자, 고동
If you beat a drum or similar instrument, you hit it in order to make a sound.

rhythm*
[riðm]

n. 리듬, 율동; 박자
A rhythm is a regular series of sounds or movements.

affect**
[əfékt]

vt. 영향을 주다; 감동시키다
If something affects a person or thing, it influences them or causes them to change in some way.

well-being
[wèl-bíːiŋ]

n. 복지, 안녕, 행복
Someone's well-being is their health and happiness.

entire^복습
[intáiər]

a. 전체의; 완전한
You use entire when you want to emphasize that you are referring to the whole of something, for example, the whole of a place, time, or population.

community^복습
[kəmjúːnəti]

n. 공동[지역] 사회, 공동체; 일반 사회, 대중
The community is all the people who live in a particular area or place.

1분에 몇 단어를 읽는지 리딩 속도를 측정해보세요.

$$\frac{723 \text{ words}}{\text{reading time (\quad) sec}} \times 60 = (\qquad) \text{ WPM}$$

Build Your Vocabulary

council복습
[káunsəl]

n. 의회, 위원회; 회의
A council is a group of people who are elected to govern a local area such as a city or, a county.

echo*
[ékou]

v. 울려 퍼지다, 메아리치다; (남의 말·의견을) 그대로 되풀이하다; n. 메아리
If a sound echoes, it is reflected off a surface and can be heard again after the original sound has stopped.

cup***
[kʌp]

vt. 손바닥으로 받다[떠내다]; 두 손을 (컵 모양으로) 둥그렇게 모아 쥐다; n. 컵, 잔
If you cup something in your hands, you make your hands into a curved dish-like shape and support it or hold it gently.

palm*
[pa:m]

① n. 손바닥 ② n. 종려나무, 야자나무
The palm of your hand is the inside part.

scratch*
[skrætʃ]

v. 긁다; 할퀴다; n. 생채기, 할큄, 찰과상
If you scratch yourself, you rub your fingernails against your skin because it is itching.

oversize
[óuvərsaiz]

a. 특대의, 너무 큰
Oversize things are too big, or much bigger than usual.

faint복습
[feint]

vi. 기절하다; n. 기절, 졸도; a. 희미한, 어렴풋한
If you faint, you lose consciousness for a short time, especially because you are hungry, or because of pain, heat, or shock.

refer**
[rifə:r]

vi. 언급하다, 나타내다
If you refer to a particular subject or person, you talk about them or mention them.

lay***
[lei]

v. (laid–laid) 놓다, 눕히다; 알을 낳다
If you lay something somewhere, you put it there in a careful, gentle, or neat way.

wrist*
[rist]

n. 손목
Your wrist is the part of your body between your hand and your arm which bends when you move your hand.

steady**
[stédi]

v. 진정시키다, 균형을 잡다; a. 확고한, 안정된; 꾸준한
If you steady yourself, you control your voice or expression, so that people will think that you are calm and not nervous.

pulse[*]
[pʌls]

n. 맥박, 고동; 파동; v. 고동치다, 맥이 뛰다
Your pulse is the regular beating of blood through your body, which you can feel when you touch particular parts of your body, especially your wrist.

pound[*]
[paund]

① v. 쿵쿵 울리다; 마구 치다, 세게 두드리다; n. 타격 ② n. 파운드(무게의 단위) ③ n. 울타리, 우리
If your heart is pounding, it is beating with an unusually strong and fast rhythm, usually because you are afraid.

immediately[**]
[imíːdiətli]

ad. 곧, 바로, 즉시
If something happens immediately, it happens without any delay.

rhythm[복습]
[riðm]

n. 리듬, 율동; 박자
A rhythm is a regular series of sounds or movements.

narrow[복습]
[nǽrou]

v. 좁히다, 작아지다; a. 좁은, 편협한
If your eyes narrow or if you narrow your eyes, you almost close them, for example because you are angry or because you are trying to concentrate on something.

mutter[*]
[mʌ́tər]

v. 중얼거리다, 불평하다; n. 중얼거림, 불평
If you mutter, you speak very quietly so that you cannot easily be heard, often because you are complaining about something.

rodent
[roudnt]

n. 설치류 동물(쥐·토끼 등)
Rodents are small mammals which have sharp front teeth. Rats, mice, and squirrels are rodents.

command[**]
[kəmǽnd]

v. 명령하다, 지휘하다, 지배하다; n. 명령, 지휘
If someone has command of a situation, they have control of it because they have, or seem to have, power or authority.

protest[**]
[próutest]

v. 항의하다, 이의를 제기하다; n. 항의
If you protest against something or about something, you say or show publicly that you object to it.

adjust[복습]
[ədʒʌ́st]

v. (옷매무새 등을) 바로 하다, 조절하다; 적응하다; 조정하다
If you adjust something such as your clothing or a machine, you correct or alter its position or setting.

shudder[*]
[ʃʌ́dəːr]

vi. 떨다, 몸서리치다; n. 떨림, 전율
If you shudder, you shake with fear, horror, or disgust, or because you are cold.

royalty[*]
[rɔ́iəlti]

n. 왕족, 왕위; 특허권 사용료
The members of royal families are sometimes referred to as royalty.

responsibility[**]
[rispɑ̀nsəbíləti]

n. 책임, 책무
If you have responsibility for something or someone, or if they are your responsibility, it is your job or duty to deal with them and to take decisions relating to them.

personal[**]
[pə́rsənl]

a. 개인의, 사사로운; 몸소 하는; 인격의, 성격의
A personal opinion, quality, or thing belongs or relates to one particular person rather than to other people.

36

distant^{**}
[dístənt]

a. 먼, (멀리) 떨어져 있는
A distant relative is one who you are not closely related to.

relative^{**}
[rélətiv]

n. 친척; a. 상대적인, 관계가 있는
Your relatives are the members of your family.

enemy[*]
[énəmi]

n. 적, 원수, 적대자
If someone is your enemy, they hate you or want to harm you.

scat
[skæt]

vi. (명령문) 저리 가라; 급히 떠나다
If you say scat to animals, you let them go away.

stamp^{**}
[stæmp]

v. (발을) 구르다, 짓밟다; (도장·스탬프 등을) 찍다; n. 우표, 인지; 도장
If you stamp or stamp your foot, you lift your foot and put it down very hard on the ground, for example because you are angry.

weep[*]
[wi:p]

v. 눈물을 흘리다, 울다; 물기를 내뿜다
If someone weeps, they cry.

ancient^{**}
[éinʃənt]

a. 옛날의, 고대의
Ancient means very old, or having existed for a long time.

sniff^{복습}
[snif]

v. 코를 훌쩍이다; 냄새를 맡다, 코를 킁킁거리다; n. 냄새 맡음
When you sniff, you breathe in air through your nose hard enough to make a sound, for example when you are trying not to cry, or in order to show disapproval.

lean^{**}
[li:n]

① v. 상체를 굽히다; 기울다; 기대다, 의지하다 ② a. 야윈, 마른
When you lean in a particular direction, you bend your body in that direction.

thunder[*]
[θʌ́ndər]

v. 소리 지르다, 외치다; 우레가 울리다; 우르릉거리며 질주하다; n. 천둥, 우레
If you thunder something, you say it loudly and forcefully, especially because you are angry.

topsy-turvy^{복습}
[tápsi-tə́:rvi]

a. 온통 뒤죽박죽인
Something that is topsy-turvy is in a confused or disorganized state.

get lost

phrasal v. (명령문) 썩 나가; 길을 잃다, 헤매다
Saying get lost is an impolite way of telling someone to go away, or of refusing something.

common sense[*]
[kámən sèns]

n. 상식(적 판단), 분별
Your common sense is your natural ability to make good judgments and to behave in a practical and sensible way.

alarm^{복습}
[əlá:rm]

vt. 놀라게 하다; 위급을 알리다; n. 놀람, 불안; 경보 (alarming a. 놀랄 만한)
If something alarms you, it makes you afraid or anxious that something unpleasant or dangerous might happen.

honor^{복습}
[ánər]

vt. 존경하다, 공경하다; n. 명예, 영예
To honor someone means to treat them or regard them with special attention and respect.

knight^{복습}
[nait]

n. (중세의) 기사
In medieval times, a knight was a man of noble birth, who served his king or lord in battle.

phrase ^{복습}
[freiz]

n. 구절; 관용구
A phrase is a short group of words that people often use as a way of saying something.

occasion***
[əkéiʒən]

n. 경우, 기회; 특별한 일, 행사
An occasion is a time when something happens, or a case of it happening.

whisper ^{복습}
[hwíspər]

v. 속삭이다; n. 속삭임; 속삭이는 소리
When you whisper, you say something very quietly.

paw ^{복습}
[pɔː]

n. (갈고리 발톱이 있는 동물의) 발; v. 앞발로 차다
The paws of an animal such as a cat, dog, or bear are its feet, which have claws for gripping things and soft pads for walking on.

bow*
[bau]

① v. 머리를 숙이다, 굽히다 ② n. 활; 곡선
When you bow, you move your head or the top half of your body forward and downward as a formal way of greeting them or showing respect.

alas**
[əlǽs]

int. (슬픔·걱정을 나타내어) 아아, 슬프도다!, 불쌍한지고!
Alas is used to express sadness or regret.

1분에 몇 단어를 읽는지 리딩 속도를 측정해보세요.

$$\frac{536 \text{ words}}{\text{reading time (} \quad \text{) sec}} \times 60 = (\quad) \text{ WPM}$$

Build Your Vocabulary

heed
[hi:d]

v. (남의 충고·경고에) 주의를 기울이다; n. 주의, 유의
If you heed someone's advice or warning, you pay attention to it and do what they suggest.

throne*
[θroun]

n. 왕좌, 왕위; vi. 왕위에 앉다, 왕권을 쥐다
You can talk about the throne as a way of referring to the position of being king, queen, or emperor.

balance**
[bǽləns]

v. 균형을 유지하다[잡다]; n. 균형, 평형; 저울; 나머지, 잔여
If you balance something somewhere, or if it balances there, it remains steady and does not fall.

spool
[spu:l]

n. (실·전선·필름 등을 감는) 릴, 얼레
A spool is a round object onto which thread, tape, or film can be wound, especially before it is put into a machine.

thread**
[θred]

n. 실, 바느질 실; vt. 실을 꿰다
A thread is a long very thin piece of material such as cotton, nylon, or silk, especially one that is used in sewing.

whisker*복습
[wískər]

n. (고양이·쥐 등의) 수염; 구레나룻
The whiskers of an animal such as a cat or a mouse are the long stiff hairs that grow near its mouth.

droop*
[dru:p]

v. 축 늘어지다, 수그러지다; 숙이다, 수그리다
If something droops, it hangs or leans downward with no strength or firmness.

dismay*
[disméi]

n. 경악, 당황; 실망, 낙담; vt. 낙담[실망]하게 하다
Dismay is a strong feeling of fear, worry, or sadness that is caused by something unpleasant and unexpected.

outrage*
[áutreidʒ]

n. 격분, 격노; vt. 격분[격노]하게 만들다
Outrage is an intense feeling of anger and shock.

dismal*
[dízməl]

a. 음침한, 음산한
Something that is dismal is bad in a sad or depressing way.

intone
[intóun]

v. (단조로운 소리로) 이야기하다, 읊조리다
If you intone something, you say it in a slow and serious way, with most of the words at one pitch.

fever**
[fí:vər]

n. 열, 발열; 열중, 열광
If you have a fever when you are ill, your body temperature is higher than usual.

lack**
[læk]

n. 부족, 결핍, 결여; v. 없다, 결핍되다, 모자라다
If there is a lack of something, there is not enough of it or it does not exist at all.

disturb**
[distə́:rb]

vt. (마음·일 등을) 방해하다, 어지럽히다 (disturbed a. 불안한)
If something disturbs you, it makes you feel upset or worried.

endanger
[indéindʒər]

vt. 위험에 빠뜨리다, 위태롭게 만들다
To endanger something or someone means to put them in a situation where they might be harmed or destroyed completely.

indisputable
[ìndispjú:təbl]

a. 반론의 여지가 없는, 부인할 수 없는, 명백한
If you say that something is indisputable, you are emphasizing that it is true and cannot be shown to be untrue.

consort
[kánsɔ:rt]

vi. (남들이 좋지 않게 생각하는 사람들과) 어울리다
If you say that someone consorts with a particular person or group, you mean that they spend a lot of time with them, and usually that you do not think this is a good thing.

allow***
[əláu]

v. 허락하다, ~하게 두다; 인정하다
If you allow something to happen, you do not prevent it.

indulge복습
[indʌ́ldʒ]

v. 맘껏 하다, 제멋대로 하게 하다; (욕망·정열 따위를) 만족시키다, 충족시키다
If you indulge in something or if you indulge yourself, you allow yourself to have or do something that you know you will enjoy.

collective*
[kəléktiv]

a. 집단의, 공동의; 집합적인
Collective actions, situations, or feelings involve or are shared by every member of a group of people.

shiver복습
[ʃívə:r]

n. 전율; v. (추위·두려움·흥분 등으로) (몸을) 떨다
When you shiver, your body shakes slightly because you are cold or frightened.

disgust*
[disgʌ́st]

n. 싫음, 혐오감; vt. 역겹게 하다, 넌더리나게 하다
Disgust is a feeling of very strong dislike or disapproval.

fellow**
[félou]

n. 친구, 동료; 녀석, 사나이
You use fellow to describe people who are in the same situation as you, or people you feel you have something in common with.

fervent
[fə́:rvənt]

a. 열렬한, 강렬한
A fervent person has or shows strong feelings about something, and is very sincere and enthusiastic about it.

obvious**
[ábviəs]

a. 명백한, 분명한 (obviously ad. 분명히, 명백하게)
If something is obvious, it is easy to see or understand.

assume**
[əsjú:m]

vt. 추정하다, 가정하다; (역할·임무 등을) 맡다
If you assume that something is true, you imagine that it is true, sometimes wrongly.

wonder복습
[wʌ́ndə:r]

v. 호기심을 가지다, 이상하게 여기다; n. 경탄할 만한 것, 경이
If you wonder at something, you are very surprised about it or think about it in a very surprised way.

nod[**] [nɔd]

v. 끄덕이다, 끄덕여 표시하다; n. (동의·인사·신호·명령의) 끄덕임
If you nod, you move your head downward and upward to show agreement, understanding, or approval.

dungeon[복습] [dʌ́ndʒən]

n. 지하 감옥; vt. 지하 감옥에 가두다
A dungeon is a dark underground prison in a castle.

pound[복습] [paund]

① v. 마구 치다, 세게 두드리다; 쿵쿵 울리다; n. 타격 ② n. 파운드(무게의 단위) ③ n. 울타리, 우리
If you pound something or pound on it, you hit it with great force, usually loudly and repeatedly.

fist[*] [fist]

vt. (주먹을) 쥐다, (주먹으로) 때리다; n. 주먹; 움켜쥠 (fisted a. 주먹을 쥔)
To fist means to make your hand closed tightly with the fingers doubled into the palm.

immediately[복습] [imí:diətli]

ad. 곧, 바로, 즉시
If something happens immediately, it happens without any delay.

vote[**] [vout]

v. 투표하다; n. 투표, 투표권
When you vote, you indicate your choice officially at a meeting or in an election, for example by raising your hand or writing on a piece of paper.

chorus[*] [kɔ́:rəs]

n. 일제히 내는 소리; 후렴; 합창, 코러스; vi. 이구동성으로 말하다; 합창하다
When there is a chorus of criticism, disapproval, or praise, that attitude is expressed by a lot of people at the same time.

oppose[**] [əpóuz]

v. 반대하다; 반항하다, 적대하다
If you oppose someone or oppose their plans or ideas, you disagree with what they want to do and try to prevent them from doing it.

reign[*] [rein]

vi. 만연하다, 널리 퍼지다; 군림하다, 지배하다; n. 지배력, 영향력; 통치, 지배
If you say, for example, that silence reigns in a place or confusion reigns in a situation, you mean that the place is silent or the situation is confused.

ashamed[**] [əʃéimd]

a. 부끄러운, 수치스러운
If someone is ashamed, they feel embarrassed or guilty because of something they do or they have done.

defend[복습] [difénd]

v. 방어하다, 지키다 (defense n. 방어, 보호)
If you defend someone or something, you take action in order to protect them.

weep[복습] [wi:p]

v. (wept-wept) 눈물을 흘리다, 울다; 물기를 내뿜다
If someone weeps, they cry.

beat[복습] [bi:t]

v. 치다, 두드리다; 패배시키다, 이기다; n. [음악] 박자, 고동
If you beat someone or something, you hit them very hard.

sin[**] [sin]

n. 죄, 죄악; v. 죄를 짓다, 나쁜 짓을 하다
A sin is any action or behavior that people disapprove of or consider morally wrong.

deny[***] [dináí]

v. 사실이 아니라고 말하다, 부인[부정]하다
When you deny something, you state that it is not true.

renounce
[rináuns]

v. (신조·행위 등을 공식적으로) 버리다[그만두다]; (직함·직책 등을) 포기[단념]하다
If you renounce a belief or a way of behaving, you decide and declare publicly that you no longer have that belief or will no longer behave in that way.

hereby
[híərbai]

ad. (문어) 이로써, 이에 의하여
You use hereby when officially or formally saying what you are doing.

decency
[dí:snsi]

n. 품위, 체면; 예의, 예절
If you say that someone did not have the decency to do something, you are criticizing them because there was a particular action which they did not do but which you believe they ought to have done.

perfidy
[pə́:rfədi]

n. (문어) 배신, 배신 행위
Perfidy is the action of betraying someone or behaving very badly toward someone.

scene**
[si:n]

n. 일, 사건, 상황; 장소, 현장; 장면; 무대
You can describe an event that you see, or that is broadcast or shown in a picture, as a scene of a particular kind.

unfold*
[ʌnfóuld]

v. 펴다, 펼치다; 열리다
If a situation unfolds, it develops and becomes known or understood.

Check Your Reading Speed

1분에 몇 단어를 읽는지 리딩 속도를 측정해보세요.

$$\frac{550 \text{ words}}{\text{reading time (}\quad\text{) sec}} \times 60 = (\quad\quad) \text{ WPM}$$

Build Your Vocabulary

wrap ^{복습}
[ræp]

v. 감싸다; 포장하다; n. 싸개, 덮개
If someone wraps their arms, fingers, or legs around something, they put them firmly around it.

assure *
[əʃúə:r]

vt. 확신하다, 보증하다 (assurance n. 확신, 보장)
If you assure someone that something is true or will happen, you tell them that it is definitely true or will definitely happen, often in order to make them less worried.

fair ^{복습}
[fɛər]

a. 아름다운, 매력적인; 공평한, 공정한; ad. 정확하게, 알맞게
If you describe someone as fair, you mean that they are attractive and pleasing in appearance.

maiden ^{복습}
[meidn]

n. 소녀, 아가씨
A maiden is a young girl or woman.

spell ^{복습}
[spel]

① n. 주문, 마법 ② v. 철자를 모두 적다[말하다]
A spell is a situation in which events are controlled by a magical power.

cripes ^{복습}
[kraips]

int. 저런, 이것 참
Cripes is an expression of surprise.

for one's sake

idiom ~ 때문에, ~를 위해서
When you do something for someone's sake, you do it in order to help them or make them happy.

pardon **
[pa:rdn]

int. 뭐라구요(상대방의 말을 되물을 때 하는 말); n. 용서, 관용; vt. 용서하다
You say 'Pardon?' or 'I beg your pardon?' when you want someone to repeat what they have just said because you have not heard or understood it.

bend **
[bend]

v. (bent–bent) 구부리다, 돌리다; 구부러지다, 휘다; n. 커브, 굽음
When you bend a part of your body such as your arm or leg, or when it bends, you change its position so that it is no longer straight.

sigh ^{복습}
[sai]

v. 한숨 쉬다; n. 한숨, 탄식
When you sigh, you let out a deep breath, as a way of expressing feelings such as disappointment, tiredness, or pleasure.

make sense

idiom 뜻이 통하다, 도리에 맞다
If something makes sense, it has a meaning that you can easily understand.

turn in

phrasal v. (도망자 용의자 등을) 고발하다, (경찰에) 넘기다
To turn someone in means to give them to someone in authority because they have done something wrong.

crawl
[krɔːl]

vi. 기어가다, 느릿느릿 가다; 우글거리다, 들끓다; n. 서행; 기어감
When you crawl, you move forward on your hands and knees.

hop
[hap]

v. 깡충깡충 뛰다; 급히 가다[움직이다]; n. 깡충 뛰기
If you hop, you move along by jumping on one foot.

tap
[tæp]

① v. 가볍게 두드리다; n. 가볍게 두드리기 ② n. 주둥이, (수도 등의) 꼭지
If you tap something, you hit it with a quick light blow or a series of quick light blows.

command
[kəmǽnd]

v. 명령하다, 지휘하다, 지배하다; n. 명령, 지휘
If someone in authority commands you to do something, they tell you that you must do it.

matter**
[mǽtər]

vi. 중요하다; n. 물질, 문제, 일
If you say that something does matter, you mean that it is important to you because it does have an effect on you or on a particular situation.

trace
[treis]

v. (선·도형 등을) 긋다, 그리다; 추적하다; n. 자취, 흔적; 극미량, 조금
If you trace something such as a pattern or a shape, for example with your finger or toe, you mark its outline on a surface.

make a fool of

idiom 놀리다, 웃음거리로 만들다
If you make a fool of someone or yourself, you make them or yourself appear stupid or ridiculous.

allow
[əláu]

v. 허락하다, ~하게 두다; 인정하다
If you allow something to happen, you do not prevent it.

fate
[feit]

n. 운명, 숙명
A person's or thing's fate is what happens to them.

Check Your Reading Speed

1분에 몇 단어를 읽는지 리딩 속도를 측정해보세요.

$$\frac{1{,}085 \text{ words}}{\text{reading time ( ) sec}} \times 60 = (\quad) \text{ WPM}$$

Build Your Vocabulary

entire 복습
[intáiər]

a. 전체의; 완전한
You use entire when you want to emphasize that you are referring to the whole of something, for example, the whole of a place, time, or population.

community 복습
[kəmjú:nəti]

n. 공동[지역] 사회, 공동체; 일반 사회, 대중
The community is all the people who live in a particular area or place.

instruct 복습
[instrʌ́kt]

vt. 지시[명령]하다; 가르치다
If you instruct someone to do something, you formally tell them to do it.

honor 복습
[ánər]

vt. 존경하다, 공경하다; n. 명예, 영예 (honored a. 명예로운)
To honor someone means to treat them or regard them with special attention and respect.

ballroom
[bɔ́:lru:m]

n. 무도장
A ballroom is a very large room that is used for dancing.

council 복습
[káunsəl]

n. 의회, 위원회; 회의
A council is a group of people who are elected to govern a local area such as a city or, a county.

atop
[ətáp]

prep. ~의 꼭대기에, 정상에
If something is atop something else, it is on top of it.

brick **
[brik]

n. 벽돌
Bricks are rectangular blocks of baked clay used for building walls, which are usually red or brown.

pile 복습
[pail]

v. 쌓아 올리다, 쌓(이)다; n. 쌓아 올린 더미; 다수
If you pile things somewhere, you put them there so that they form a pile.

spread ***
[spred]

v. (spread–spread) 펴(지)다, 뻗다, 펼치다; 뿌리다; n. 퍼짐, 폭, 넓이
If people or things are spread out, they are a long way apart.

cling *
[kliŋ]

vi. (clung–clung) 매달리다, 달라붙다
If you cling to someone or something, you hold onto them tightly.

whisper 복습
[hwíspə:r]

v. 속삭이다; n. 속삭임; 속삭이는 소리
When you whisper, you say something very quietly.

pull away

idiom (~에서) (몸을) 빼다, 이탈하다; [차가] 움직이기 시작하다, 떠나다
If you pull away from someone or something, you move quickly away from them.

disgust᛫
[disgʌ́st]

n. 싫음, 혐오감; vt. 역겹게 하다, 넌더리나게 하다
Disgust is a feeling of very strong dislike or disapproval.

thrill᛫
[θril]

n. 전율, 스릴, 오싹함; v. 오싹하(게 하)다; 설레게 하다
If something gives you a thrill, it gives you a sudden feeling of great excitement, pleasure, or fear.

seek᛫
[siːk]

v. 추구하다, 얻으려 하다, 찾다 (seeker n. ~을 찾는 사람)
When someone seeks something, they try to obtain it.

paw᛫
[pɔː]

n. (갈고리 발톱이 있는 동물의) 발; v. 앞발로 차다
The paws of an animal such as a cat, dog, or bear are its feet, which have claws for gripping things and soft pads for walking on.

distinctive᛫
[distíŋktiv]

a. 독특한, 뚜렷한 구별이 되는
Something that is distinctive has a special quality or feature which makes it easily recognizable and different from other things of the same type.

let go of

idiom (쥐고 있던 것을) 놓다, ~에서 손을 놓다
To let go of someone or something means to stop holding them.

gaze᛫
[geiz]

n. 주시, 응시; vi. 응시하다, 뚫어지게 보다
You can talk about someone's gaze as a way of describing how they are looking at something, especially when they are looking steadily at it.

delightful᛫
[diláitfəl]

a. 기쁨을 주는, 정말 기분 좋은
If you describe something or someone as delightful, you mean they are very pleasant.

phrase᛫
[freiz]

n. 구절; 관용구
A phrase is a short group of words that people often use as a way of saying something.

trial᛫
[traiəl]

n. 재판, 공판; 시험, 실험
A trial is a formal meeting in a law court, at which a judge and jury listen to evidence and decide whether a person is guilty of a crime.

conduct᛫᛫
[kándʌkt]

v. 수행하다, 지도하다; 행동하다, 처신하다; 인도하다, 안내하다
When you conduct an activity or task, you organize it and carry it out.

orderly᛫
[ɔ́ːrdərli]

a. 정돈된, 단정한; 질서를 지키는, 예의 바른
(in an orderly fashion idiom 차분하게)
If something is done in an orderly fashion or manner, it is done in a well-organized and controlled way.

civilized᛫
[sívəlàizd]

a. 교양 있는, 품위 있는; 문명적인, 개화된
If you describe a person or their behavior as civilized, you mean that they are polite and reasonable.

46

throat^{복습}
[θrout]

n. 목구멍, 목 (clear one's throat idiom 목을 가다듬다, 헛기침하다)
Your throat is the back of your mouth and the top part of the tubes that go down into your stomach and your lungs.

frighten^{복습}
[fraitn]

v. 놀라게 하다, 섬뜩하게 하다; 기겁하다 (frightened a. 겁먹은, 무서워하는)
If something or someone frightens you, they cause you to suddenly feel afraid, anxious, or nervous.

thud
[θʌd]

v. (심장이) 고동치다, 두근거리다; 쿵 떨어지다; n. 쿵(무거운 물건이 떨어지는 소리)
When your heart thuds, it beats strongly and rather quickly, for example because you are very frightened or very happy.

defend^{복습}
[difénd]

v. 방어하다, 지키다
If you defend someone or something, you take action in order to protect them.

rumor[*]
[rú:mər]

n. 소문, 루머; vt. 소문을 내다
A rumor is a story or piece of information that may or may not be true, but that people are talking about.

egregious
[igrí:dʒəs]

a. 지독한, 어처구니없는
Egregious means very bad indeed.

shift[*]
[ʃift]

v. 옮기다, 이동하다; n. 교대 근무; 교체, 순환
If you shift something or if it shifts, it moves slightly.

gasp^{복습}
[gæsp]

n. (숨이 막히는 듯) 헉 하는 소리를 냄; v. 숨이 턱 막히다, 헉 하고 숨을 쉬다
A gasp is a short quick breath of air that you take in through your mouth, especially when you are surprised, shocked, or in pain.

arise[*]
[əráiz]

vi. (arose–arisen) 생기다, 발생하다; (무엇의 결과로) 유발되다
If a situation or problem arises, it begins to exist or people start to become aware of it.

assemble[*]
[əsémbl]

v. 모으다, 모이다, 집합하다
When people assemble or when someone assembles them, they come together in a group, usually for a particular purpose such as a meeting.

roar[*]
[rɔːr]

vi. 고함치다, 으르렁거리다; n. 외치는 소리, 왁자지껄함; 으르렁거리는 소리
If someone roars, they shout something in a very loud voice.

sacred[*]
[séikrid]

a. 성스러운, 신성한; 종교적인
You can describe something as sacred when it is regarded as too important to be changed or interfered with.

raise^{***}
[reiz]

vt. (소리를) 높이다, 크게 외치다; 들(어 올리)다
If you raise your voice, you speak more loudly, usually because you are angry.

deny^{복습}
[dinái]

v. 사실이 아니라고 말하다, 부인[부정]하다
When you deny something, you state that it is not true.

charge^{**}
[ʧɑːrʤ]

n. 혐의, 고발, 책임, 담당; v. 비난하다, 고소하다; 맡기다; 청구하다
A charge is a formal accusation that someone has committed a crime.

punish [복습]
[pʌ́niʃ]

v. 처벌하다, 벌주다
To punish someone means to make them suffer in some way because they have done something wrong.

ancient [복습]
[éinʃənt]

a. 옛날의, 고대의
Ancient means very old, or having existed for a long time.

decree
[dikríː]

n. 법령, 판결; v. (법령에 의하여) 명령하다, 선언하다
A decree is an official order or decision, especially one made by the ruler of a country.

sink***
[siŋk]

v. (sank—sunk) (마음 등이) 가라앉다, 낙심하다; 가라앉히다, 침몰하다
If your heart or your spirits sink, you become depressed or lose hope.

tip**
[tip]

① n. (뾰족한) 끝 ② v. 뒤집어엎다, 기울이다 ③ n. 팁, 사례금
The tip of something long and narrow is the end of it.

stain [복습]
[stein]

v. 착색[염색]하다; 더러워지다, 얼룩지게 하다; n. 얼룩, 오점
If a liquid stains something, the thing becomes colored or marked by the liquid.

renounce [복습]
[rináuns]

v. (신조·행위 등을 공식적으로) 버리다[그만두다]; (직함·직책 등을) 포기[단념]하다
If you renounce a belief or a way of behaving, you decide and declare publicly that you no longer have that belief or will no longer behave in that way.

repent*
[ripént]

v. 후회하다, 뉘우치다, 유감으로 생각하다
If you repent, you show or say that you are sorry for something wrong you have done.

bellow
[bélou]

n. 울부짖기, 포효; v. (우렁찬 소리로) 고함치다, 큰 소리로 울다
If someone bellows, they shout angrily in a loud, deep voice.

collective [복습]
[kəléktiv]

a. 집단의, 공동의; 집합적인
Collective actions, situations, or feelings involve or are shared by every member of a group of people.

outrage [복습]
[áutreidʒ]

n. 격분, 격노; vt. 격분[격노]하게 만들다
Outrage is an intense feeling of anger and shock.

surge*
[səːrdʒ]

v. 쇄도하다, 밀어닥치다; n. (파도 같은) 쇄도, 돌진
If a crowd of people surge forward, they suddenly move forward together.

pound [복습]
[paund]

① v. 쿵쿵 울리다; 마구 치다, 세게 두드리다; n. 타격 ② n. 파운드(무게의 단위) ③ n. 울타리, 우리
If you pound something or pound on it, you hit it with great force, usually loudly and repeatedly.

thread [복습]
[θred]

n. 실, 바느질 실; vt. 실을 꿰다
A thread is a long very thin piece of a material such as cotton, nylon, or silk, especially one that is used in sewing.

master**
[mǽstər]

n. 대가, 명인, 정통한 사람; vt. 숙달하다, 터득하다
If you say that someone is a master of a particular activity, you mean that they are extremely skilled at it.

48

marvel*
[máːrvəl]

v. 놀라다, 경탄하다; 이상하게 여기다; n. 놀라운 일, 경이
If you marvel at something, you express your great surprise, wonder, or admiration.

bravery*
[bréiːvəri]

n. 용기, 용맹
Bravery is brave behavior or the quality of being brave.

admire**
[ædmáiər]

v. 감탄하다, 칭찬하다
If you admire someone or something, you like and respect them very much.

defiance
[difáiəns]

n. 저항, 반항; 도전
Defiance is behavior or an attitude which shows that you are not willing to obey someone.

faint복습
[feint]

vi. 기절하다; n. 기절, 졸도; a. 희미한, 어렴풋한
If you faint, you lose consciousness for a short time, especially because you are hungry, or because of pain, heat, or shock.

1분에 몇 단어를 읽는지 리딩 속도를 측정해보세요.

$$\frac{614 \text{ words}}{\text{reading time } (\quad) \text{ sec}} \times 60 = (\qquad) \text{ WPM}$$

Build Your Vocabulary

rhythm ^{복습}
[riðm]

n. 리듬, 율동; 박자
A rhythm is a regular series of sounds or movements.

ominous
[ámənəs]

a. 불길한, 나쁜 징조의
If you describe something as ominous, you mean that it worries you because it makes you think that something unpleasant is going to happen.

spool ^{복습}
[spu:l]

n. (실·전선·필름 등을 감는) 릴, 얼레
A spool is a round object onto which thread, tape, or film can be wound, especially before it is put into a machine.

dungeon ^{복습}
[dʌ́ndʒən]

n. 지하 감옥; vt. 지하 감옥에 가두다
A dungeon is a dark underground prison in a castle.

blink*
[bliŋk]

v. 눈을 깜박거리다; (등불·별 등이) 깜박이다; n. 깜박거림
When you blink or when you blink your eyes, you shut your eyes and very quickly open them again.

wonder ^{복습}
[wʌ́ndə:r]

v. 호기심을 가지다, 이상하게 여기다; n. 경탄할 만한 것, 경이
If you wonder about something, you think about it, either because it interests you and you want to know more about it, or because you are worried or suspicious about it.

knight ^{복습}
[nait]

n. (중세의) 기사
In medieval times, a knight was a man of noble birth, who served his king or lord in battle.

maiden ^{복습}
[meidn]

n. 소녀, 아가씨
A maiden is a young girl or woman.

rescue ^{복습}
[réskju:]

vt. 구조하다, 구출하다; n. 구출, 구원
If you rescue someone, you get them out of a dangerous or unpleasant situation.

master ^{복습}
[mǽstər]

n. 대가, 명인, 정통한 사람; vt. 숙달하다, 터득하다
If you say that someone is a master of a particular activity, you mean that they are extremely skilled at it.

chilling
[tʃíliŋ]

a. 냉담한, 무서운, 으스스한
If you describe something as chilling, you mean it is frightening.

possibility[**]
[pàsəbílətí]

n. 가능성
If you say there is a possibility that something is the case or that something will happen, you mean that it might be the case or it might happen.

murmur[*]
[mə́:rmə:r]

v. 중얼거리다; 투덜거리다; n. 중얼거림
If you murmur something, you say it very quietly, so that not many people can hear what you are saying.

get to one's feet

idiom 벌떡 일어서다
If you get or rise to your feet, you stand up.

hind[복습]
[haind]

a. 뒤쪽의, 후방의
An animal's hind legs are at the back of its body.

appreciate[**]
[əprí:ʃièit]

vt. 고맙게 생각하다; 평가하다, 감상하다
If you appreciate something that someone has done for you or is going to do for you, you are grateful for it.

unwind
[ʌnwáind]

v. (unwound–unwound) (감겨 있는 것을) 풀다; (긴장을) 풀다, 풀리다
If you unwind a length of something that is wrapped round something else or round itself, you loosen it and make it straight.

length[**]
[leŋθ]

n. 길이; (무엇이 계속되는) 시간[기간]
The length of something is the amount that it measures from one end to the other along the longest side.

loop[*]
[lu:p]

n. 고리, 올가미; v. 고리로 만들다; 원호를 그리며 움직이다
A loop is a curved or circular shape in something long, for example in a piece of string.

mutter[복습]
[mʌ́tər]

v. 중얼거리다, 불평하다; n. 중얼거림, 불평
If you mutter, you speak very quietly so that you cannot easily be heard, often because you are complaining about something.

lean[복습]
[li:n]

① v. 상체를 굽히다; 기울다; 기대다, 의지하다 ② a. 야윈, 마른
When you lean in a particular direction, you bend your body in that direction.

celery[*]
[séləri]

n. [식물] 셀러리
Celery is a vegetable with long pale green stalks. It is eaten raw in salads.

breath[복습]
[breθ]

n. 숨, 호흡
Your breath is the air that you let out through your mouth when you breathe.

tighten[**]
[taitn]

v. 단단히 죄다, 팽팽하게 하다, 단단해지다
If you tighten a rope or chain, or if it tightens, it is stretched or pulled hard until it is straight.

nod[복습]
[nɔd]

v. 끄덕이다, 끄덕여 표시하다; n. (동의·인사·신호·명령의) 끄덕임
If you nod, you move your head downward and upward to show agreement, understanding, or approval.

fairy tale
[fέəri tèil]

n. 동화, 옛날이야기
A fairy tale is a story for children involving magical events and imaginary creatures.

courtly
[kɔ́:rtli]

a. 예의 바른, 공손한[정중한] (courtly love n. 기사도적인 사랑)
Courtly love is a tradition represented in Western European literature between the 12th and the 14th centuries, idealizing love between a knight and a revered lady.

bravery^{복습}
[bréi:vəri]

n. 용기, 용맹
Bravery is brave behavior or the quality of being brave.

courtesy*
[kɔ́:rtəsi]

n. 정중, 예의, 친절
If you refer to the courtesy of doing something, you are referring to a polite action.

devotion*
[divóuʃən]

n. 헌신, 전념
Devotion is great love, affection, or admiration for someone.

fellow^{복습}
[félou]

n. 친구, 동료; 녀석, 사나이
You use fellow to describe people who are in the same situation as you, or people you feel you have something in common with.

knot**
[nat]

v. 매다, 얽히(게 하)다; n. 매듭, 얽힘; 나무 마디
If you knot a piece of string, rope, cloth, or other material, you pass one end or part of it through a loop and pull it tight.

roar^{복습}
[rɔ:r]

n. 외치는 소리, 왁자지껄함; 으르렁거리는 소리; vi. 고함치다, 으르렁거리다
If someone roars, they shout something in a very loud voice.

approval**
[əprú:vəl]

n. 찬성, 동의; 승인
If someone or something has your approval, you like and admire them.

square***
[skwɛər]

v. (몸을) 똑바로 펴다; 네모지게 하다; n. 정사각형; 광장
If you square up, you pull your shoulders up and back because you feel determined to do something.

1분에 몇 단어를 읽는지 리딩 속도를 측정해보세요.

$$\frac{616 \text{ words}}{\text{reading time ( ) sec}} \times 60 = (\quad) \text{ WPM}$$

Build Your Vocabulary

retreat*
[ritríːt]

v. 물러서다, 퇴각하다; n. 퇴각; 은퇴
If you retreat, you move away from something or someone.

expectant
[ikspéktənt]

a. 기다리는, 기대하고 있는
If someone is expectant, they are excited because they think something interesting is about to happen.

council복습
[káunsəl]

n. 의회, 위원회; 회의
A council is a group of people who are elected to govern a local area such as a city or, a county.

perch*
[pəːrʧ]

v. (높은 곳에) 앉(히)다, 놓다; n. (새의) 횃대; 높은 자리
To perch somewhere means to be on the top or edge of something.

brick복습
[brik]

n. 벽돌
Bricks are rectangular blocks of baked clay used for building walls, which are usually red or brown.

burly
[bə́ːrli]

a. 억센, 건장한
A burly man has a broad body and strong muscles.

slit*
[slit]

n. 갈라진 틈, 틈새; v. 잘라 내다, 가느다랗게 베다
A slit is a long narrow opening in something.

escort*
[éskɔːrt]

vt. 호송하다, 호위하다; 안내하다; n. 호위, 호송
If you escort someone somewhere, you accompany them there.

spot**
[spat]

vt. 발견하다, 분별하다; n. 반점, 얼룩; 장소, 지점
If you spot something or someone, you notice them.

in honor of

idiom ~에게 경의를 표하여
In honor of someone or something means in order to show respect and admiration for them.

tremendous*
[triméndəs]

a. 거대한, 대단한; 엄청난, 무서운
You use tremendous to emphasize how strong a feeling or quality is, or how large an amount is.

makeup복습
[méikʌp]

n. 화장, 분장; 조립, 구성
Makeup consists of things such as lipstick, eye shadow, and powder which some women put on their faces to make themselves look more attractive or which actors use to change or improve their appearance.

hood[*]
[hud]

n. 복면; 두건; 자동차 보닛, 덮개 (hooded a. 복면을 한)
A hooded person is wearing a hood or a piece of clothing pulled down over their face, so they are difficult to recognize.

concentrate[**]
[kánsəntrèit]

v. 집중하다, 전념하다
If you concentrate on something, you give all your attention to it.

tremble[복습]
[trembl]

v. 떨(리)다, 진동하다, 흔들리다
If you tremble, you shake slightly because you are frightened or cold.

dramatic[복습]
[drəmǽtik]

a. 극적인, 놀라운; 과장된, 호들갑스러운
A dramatic action, event, or situation is exciting and impressive.

timing
[táimiŋ]

n. 타이밍, 알맞은 시간 택하기; 시간 조절
Timing is the skill or action of judging the right moment in a situation or activity at which to do something.

beat someone to it

idiom 남의 선수를 치다, 남을 앞지르다
If you intend to do something but someone beats you to it, they do it before you do.

execute[**]
[éksikjuːt]

vt. 실행하다, 수행하다; 처형하다
If you execute a difficult action or movement, you successfully perform it.

flawless
[flɔ́ːlis]

a. 흠 없는, 나무랄 데 없는, 완전한
If you say that something or someone is flawless, you mean that they are extremely good and that there are no faults or problems with them.

swoon
[swuːn]

n. 기절, 졸도; 황홀; vi. 황홀해지다; 기절하다
If you swoon, you lose your consciousness and faint.

matter[복습]
[mǽtər]

vi. 중요하다; n. 물질, 문제, 일
If you say that something does matter, you mean that it is important to you because it does have an effect on you or on a particular situation.

tug[*]
[tʌg]

v. (세게) 당기다, 끌다; 노력[분투]하다; n. 힘껏 당김; 분투, 노력
If you tug something or tug at it, you give it a quick and usually strong pull.

part[***]
[paːrt]

v. (두 사물·부분이) 갈라지다[벌어지다]; (~와) 헤어지다; n. 부분
If things that are next to each other part or if you part them, they move in opposite directions, so that there is a space between them.

chant[*]
[ʧænt]

v. (단조로운 말투로) 반복해 말하다, 일제히 외치다; 노래를 부르다; n. (규칙적으로 반복되는) 문구; 노래
If you chant something or if you chant, you repeat the same words over and over again.

beat[복습]
[biːt]

n. [음악] 박자, 고동; v. 치다, 두드리다; 패배시키다, 이기다 (drumbeat n. 북소리)
The beat of a piece of music is the main rhythm that it has.

definition[*]
[dèfəníʃən]

n. 정의, 설명; 한정, 명확함
A definition is a statement giving the meaning of a word or expression, especially in a dictionary.

bother[*]
[báðər]

v. 일부러 ~하다, 애를 쓰다; 귀찮게 하다, 괴롭히다
If you do not bother to do something or if you do not bother with it, you do not do it, consider it, or use it because you think it is unnecessary or because you are too lazy.

farewell[*]
[fɛərwél]

int. 안녕! 잘 가시오!; n. 작별(인사), 고별
Farewell means the same as goodbye.

oversize[복습]
[óuvərsaiz]

a. 특대의, 너무 큰
Oversize things are too big, or much bigger than usual.

a great deal of

idiom 다량의, 많은
If you say that you need or have a great deal of or a good deal of a particular thing, you are emphasizing that you need or have a lot of it.

comfort[**]
[kʌ́mfərt]

n. 위로, 위안; vt. 위로[위안]하다
If you refer to a person, thing, or idea as a comfort, you mean that it helps you to stop worrying or makes you feel less unhappy.

sorrow[*]
[sárou]

n. 슬픔, 비통; 후회
Sorrow is a feeling of deep sadness or regret.

absolute[*]
[ǽbsəlùːt]

a. 절대적인, 무조건의; 완전한 (absolutely ad. 절대적으로, 무조건)
Absolute means total and complete.

1분에 몇 단어를 읽는지 리딩 속도를 측정해보세요.

$$\frac{574 \text{ words}}{\text{reading time ( ) sec}} \times 60 = (\quad) \text{ WPM}$$

Build Your Vocabulary

thread ^{복습}
[θred]

n. 실, 바느질 실; vt. 실을 꿰다
A thread is a long very thin piece of a material such as cotton, nylon, or silk, especially one that is used in sewing.

choke **
[ʧouk]

v. 질식시키다, 숨이 막히다; n. 질식
When you choke or when something chokes you, you cannot breathe properly or get enough air into your lungs.

tug ^{복습}
[tʌg]

v. (세게) 당기다, 끌다; 노력[분투]하다; n. 힘껏 당김; 분투, 노력
If you tug something or tug at it, you give it a quick and usually strong pull.

bark ^{복습}
[ba:rk]

v. 고함치다; (개가) 짖다; n. 짖는 소리
If you bark at someone, you shout at them aggressively in a loud, rough voice.

hood ^{복습}
[hud]

n. 복면; 두건; 자동차 보닛, 덮개
A hood is a piece of clothing pulled down over a person's face in order to make others difficult to recognize it.

echo ^{복습}
[ékou]

v. (남의 말·의견을) 그대로 되풀이하다; 울려 퍼지다, 메아리치다; n. 메아리
If you echo someone's words, you repeat them or express agreement with their attitude or opinion.

poke *
[pouk]

v. (손가락 등으로) 쿡 찌르다; n. 찌르기, 쑤시기
If you poke someone or something, you quickly push them with your finger or with a sharp object.

fling **
[fliŋ]

vt. (flung-flung) 내던지다; 내밀다; 던지다; n. 내던지기, 돌진
If you fling something somewhere, you throw it there using a lot of force.

marble *
[ma:rbl]

n. 대리석; 구슬
Marble is a type of very hard rock which feels cold when you touch it and which shines when it is cut and polished.

drape
[dreip]

n. (pl.) 덮는 천, 두꺼운 커튼; vt. 걸치다, 씌우다; 주름을 잡아 예쁘게 덮다
Drapes are pieces of heavy fabric that you hang from the top of a window and can close to keep the light out or stop people looking in.

patch ^{복습}
[pæʧ]

n. (주변과는 다른 조그만) 부분; 헝겊 조각; 반창고; v. 헝겊을 대고 깁다
A patch on a surface is a part of it which is different in appearance from the area around it.

56

pool **
[pu:l]

n. 웅덩이, (액체·빛이) 고여 있는 곳 (a poof of shade n. 음지)
A pool of liquid or light is a small area of it on the ground or on a surface.

shade **
[ʃeid]

n. (시원한) 그늘; 색조, 음영; vt. 그늘지게 하다
Shade is an area of darkness under or next to an object such as a tree, where sunlight does not reach.

clap *
[klæp]

v. 박수를 치다; n. 박수 (소리); 쿵[탁] 하는 소리
When you clap, you hit your hands together to show appreciation or attract attention.

aware **
[əwέər]

a. 알고 있는, 의식하고 있는, 알아차린 (unaware a. 알지 못하는)
If you are aware of something, you know about it.

fate 복습
[feit]

n. 운명, 숙명
A person's or thing's fate is what happens to them.

unbearable
[ʌnbέərəbəl]

a. 참을 수 없는, 견딜 수 없는
If you describe something as unbearable, you mean that it is so unpleasant, painful, or upsetting that you feel unable to accept it or deal with it.

stamp 복습
[stæmp]

v. (발을) 구르다, 짓밟다; (도장·스탬프 등을) 찍다; n. 우표, 인지; 도장
If you stamp or stamp your foot, you lift your foot and put it down very hard on the ground, for example because you are angry.

frustrate *
[frʌstreit]

v. 좌절시키다, 불만스럽게 만들다; 방해하다 (frustration n. 실망, 좌절)
If something frustrates you, it upsets or angers you because you are unable to do anything about the problems it creates.

irritable
[irətəbl]

a. 화를 잘 내는, 성미가 급한 (irritably ad. 성질내며, 화를 내며)
If you are irritable, you are easily annoyed.

shudder 복습
[ʃʌdəːr]

vi. 떨다, 몸서리치다; n. 떨림, 전율
If you shudder, you shake with fear, horror, or disgust, or because you are cold.

shrink *
[ʃriŋk]

v. (shrunk/shrank–shrunken/shrunk) 줄어들다, 오그라지다; 움츠리다
If something shrinks or something else shrinks it, it becomes smaller.

pebble *
[pebl]

n. 조약돌, 자갈
A pebble is a small, smooth, round stone which is found on beaches and at the bottom of rivers.

leap *
[li:p]

v. (leapt/leaped–leapt/leaped) (심장이) 뛰다, 고동치다; 껑충 뛰다, 뛰어넘다; n. 뜀, 도약
If you leap, you jump high in the air or jump a long distance.

recall *
[rikɔ́:l]

vt. 생각해내다, 상기하다; 소환하다; n. 회상, 상기
When you recall something, you remember it and tell others about it.

perfidy 복습
[pə́:rfədi]

n. (문어) 배신, 배신 행위
Perfidy is the action of betraying someone or behaving very badly toward someone.

progress[**]
[prəgrés]

vi. 진행되다, 나아가다; 진보하다; n. 전진, 진행; 진보, 향상
If events progress, they continue to happen gradually over a period of time.

appropriate[*]
[əpróupriət]

a. 적당한, 적절한, 알맞은; vt. 사용하다, 충당하다
Something that is appropriate is suitable or acceptable for a particular situation.

narrow[복습]
[nǽrou]

a. 좁은, 편협한; v. 좁히다, 작아지다
Something that is narrow measures a very small distance from one side to the other, especially compared to its length or height.

steep[*]
[stiːp]

a. 가파른, 비탈진; 급격한
A steep slope rises at a very sharp angle and is difficult to go up.

contemplate[*]
[kántəmplèit]

v. 응시하다, 눈여겨 보다; 심사숙고하다, 신중히 생각하다
If you contemplate something or someone, you look at them for a long time.

abyss
[əbís]

n. 심연, 깊은 구멍
An abyss is a very deep hole in the ground.

hind[복습]
[haind]

a. 뒤쪽의, 후방의
An animal's hind legs are at the back of its body.

announce[**]
[ənáuns]

vt. 알리다, 공고하다, 전하다
If you announce a piece of news or an intention, especially something that people may not like, you say it loudly and clearly, so that everyone you are with can hear it.

punish[복습]
[pʌ́niʃ]

v. 처벌하다, 벌주다 (punishment n. 처벌)
To punish someone means to make them suffer in some way because they have done something wrong.

according to

prep. ~에 따르면, ~에 따라
If someone says that something is true according to a particular person, book, or other source of information, they are indicating where they got their information.

establish[***]
[istǽbliʃ]

vt. 제정하다, 규정하다; 수립하다, 설립하다
If someone establishes something such as an organization, a type of activity, or a set of rules, they create it or introduce it in such a way that it is likely to last for a long time.

phrase[복습]
[freiz]

n. 구절; 관용구
A phrase is a short group of words that people often use as a way of saying something.

consider[복습]
[kənsídər]

v. 고려하다, 숙고하다
If you consider something, you think about it carefully.

imply[*]
[implái]

vt. 함축하다, 암시하다 (implication n. 함축, 암시)
If you imply that something is the case, you say something which indicates that it is the case in an indirect way.

tumble[**]
[tʌmbl]

v. 굴러 떨어지다, 넘어지다; n. 추락; 폭락
If someone or something tumbles somewhere, they fall there with a rolling or bouncing movement.

whisker[복습]
[wískər]

n. (고양이·쥐 등의) 수염; 구레나룻
The whiskers of an animal such as a cat or a mouse are the long stiff hairs that grow near its mouth.

cling[복습]
[kliŋ]

vi. (clung–clung) 매달리다, 달라붙다
If you cling to someone or something, you hold onto them tightly.

pinwheel
[pínhwi:l]

v. 바람개비처럼 돌다; n. (장난감) 바람개비
If something pinwheels, it revolves rapidly like a pinwheel.

descend*
[disénd]

v. 내려가다; (어둠 등이) 내려앉다; 전해지다, 유래하다
If you descend, you move downward from a higher to a lower level.

Check Your Reading Speed

1분에 몇 단어를 읽는지 리딩 속도를 측정해보세요.

$$\frac{421 \text{ words}}{\text{reading time ( ) sec}} \times 60 = (\qquad) \text{ WPM}$$

Build Your Vocabulary

get to one's feet 복습	**idiom** 벌떡 일어서다 If you get or rise to your feet, you stand up.
aware 복습 [əwéər]	**a.** 알고 있는, 의식하고 있는, 알아차린 If you are aware of something, you know about it.
**foul* [faul]	**a.** 악취가 나는, (성격·맛 등이) 더러운 If you describe something as foul, you mean it is dirty and smells or tastes unpleasant.
extreme [ikstrí:m]	**a.** 지나친, 과도한; 극단의, 극도의 (**extremely** ad. 극도로, 매우) Extreme means very great in degree or intensity.
**insult* [insʌ́lt]	**vt.** 모욕하다, 창피주다; **n.** 모욕(적인 말·행동) (**insulting** a. 모욕적인) If someone insults you, they say or do something that is rude or offensive.
dungeon 복습 [dʌ́ndʒən]	**n.** 지하 감옥; **vt.** 지하 감옥에 가두다 A dungeon is a dark underground prison in a castle.
stink [stiŋk]	**v.** (stank–stunk) (고약한) 냄새가 나다, 악취가 풍기다; **n.** 악취 To stink means to smell extremely unpleasant.
despair 복습 [dispέər]	**n.** 절망, 자포자기; **vi.** 절망하다 Despair is the feeling that everything is wrong and that nothing will improve.
**encounter* [inkáuntər]	**v.** 만나다, 마주치다; **n.** 마주침 If you encounter problems or difficulties, you experience them.
awful [ɔ́:fəl]	**a.** 몹시 나쁜, 무서운, 지독한 If you say that something is awful, you mean that it is extremely unpleasant, shocking, or bad.
encompass [inkʌ́mpəs]	**vt.** 에워싸다; 포함하다, 아우르다 To encompass a place means to completely surround or cover it.
physical [fízikəl]	**a.** 물리적인, 물질의; 신체의, 육체의 Physical things are real things that can be touched and seen, rather than ideas or spoken words.
paw 복습 [pɔ:]	**n.** (갈고리 발톱이 있는 동물의) 발; **v.** 앞발로 차다 The paws of an animal such as a cat, dog, or bear are its feet, which have claws for gripping things and soft pads for walking on.

60

alarm^{복습}
[əlá:rm]

vt. 놀라게 하다; 위급을 알리다; n. 놀람, 불안; 경보 (alarming a. 놀랄 만한)
If something alarms you, it makes you afraid or anxious that something unpleasant or dangerous might happen.

exist^{복습}
[igzíst]

v. 존재하다, 실재하다
If something exists, it is present in the world as a real thing.

echo^{복습}
[ékou]

v. 울려 퍼지다, 메아리치다; (남의 말·의견을) 그대로 되풀이하다; n. 메아리
If a sound echoes, it is reflected off a surface and can be heard again after the original sound has stopped.

perfidy^{복습}
[pə́:rfədi]

n. (문어) 배신, 배신 행위
Perfidy is the action of betraying someone or behaving very badly toward someone.

assure^{복습}
[əʃúə:r]

vt. 확신하다, 보증하다
If you assure someone that something is true or will happen, you tell them that it is definitely true or will definitely happen, often in order to make them less worried.

beloved*
[bilʌ́vd]

a. 가장 사랑하는, 소중한
A beloved person, thing, or place is one that you feel great affection for.

immediately^{복습}
[imí:diətli]

ad. 곧, 바로, 즉시
If something happens immediately, it happens without any delay.

swallow^{**}
[swálou]

v. 삼키다, 목구멍으로 넘기다; (초조해서) 마른침을 삼키다
If you swallow something, you cause it to go from your mouth down into your stomach.

shiver^{복습}
[ʃívə:r]

v. (추위·두려움·흥분 등으로) (몸을) 떨다; n. 전율
When you shiver, your body shakes slightly because you are cold or frightened.

sneeze^{복습}
[sni:z]

vi. 재채기하다; n. 재채기
When you sneeze, you suddenly take in your breath and then blow it down your nose noisily without being able to stop yourself, for example because you have a cold.

chatter^{**}
[tʃǽtər]

v. (이가 공포·추위로) 딱딱 맞부딪치다; 수다를 떨다, 재잘거리다; n. 재잘거림, 수다
If your teeth chatter, they keep knocking together because you are very cold or very nervous.

long^{**}
[lɔːŋ]

① vi. 간절히 바라다, 갈망하다 ② a. 긴, 오랜
If you long for something, you want it very much.

handkerchief^{복습}
[hǽŋkərtʃif]

n. 손수건
A handkerchief is a small square piece of fabric which you use for blowing your nose.

grab*
[græb]

v. 움켜쥐다, 부여잡다; n. 부여잡기
If you grab something such as food, drink, or sleep, you manage to get some quickly.

frighten 복습
[fraitn]

v. 놀라게 하다, 섬뜩하게 하다; 기겁하다 (frightening a. 두려운, 끔찍한)
If something or someone frightens you, they cause you to suddenly feel afraid, anxious, or nervous.

locate*
[lóukeit]

vt. 놓다, 두다; (물건의 위치 등을) 알아내다; (어떤 장소에) 정하다
If you locate something in a particular place, you put it there or build it there.

absolute 복습
[ǽbsəlù:t]

a. 완전한; 절대적인, 무조건의
Absolute means total and complete.

faint 복습
[feint]

vi. 기절하다; n. 기절, 졸도; a. 희미한, 어렴풋한
If you faint, you lose consciousness for a short time, especially because you are hungry, or because of pain, heat, or shock.

deem
[di:m]

vt. ~으로 생각하다, 간주하다
If something is deemed to have a particular quality or to do a particular thing, it is considered to have that quality or do that thing.

reasonable
[rí:zənəbl]

a. 이치에 맞는, 분별 있는, 합당한
If you say that a decision or action is reasonable, you mean that it is fair and sensible.

master 복습
[mǽstər]

n. 대가, 명인, 정통한 사람; vt. 숙달하다, 터득하다
If you say that someone is a master of a particular activity, you mean that they are extremely skilled at it.

honor 복습
[ánər]

n. 명예, 영예; vt. 존경하다, 공경하다
An honor is a special award that is given to someone, usually because they have done something good or because they are greatly respected.

courtesy 복습
[kə́:rtəsi]

n. 정중, 예의, 친절
If you refer to the courtesy of doing something, you are referring to a polite action.

devotion 복습
[divóuʃən]

n. 헌신, 전념
Devotion is great love, affection, or admiration for someone.

bravery 복습
[bréi:vəri]

n. 용기, 용맹
Bravery is brave behavior or the quality of being brave.

armor*
[á:rmər]

n. 갑옷, 철갑; vt. ~에게 갑옷을 입히다
In former times, armor was special metal clothing that soldiers wore for protection in battle.

throat 복습
[θrout]

n. 목구멍, 목 (clear one's throat idiom 목을 가다듬다, 헛기침하다)
Your throat is the back of your mouth and the top part of the tubes that go down into your stomach and your lungs.

let go of 복습

idiom (쥐고 있던 것을) 놓다, ~에서 손을 놓다
To let go of someone or something means to stop holding them.

comfort 복습
[kʌ́mfərt]

vt. 위로[위안]하다; n. 위로, 위안
If you comfort someone, you make them feel less worried, unhappy, or upset, for example by saying kind things to them.

boom[*]
[buːm]

v. (소리가) 울려 퍼지다, 쿵 하는 소리를 내다; n. 쿵 울리는 소리; 인기, 붐
When something such as someone's voice, a cannon, or a big drum booms, it makes a loud, deep sound that lasts for several seconds.

assume^{복습}
[əsjúːm]

vt. 추정하다, 가정하다; (역할·임무 등을) 맡다
If you assume that something is true, you imagine that it is true, sometimes wrongly.

overwork
[óuvərwəːrk]

v. 지나치게 하다, 혹사하다; n. 과로, 초과 노동 (overworked a. 과로한)
If you overwork or if someone overworks you, you work too hard, and are likely to become very tired or ill.

1분에 몇 단어를 읽는지 리딩 속도를 측정해보세요.

$$\frac{895 \text{ words}}{\text{reading time ( ) sec}} \times 60 = (\quad) \text{ WPM}$$

Build Your Vocabulary

cup^{복습}
[kʌp]

vt. 손바닥으로 받다[떠내다]; 두 손을 (컵 모양으로) 동그랗게 모아 쥐다; n. 컵, 잔
If you cup something in your hands, you make your hands into a curved dish-like shape and support it or hold it gently.

calloused
[kǽləst]

a. (피부에) 못[굳은살]이 박힌
A foot or hand that is calloused is covered in calluses.

stare^{복습}
[stɛər]

v. 응시하다, 뚫어지게 보다
If you stare at someone or something, you look at them for a long time.

match^{**}
[mætʃ]

① n. 성냥 ② vt. ~에 필적하다, 대등하다; 조화하다, 어울리다; n. 상대, 경기
A match is a small wooden stick with a substance on one end that produces a flame when you rub it along the rough side of a matchbox.

mark^{복습}
[maːrk]

v. 표시하다, 나타내다; n. 표시, 부호; 표적, 목표물
If something marks a surface, or if the surface marks, the surface is damaged by marks or a mark.

sputter
[spʌ́tər]

v. 펑펑[탁탁] 소리를 내다; 흥분하여 말하다, 식식거리며 말하다
If something such as an engine or a flame sputters, it works or burns in an uneven way and makes a series of soft popping sounds.

ankle[*]
[ǽŋkl]

n. 발목
Your ankle is the joint where your foot joins your leg.

descend^{복습}
[disénd]

v. (어둠 등이) 내려앉다; 내려가다; 전해지다, 유래하다
When night, dusk, or darkness descends, it starts to get dark.

beleaguer
[bilíːgər]

v. 포위하다, 둘러싸다; 괴롭히다 (beleaguered a. 포위된)
A beleaguered person, organization, or project is experiencing a lot of difficulties, opposition, or criticism.

rhythm^{복습}
[ríðm]

n. 리듬, 율동; 박자
A rhythm is a regular series of sounds or movements.

whisper^{복습}
[hwíspəːr]

v. 속삭이다; n. 속삭임; 속삭이는 소리
When you whisper, you say something very quietly.

jailer
[dʒéilər]

n. 교도관, 간수
A jailer is a person who is in charge of a jail and the prisoners in it.

64

bury[*][*]
[béri]

vt. 묻다, 파묻다, 매장하다
To bury a dead person means to put their body into a grave and cover it with earth.

decade[*]
[díkéid]

n. 10년
A decade is a period of ten years.

century[*][*]
[séntʃəri]

n. 1세기, 100년
A century is any period of a hundred years.

eon
[í:ən]

n. 무한히 긴 시기; [지질학] 이온(연대 측정의 단위, 10억 년)
An eon is an extremely long period of time.

eternity
[itə́:rnəti]

n. 영원, 무궁; 불사, 불멸
Eternity is time without an end or a state of existence outside time, especially the state which some people believe they will pass into after they have died.

irony[*]
[áiərəni]

n. 반어, 비꼬기, 역설적인 점[상황]
Irony is a subtle form of humor which involves saying things that you do not mean.

treacherous
[trétʃərəs]

a. 배반하는, 반역하는, 불충한
If you describe someone as treacherous, you mean that they are likely to betray you and cannot be trusted.

release[*]
[rilí:s]

vt. 놓아주다, 해방시키다, 풀어놓다; n. 석방
If a person or animal is released from somewhere where they have been looked after, they are set free or allowed to go.

twist[*][*]
[twist]

v. 비틀다, 돌리다, 꼬다; n. 뒤틀림; 엉킴; 변화
If you twist something, you turn it so that it moves around in a circular direction.

false[*][*]
[fɔ:ls]

a. 가짜의, 모조의; 틀린, 정확하지 않은
You use false to describe objects which are artificial but which are intended to look like the real thing or to be used instead of the real thing.

doorway[*]
[dɔ́:rwèi]

n. 문간, 현관, 출입구
A doorway is a space in a wall where a door opens and closes.

swallow[복습]
[swálou]

v. 삼키다, 목구멍으로 넘기다; (초조해서) 마른침을 삼키다
If you swallow something, you cause it to go from your mouth down into your stomach.

maze
[meiz]

n. 미로, 미궁; vt. 당혹하게 하다
A maze is a complex system of passages or paths between walls or hedges and is designed to confuse people who try to find their way through it, often as a form of amusement.

beg[*]
[beg]

vt. 부탁[간청]하다; 빌다, 구걸하다
If you beg someone to do something, you ask them very anxiously or eagerly to do it.

drag[*]
[dræg]

v. 끌(리)다, 끌고 오다; (발을) 질질 끌다; n. 견인, 끌기; 빨아들이기
If you drag something, you pull it along the ground, often with difficulty.

muck
[mʌk]

n. 쓰레기, 오물; 거름, 퇴비; **vt.** 실패하다, 망쳐놓다
Muck is dirt or some other unpleasant substance.

filth
[filθ]

n. 오물, 쓰레기; 타락
Filth is a disgusting amount of dirt.

file
[fail]

① v. (줄로) 다듬다; n. (손톱)줄; 마무리, 끝손질
② v. 줄지어 가다; 파일에 철하다, 정리 보관하다; n. 파일, (신문·서류 등의) 철
If you file an object, you smooth it, shape it, or cut it with a hand tool which is used for rubbing hard objects.

piece by piece

idiom 조금씩; 서서히
If you take something out piece by piece, you take one part at a time.

strip*
[strip]

v. 벗다, 벗기다, 떼어내다; n. 좁고 긴 땅; 길고 가느다란 조각
To strip something means to remove everything that covers it.

fur*
[fəːr]

n. 부드러운 털; 모피
Fur is the thick and usually soft hair that grows on the bodies of many mammals.

flesh**
[fleʃ]

n. 살; 육체; **vt.** (칼 등을) 살에 찌르다
Flesh is the soft part of a person's or animal's body between the bones and the skin.

tragic*
[trǽdʒik]

a. 비극의, 비참한
A tragic event or situation is extremely sad, usually because it involves death or suffering.

duty**
[djúːti]

n. 의무, 임무
If you say that something is your duty, you believe that you ought to do it because it is your responsibility.

serve복습
[səːrv]

v. 섬기다, 복무하다; 제공하다, 시중 들다; n. 서브
If you serve your country, an organization, or a person, you do useful work for them.

hark
[haːrk]

v. (명령문) 주의 깊게 듣다, 귀를 기울이다; (사냥개에 대한 명령) 가라
If you say hark to someone, you order them to listen.

strike***
[straik]

v. (struck–struck) (성냥을) 긋다; 치다, 때리다; 부딪치다, 충돌하다; n. 공격
When you strike a match, you make it produce a flame by moving it quickly against something rough.

flame**
[fleim]

n. 불꽃, 화염; v. 타오르다; 빛나다, 반짝이다; (얼굴이) 확 붉어지다
A flame is a hot bright stream of burning gas that comes from something that is burning.

illuminate*
[ilúːmənèit]

vt. 비추다, 밝히다
To illuminate something means to shine light on it and to make it brighter and more visible.

massive*
[mǽsiv]

a. 거대한, 육중한
Something that is massive is very large in size, quantity, or extent.

tower*
[tauər]

vi. 솟다; (~보다) 뛰어나다; n. 탑 (towering a. 몹시 높은)
If you describe something such as a mountain or cliff as towering, you mean that it is very tall and therefore impressive.

teeter
[tíːtər]

v. 위아래로 움직이다, 흔들리다; 시소를 타다; n. 시소
If someone or something teeters, they shake in an unsteady way, and seem to be about to lose their balance and fall over.

pile복습
[pail]

n. 쌓아 올린 더미; 다수; v. 쌓아 올리다, 쌓(이)다
A pile of things is a mass of them that is high in the middle and has sloping sides.

kettle*
[ketl]

n. 솥, 냄비; 주전자
A kettle is a metal pot for boiling or cooking things in.

monument*
[mánjumənt]

n. 기념비, 기념물
A monument is something such as a castle or bridge which was built a very long time ago and is regarded as an important part of a country's history.

evidence*
[évədəns]

n. 증거, 흔적; vt. 증명하다
Evidence is anything that you see, experience, read, or are told that causes you to believe that something is true or has really happened.

monstrosity
[manstrásəti]

n. 기괴[거대]한 것, 괴물; 기괴함
If you describe something, especially something large, as a monstrosity, you mean that you think it is extremely ugly.

junk*
[dʒʌŋk]

n. 쓰레기, 폐물, 고물
Junk is old and used goods that have little value and that you do not want any more.

heap*
[hiːp]

n. 더미, 쌓아 올린 것; 많음, 다수; vt. 쌓아 올리다
A heap of things is a pile of them, especially a pile arranged in a rather untidy way.

precious*
[préʃəs]

a. 귀한, 소중한
If you say that something such as a resource is precious, you mean that it is valuable and should not be wasted or used badly.

leathery
[léðəri]

a. 가죽 같은, 가죽 빛의
If the texture of something, for example someone's skin, is leathery, it is tough and hard, like leather.

timeworn
[táimwɔːrn]

a. 오래되어 낡은, 낡아빠진; 케케묵은, 진부한
Something that is timeworn is old or has been used a lot over a long period of time.

reduce*
[ridjúːs]

v. (~으로) 바꾸다, 변형시키다; 줄(이)다; 진압하다
If something is changed to a different or less complicated form, you can say that it is reduced to that form.

particular*
[pərtíkjələr]

a. 특정한, 특별한, 특유의 (in particular idiom 특히)
You use particular to emphasize that you are talking about one thing or one kind of thing rather than other similar ones.

Book the Second
(Chapter Sixteen to Chapter Twenty-three)

1. How did Roscuro react to light after Gregory lit the match near his face?

   A. He was blinded and could not see anything after that.

   B. He was fascinated with light and tried to find more light.

   C. He was frightened by light and tried to avoid more light.

   D. He was sad due to the light's brightness and cried.

2. What did Botticelli say was the meaning of life?

   A. The suffering of others

   B. The helping of others

   C. The generosity of others

   D. The solitude of others

3. What were the small comforts given to the prisoner?

   A. A red hat

   B. A red candle

   C. A red container

   D. A red cloth

4. What did Botticelli tell Roscuro to do with the new prisoner?

   A. He told Roscuro to tell the prisoner a story.

   B. He told Roscuro to bring some soup to the prisoner.

   C. He told Roscuro to take the red cloth from the prisoner.

   D. He told Roscuro to bite the rope around the prisoner's legs.

5. What crime did the prisoner commit to end up in the dungeon?

   A. He stole six cows.

   B. He stole seven sheep.

   C. He sold his son and wife.

   D. He sold his daughter and wife.

6. How did Roscuro feel after taking the red cloth from the prisoner?

   A. He was disappointed and gave it back to the prisoner.

   B. He was disappointed and realized he wanted the light instead.

   C. He was satisfied and wore it like a cape.

   D. He was satisfied and never wanted to seek the light again.

7. Why had Roscuro never seen happy people before?

   A. Nobody in the castle was happy.

   B. He had never seen any humans before.

   C. He only knew the miserable people in the dungeon.

   D. He could not see clearly in the dark dungeon.

8. How did Roscuro first feel when he saw the princess?

   A. He thought she was lovely and like light.

   B. He thought she was lovely and like a flower.

   C. He thought she was spoiled and like jewelry.

   D. He thought she was beautiful and like a candle.

9. Why did Roscuro climb to the chandelier?

   A. He wanted to find a way back to the dungeon.

   B. He wanted people to notice him.

   C. He wanted to get closer to the candles.

   D. He wanted to view the whole party.

10. How did Roscuro feel when he heard the princess call him a rat?

   A. He felt it was a compliment but felt embarrassed being called it.

   B. He felt it was a beautiful word and liked being called it.

   C. He felt it was an ugly word and did not like being called it.

   D. He felt that he was more like a mouse than a rat.

11. What happened when the queen saw Roscuro in her soup?

   A. The queen let him have it and got a new bowl of soup.

   B. The queen screamed and threw the bowl of soup off the table.

   C. The queen mistook him for a bug instead of a rat.

   D. The queen stated that there was a rat in her soup and died.

12. What did Roscuro see as he left that caused his heart to break?

   A. The princess staring at him with sorrow and pain

   B. The princess staring at him with love and joy

   C. The princess glaring at him with confusion and shock

   D. The princess glaring at him with disgust and anger

13. What beautiful object did Roscuro take from the banquet hall?

   A. The king's soupspoon

   B. The queen's soupspoon

   C. The queen's royal crown

   D. The queen's diamond necklace

14. In addition to something beautiful, what else did Roscuro say he would have?
    A. Revenge
    B. The princess
    C. Light
    D. Rewards

15. Which of the following did the king outlaw and why?
    A. He outlawed banquets because the queen died at a banquet.
    B. He outlawed soup because the queen died while eating soup.
    C. He outlawed rats because rats spread disease among humans.
    D. He outlawed plates because Roscuro had fallen on top of one.

16. As Despereaux listened to the music for the first time, what was happening outside the castle?
    A. Roscuro was gathering an army of rats to kidnap the princess.
    B. The Mouse Council was having a vote to decide what to do with Despereaux.
    C. A wagon carrying spoons, bowls, kettles, and a young girl was headed to the castle.
    D. People were bringing cats to the king in order to get rid of the rats.

1분에 몇 단어를 읽는지 리딩 속도를 측정해보세요.

$$\frac{1{,}140 \text{ words}}{\text{reading time ( ) sec}} \times 60 = (\quad) \text{ WPM}$$

Build Your Vocabulary

filth^{복습}
[filθ]

n. 오물, 쓰레기; 타락
Filth is a disgusting amount of dirt.

definition^{복습}
[dèfəníʃən]

n. 정의, 설명; 한정, 명확함
A definition is a statement giving the meaning of a word or expression, especially in a dictionary.

arrange^{복습}
[əréindʒ]

v. 가지런히 하다, 배열하다; 준비하다 (arrangement n. 배열)
If you arrange things somewhere, you place them in a particular position, usually in order to make them look attractive or tidy.

humor**
[hjú:mər]

n. 유머, 익살; vt. 맞장구치다, 비위를 맞춰주다
Someone who has a sense of humor often finds things amusing, rather than being serious all the time.

prophecy
[práfəsi]

n. 예언
A prophecy is a statement in which someone says they strongly believe that a particular thing will happen.

come upon

idiom ~을 우연히 만나다[발견하다]
If you come upon something, you meet or encounter it unexpectedly.

length^{복습}
[leŋθ]

n. 길이; (무엇이 계속되는) 시간[기간]
The length of something is the amount that it measures from one end to the other along the longest side.

nibble^{복습}
[nibl]

v. 조금씩 물어뜯다, 갉아먹다; n. 조금씩 물어뜯기, 한 입 분량
If you nibble food, you eat it by biting very small pieces of it.

boom^{복습}
[bu:m]

v. (소리가) 울려 퍼지다, 쿵 하는 소리를 내다; n. 쿵 울리는 소리; 인기, 붐
When something such as someone's voice, a cannon, or a big drum booms, it makes a loud, deep sound that lasts for several seconds.

suspend*
[səspénd]

v. 매달다, 걸다; 중지하다
If something is suspended from a high place, it is hanging from that place.

upside down
[ʌ́psàid dáun]

ad. 거꾸로, 뒤집혀
If something has been moved upside down, it has been turned round so that the part that is usually lowest is above the part that is usually highest.

smart-alecky
[smá:rt-æ̀liki]

a. 잘난 체하는, 똑똑한 체하는, 자만심이 강한
If you describe someone as smart-alecky, you dislike the fact that they think they are very clever and always have an answer for everything.

mess*
[mes]

v. 망쳐놓다, 방해하다; n. 엉망진창, 난잡함
If you mess with something, you use or treat it carelessly, causing damage.

match^{복습}
[mætʃ]

① n. 성냥 ② vt. ~에 필적하다, 대등하다; 조화하다, 어울리다; n. 상대, 경기
A match is a small wooden stick with a substance on one end that produces a flame when you rub it along the rough side of a matchbox.

thumb**
[θʌm]

n. 엄지손가락; v. (책을) 엄지손가락으로 넘기다
Your thumb is the short thick part on the side of your hand next to your four fingers.

brilliant^{복습}
[bríljənt]

a. 빛나는, 반짝이는; 훌륭한, 멋진
You describe light, or something that reflects light, as brilliant when it shines very brightly.

flame^{복습}
[fleim]

n. 불꽃, 화염; v. 타오르다; 빛나다, 반짝이다; (얼굴이) 확 붉어지다
A flame is a hot bright stream of burning gas that comes from something that is burning.

alas^{복습}
[əlǽs]

int. (슬픔·걱정을 나타내어) 아아, 슬프도다!, 불쌍한지고!
Alas is used to express sadness or regret.

explode*
[iksplóud]

v. 폭발하다, 격발하다; 폭발시키다
If an object such as a bomb explodes or if someone or something explodes it, it bursts loudly and with great force, often causing damage or injury.

off-limits

n. 출입금지(구역)
If a place is off-limits to someone, they are not allowed to go there.

apologize**
[əpálədʒàiz]

v. 사과하다, 사죄하다
When you apologize to someone, you say that you are sorry that you have hurt them or caused trouble for them.

chew*
[tʃuː]

v. 씹다, 씹어서 으깨다, 물다
If a person or animal chews an object, they bite it with their teeth.

whisker^{복습}
[wískər]

n. (고양이·쥐 등의) 수염; 구레나룻
The whiskers of an animal such as a cat or a mouse are the long stiff hairs that grow near its mouth.

jailer^{복습}
[dʒéilər]

n. 교도관, 간수
A jailer is a person who is in charge of a jail and the prisoners in it.

release^{복습}
[rilíːs]

vt. 놓아주다, 해방시키다, 풀어놓다; n. 석방
If a person or animal is released from somewhere where they have been looked after, they are set free or allowed to go.

fling^{복습}
[fliŋ]

vt. (flung–flung) 내던지다; 내밀다, 던지다; n. 내던지기, 돌진
If you fling something somewhere, you throw it there using a lot of force.

beat^{복습}
[biːt]

v. 치다, 두드리다; 패배시키다, 이기다; n. [음악] 박자, 고동
When your heart or pulse beats, it continually makes regular rhythmic movements.

abnormal*
[æbnɔ́ːrməl]

a. 보통과 다른, 비정상적인
Someone or something that is abnormal is unusual, especially in a way that is worrying.

inordinate
[inɔ́ːrdənət]

a. 과도한, 지나친
If you describe something as inordinate, you are emphasizing that it is unusually or excessively great in amount or degree.

illuminate^{복습}
[ilúːmənèit]

vt. 비추다, 밝히다 (illumination n. (불)빛, 조명)
To illuminate something means to shine light on it and to make it brighter and more visible.

lookout*
[lúkàut]

n. 경계, 감시; 전망, 예상
(be on the lookout for idiom ~을 망보고 있다, 경계하고 있다)
If you are on the lookout for something, you are searching for it.

glimmer
[glímər]

n. 희미한 빛; vi. 희미하게 빛나다, 깜빡이다
A glimmer is a faint, gentle, often unsteady light.

shimmer
[ʃímər]

n. 어른거리는 빛; vi. 희미하게 반짝이다, 빛나다
A shimmer is a faint, unsteady light.

long^{복습}
[lɔːŋ]

① vi. 간절히 바라다, 갈망하다 ② a. 긴, 오랜
If you long for something, you want it very much.

inexplicable
[inéksplikəbl]

a. 설명할 수 없는, 해석할 수 없는 (inexplicably ad. 불가사의하게도)
If something is inexplicable, you cannot explain why it happens or why it is true.

despair^{복습}
[dispéər]

vi. 절망하다; n. 절망, 자포자기
If you despair of something, you feel that there is no hope that it will happen or improve.

sentiment*
[séntəmənt]

n. 심정, 감정; 정서, 감상
A sentiment that people have is an attitude which is based on their thoughts and feelings.

have nothing to do with

idiom ~와 관계가 없다
To have nothing to do with something means not to be connected or concerned with it.

specific**
[spisífik]

a. 명확한, 구체적인; 특정의 (specifically ad. 명확하게, 특히)
You use specific to refer to a particular fixed area, problem, or subject.

reduce^{복습}
[ridjúːs]

v. (~으로) 바꾸다, 변형시키다; 줄(이)다; 진압하다
If something is changed to a different or less complicated form, you can say that it is reduced to that form.

weep^{복습}
[wiːp]

v. 눈물을 흘리다, 울다; 물기를 내뿜다
If someone weeps, they cry.

wail
[weil]

v. 울부짖다, 통곡하다; n. 울부짖음, 통곡
If someone wails, they make long, loud, high-pitched cries which express sorrow or pain.

74

beg ^{복습}
[beg]

vt. 부탁[간청]하다; 빌다, 구걸하다
If you beg someone to do something, you ask them very anxiously or eagerly to do it.

delightful ^{복습}
[diláitfəl]

a. 기쁨을 주는, 정말 기분 좋은
If you describe something or someone as delightful, you mean they are very pleasant.

invest *
[invést]

vt. 부여하다; (돈·자본을) 투자하다; (시간·노력 등을) 쏟다
To invest someone with rights or responsibilities means to give them those rights or responsibilities legally or officially.

swing **
[swiŋ]

v. (swung-swung) 휘두르다; (한 점을 축으로 하여) 빙 돌다, 휙 움직이다;
n. 휘두르기, 스윙; 흔들기
If something swings in a particular direction or if you swing it in that direction, it moves in that direction with a smooth, curving movement.

extraordinary *
[ikstrɔ́:rdənèri]

a. 놀라운, 비상한 (extraordinarily ad. 비상하게, 엄청나게)
If you describe something as extraordinary, you mean that it is very unusual or surprising.

locket
[lákit]

n. 로켓(사진 등을 넣어 목걸이에 다는 작은 갑)
A locket is a piece of jewelry containing something such as a picture, which a woman wears on a chain around her neck.

braid *
[breid]

vt. (머리·끈 등을) 꼬다, 땋다; n. 끈[땋은] 끈, 노끈; 땋은 머리
If you braid hair or a group of threads, you twist three or more lengths of the hair or threads over and under each other to make one thick length.

torture *
[tɔ́:rtʃər]

vt. 고문하다, 고통을 주다; n. 고문, 고뇌
To torture someone means to cause them to suffer mental pain or anxiety.

convince *
[kənvíns]

vt. 확신[납득]시키다, 설득하다
If someone or something convinces you of something, they make you believe that it is true or that it exists.

encourage **
[inkə́:ridʒ]

vt. 용기를 북돋우다, 장려하다
If you encourage someone, you give them confidence, hope, or support.

confess **
[kənfés]

v. 고백하다, 자백하다, 인정하다
If someone confesses to doing something wrong, they admit that they did it.

sin ^{복습}
[sin]

n. 죄, 죄악; v. 죄를 짓다, 나쁜 짓을 하다
A sin is any action or behavior that people disapprove of or consider morally wrong.

grant **
[grænt]

vt. 주다, 수여하다; 승인하다; n. 허가, 인가
If someone in authority grants you something, or if something is granted to you, you are allowed to have it.

deny ^{복습}
[dinái]

v. 사실이 아니라고 말하다, 부인[부정]하다
When you deny something, you state that it is not true.

withhold
[wiðhóuld]

vt. 보류하다, 억제하다
If you withhold something that someone wants, you do not let them have it.

lecture*
[lékʧər]

n. 훈계, 설교; 강의, 강연; v. 설교[훈계]하다; 강의하다
A lecture is a talk someone gives in order to teach people about a particular subject, usually at a university or college.

breath복습
[breθ]

n. 숨, 호흡 (catch one's breath idiom 숨을 가다듬다)
Your breath is the air that you let out through your mouth when you breathe.

sway*
[swei]

v. 흔들(리)다, 움직이다; 동요하다; 설득하다; n. 동요
When people or things sway, they lean or swing slowly from one side to the other.

wipe*
[waip]

vt. 닦다, 닦아 내다; n. 닦기
If you wipe something, you rub its surface to remove dirt or liquid from it.

sigh복습
[sai]

v. 한숨 쉬다; n. 한숨, 탄식
When you sigh, you let out a deep breath, as a way of expressing feelings such as disappointment, tiredness, or pleasure.

content*
[kəntént]

a. 만족하여; vt. ~에게 만족을 주다, 만족시키다 (contentment n. 만족)
If you are content, you are fairly happy or satisfied.

motion*
[móuʃən]

n. (사물의) 운동, 움직임; 동작, 몸짓; v. 몸짓으로 알리다
If a process or event is set in motion, it is happening or beginning to happen.

induce*
[indjúːs]

vt. 야기하다, 일으키다; 꾀다, 설득하여 ~하게 하다
To induce a state or condition means to cause it.

physical복습
[fízikəl]

a. 신체의, 육체의; 물리적인, 물질의
Physical qualities, actions, or things are connected with a person's body, rather than with their mind.

terror*
[térər]

n. 공포, 두려움; 테러 (행위)
A terror is something that makes you very frightened.

chock-full
[ʧák-ful]

a. ~으로 가득 찬, 꽉 들어찬
Something that is chock-full is completely full.

current*
[kɔ́ːrənt]

a. 현행의, 지금의, 현재의; 유행하는; n. 해류, 기류; 흐름 (currently ad. 현재는)
Current means happening, being used, or being done at the present time.

sooner or later

idiom 머지않아, 조만간
Sooner or later means at some time in the future, even if you are not sure exactly when.

guarantee*
[gærəntíː]

vt. 보증하다, 단언하다; n. 보증, 개런티
If you guarantee something, you promise that it will definitely happen, or that you will do or provide it for someone.

76

look forward to

idiom ~을 고대하다

If you look forward to something, you feel excited about it that is going to happen because you expect to enjoy it.

concern**
[kənsə́ːrn]

vt. 걱정하다, 염려하다; ~에 관계하다; n. 염려; 관심

If you concern yourself with something, you give it attention because you think that it is important.

fit*
[fit]

v. 꼭 맞다, 잘 어울리다; 맞추다, 끼우다; a. 알맞은, 적합한

If something fits something else or fits into it, it goes together well with that thing or is able to be part of it.

neat**
[niːt]

a. 산뜻한, 깔끔한; 뛰어난, 훌륭한 (neatly ad. 깔끔하게)

A neat place, thing, or person is tidy and smart, and has everything in the correct place.

1분에 몇 단어를 읽는지 리딩 속도를 측정해보세요.

$$\frac{685 \text{ words}}{\text{reading time (} \quad \text{) sec}} \times 60 = (\quad) \text{ WPM}$$

Build Your Vocabulary

dungeon^{복습}
[dʌ́ndʒən]

n. 지하 감옥; vt. 지하 감옥에 가두다
A dungeon is a dark underground prison in a castle.

slam*
[slæm]

v. 쾅 닫(히)다; 세게 놓다, 세게 치다; n. 쾅 (하는 소리)
If you slam a door or window or if it slams, it shuts noisily and with great force.

shaft*
[ʃæft]

n. 한 줄기의 광선[빛]; (도끼·골프채 등의) 자루, 손잡이
A shaft of light is a beam of light, for example sunlight shining through an opening.

paw^{복습}
[pɔː]

n. (갈고리 발톱이 있는 동물의) 발; v. 앞발로 차다
The paws of an animal such as a cat, dog, or bear are its feet, which have claws for gripping things and soft pads for walking on.

gasp^{복습}
[gæsp]

v. 숨이 턱 막히다, 헉 하고 숨을 쉬다; n. (숨이 막히는 듯) 헉 하는 소리를 냄
When you gasp, you take a short quick breath through your mouth, especially when you are surprised, shocked, or in pain.

wonder^{복습}
[wʌ́ndər]

n. 경탄할 만한 것, 경이; v. 호기심을 가지다, 이상하게 여기다
If you say that it is a wonder that something happened, you mean that it is very surprising and unexpected.

comfort^{복습}
[kʌ́mfərt]

n. 위로, 위안; vt. 위로[위안]하다
Comfort is what you feel when worries or unhappiness stop.

suspend^{복습}
[səspénd]

v. 매달다, 걸다; 중지하다
If something is suspended from a high place, it is hanging from that place.

glow*
[glou]

vi. 빛을 내다, 빛나다; n. 빛, 밝음
If something glows, it produces a dull, steady light.

bend^{복습}
[bend]

v. (bent–bent) 구부리다, 돌리다; 구부러지다, 휘다; n. 커브, 굽음
When you bend a part of your body such as your arm or leg, or when it bends, you change its position so that it is no longer straight.

drape^{복습}
[dreip]

vt. 걸치다, 씌우다; 주름을 잡아 예쁘게 덮다; n. (pl.) 덮는 천, 두꺼운 커튼
If you drape a piece of cloth somewhere, you place it there so that it hangs down in a casual and graceful way.

cloak*
[klouk]

n. 소매 없는 외투, 망토; vt. 입고 있다; 가리다, 은폐하다
A cloak is a long, loose, sleeveless piece of clothing which people used to wear over their other clothes when they went out.

leak *
[liːk]

v. (액체·기체가) 새게 하다, 새다; n. (액체·기체가) 새는 곳; 누출, 누수
If a container leaks, there is a hole or crack in it which lets a substance such as liquid or gas escape.

hideous *
[hídiəs]

a. 끔찍한, 오싹한, 흉측한 (hideously ad. 소름 끼칠 만큼)
If you say that someone or something is hideous, you mean that they are very ugly or unattractive.

ridiculous 복습
[ridíkjuləs]

a. 터무니없는; 웃기는, 우스꽝스러운
If you say that something or someone is ridiculous, you mean that they are very foolish.

intent 복습
[intént]

① a. 몰두하는, 여념이 없는 (intently ad. 골똘하게) ② n. 의지, 의향
If you are intent on doing something, you are eager and determined to do it.

obsession
[əbséʃən]

n. 강박 관념, 망상, 집념
If you say that someone has an obsession with a person or thing, you think they are spending too much time thinking about them.

tiresome *
[táiərsəm]

a. 지겨운, 따분한; 성가신, 짜증스러운
If you describe someone or something as tiresome, you mean that you find them irritating or boring.

but ***
[bət]

n. 이의; conj. 그러나
You use buts in expressions like 'no buts' and 'ifs and buts' to refer to reasons someone gives for not doing something, especially when you do not think that they are good reasons.

domain
[douméin]

n. 영역, 영토
A domain is a particular field of thought, activity, or interest, especially one over which someone has control, influence, or rights.

locket 복습
[lákit]

n. 로켓(사진 등을 넣어 목걸이에 다는 작은 갑)
A locket is a piece of jewelry containing something such as a picture, which a woman wears on a chain around her neck.

swing 복습
[swiŋ]

v. 휘두르다; (한 점을 축으로 하여) 빙 돌다, 획 움직이다; n. 휘두르기, 스윙; 흔들기
If something swings in a particular direction or if you swing it in that direction, it moves in that direction with a smooth, curving movement.

spit *
[spit]

v. (spat/spit–spat/spit) (침을) 뱉다, 토하다; 내뱉듯이 말하다; n. 침
If someone spits, they force an amount of liquid out of their mouth, often to show hatred or contempt.

despicable
[dispíkəbl]

a. 야비한, 비열한
If you say that a person or action is despicable, you are emphasizing that they are extremely nasty, cruel, or evil.

opposite **
[ápəzit]

n. 정반대의 일[것]; a. 반대편의, 맞은편의; 정반대의; ad. 정반대의 위치에
The opposite of someone or something is the person or thing that is most different from them.

strive *
[straiv]

vi. 노력하다, 분투하다
If you strive to do something or strive for something, you make a great effort to do it or get it.

sliver
[slívə:r]

n. 찢어진 조각, 가느다란 조각; vt. 가늘고 길게 베다[찢다]
A sliver of something is a small thin piece or amount of it.

shine^{복습}
[ʃain]

v. (shone-shone) 빛나(게 하)다, 반짝이다; n. 빛, 빛남, 광채
Something that shines is very bright and clear because it is reflecting light.

torture^{복습}
[tɔ́:rtʃər]

vt. 고문하다, 고통을 주다; n. 고문, 고뇌
To torture someone means to cause them to suffer mental pain or anxiety.

crave
[kreiv]

v. 갈망하다, 간절히 원하다
If you crave something, you want to have it very much.

cheat**
[tʃi:t]

v. 속이다; 규칙을 어기다; n. 사기
When someone cheats, they do not obey a set of rules which they should be obeying, for example in a game or exam.

spin**
[spin]

v. 돌다, 회전시키다; (실을) 잣다, (이야기를) 지어내다; n. 회전
If something spins or if you spin it, it turns quickly around a central point.

backdrop
[bǽkdràp]

n. 배경, 배경막; vt. 배경막을 달다
A backdrop is a large piece of cloth, often with scenery painted on it, that is hung at the back of a stage while a play is being performed.

1분에 몇 단어를 읽는지 리딩 속도를 측정해보세요.

$$\frac{777 \text{ words}}{\text{reading time ( ) sec}} \times 60 = (\quad) \text{ WPM}$$

Build Your Vocabulary

torment＊
[tɔ:rmént]

vt. 괴롭히다, 고문하다; n. 고통, 고뇌
If you torment a person or animal, you annoy them in a playful, rather cruel way for your own amusement.

stretch^{복습}
[stretʃ]

v. 쭉 펴다, 뻗다; 뻗어 있다; 늘이다; n. 뻗침
When you stretch, you put your arms or legs out straight and tighten your muscles.

chain＊＊
[tʃein]

v. (사슬로) 묶다; n. 사슬, 쇠줄; 일련
If a person or thing is chained to something, they are fastened to it with a chain.

drape^{복습}
[dreip]

vt. 걸치다, 씌우다; 주름을 잡아 예쁘게 덮다; n. (pl.) 덮는 천, 두꺼운 커튼
If you drape a piece of cloth somewhere, you place it there so that it hangs down in a casual and graceful way.

squeeze^{복습}
[skwi:z]

v. (억지로) 비집고 들어가다; (꼭) 짜다, 쥐다; n. (꼭) 짜기
If you squeeze a person or thing somewhere or if they squeeze there, they manage to get through or into a small space.

creep^{복습}
[kri:p]

vi. (crept–crept) 살금살금 걷다, 기다; n. 포복
When people or animals creep somewhere, they move quietly and slowly.

damp＊
[dæmp]

a. 축축한, 습기 있는; n. 습기
Something that is damp is slightly wet.

weep^{복습}
[wi:p]

v. 물기를 내뿜다; 눈물을 흘리다, 울다 (weeping a. 물이 새어나오는)
If something as soil, a rock, a plant stem, or a sore weeps, water or liquid comes from it.

cell＊＊
[sel]

n. 독방, 독실; 작은 방; 세포
A cell is a small room in which a prisoner is locked.

delighted＊
[diláitid]

a. 아주 기뻐하여, 즐거워하는
If you are delighted, you are extremely pleased and excited about something.

match^{복습}
[mætʃ]

① n. 성냥 ② vt. ~에 필적하다, 대등하다; 조화하다, 어울리다; n. 상대, 경기
A match is a small wooden stick with a substance on one end that produces a flame when you rub it along the rough side of a matchbox.

stare^{복습} [stɛər]	v. 응시하다, 뚫어지게 보다 If you stare at someone or something, you look at them for a long time.
long^{복습} [lɔːŋ]	① vi. 간절히 바라다, 갈망하다 (longingly ad. 간절히) ② a. 긴, 오랜 If you long for something, you want it very much.
congratulate^{**} [kəngrǽtʃulèit]	vt. 축하하다 If you congratulate someone, you say something to show you are pleased that something nice has happened to them.
astute [əstjúːt]	a. 통찰력 있는, 기민한; 약삭빠른, 영악한 If you describe someone as astute, you think they show an understanding of behavior and situations, and are skillful at using this knowledge to their own advantage.
observe^{복습} [əbzɔ́ːrv]	v. 관찰하다, 목격하다; 알다, 알아채다 (observation n. 관찰, 감시) If you observe a person or thing, you watch them carefully, especially in order to learn something about them.
for one's sake^{복습}	idiom ~ 때문에, ~를 위해서 When you do something for someone's sake, you do it in order to help them or make them happy.
company^{***} [kʌ́mpəni]	n. 친구, 동료; 교제; 회사; v. 사귀다; 따르다, 동행하다 (keep a person company idiom 남의 상대가 되다) If you keep someone company, you spend time with them and stop them feeling lonely or bored.
crawl^{복습} [krɔːl]	vi. 기어가다, 느릿느릿 가다; 우글거리다; 들끓다; n. 서행; 기어감 When you crawl, you move forward on your hands and knees.
solace [sáləs]	n. 위안, 위로; v. 위안[위로]하다 Solace is a feeling of comfort that makes you feel less sad.
sympathetic[*] [simpəθétik]	a. 동정심 있는, 인정 있는; 마음에 드는 If you are sympathetic to someone who is in a bad situation, you are kind to them and show that you understand their feelings.
confess^{복습} [kənfés]	v. 고백하다, 자백하다, 인정하다 If someone confesses to doing something wrong, they admit that they did it.
sin^{복습} [sin]	n. 죄, 죄악; v. 죄를 짓다, 나쁜 짓을 하다 A sin is any action or behavior that people disapprove of or consider morally wrong.
kid^{**} [kid]	① v. 놀리다, 장난치다; 속이다 ② n. 어린이 If you are kidding, you are saying something that is not really true, as a joke.
pretend^{***} [priténd]	v. 가장하다, ~인 체하다; a. 가짜의 If you pretend that something is the case, you act in a way that is intended to make people believe that it is the case, although in fact it is not.
desperate^{**} [déspərət]	a. 절망적인, 자포자기의; 필사적인 A desperate situation is very difficult, serious, or dangerous.

throat^{복습}
[θrout]

n. 목구멍, 목 (clear one's throat idiom 목을 가다듬다, 헛기침하다)
Your throat is the back of your mouth and the top part of the tubes that go down into your stomach and your lungs.

steal***
[sti:l]

v. 훔치다, 도둑질하다; n. 도둑질, 절도
If you steal something from someone, you take it away from them without their permission and without intending to return it.

theft
[θeft]

n. 도둑질, 절도
Theft is the crime of stealing.

crime**
[kraim]

n. 범죄, 죄
A crime is an illegal action or activity for which a person can be punished by law.

trade***
[treid]

v. 교환하다; 장사하다; n. 교환, 무역; 직업
When people, firms, or countries trade, they buy, sell, or exchange goods or services between themselves.

tablecloth*
[téiblklɔ:θ]

n. 식탁보, 테이블보
A tablecloth is a cloth used to cover a table.

hen*
[hen]

n. 암탉
A hen is a female chicken. People often keep hens in order to eat them or sell their eggs.

handful*
[hǽndfùl]

n. 한 움큼, 한 줌; 소량, 소수
A handful of something is the amount of it that you can hold in your hand.

cigarette*
[sìgərét]

n. 담배
Cigarettes are small tubes of paper containing tobacco which people smoke.

alarm^{복습}
[əlá:rm]

vt. 놀라게 하다; 위급을 알리다; n. 놀람, 불안; 경보 (alarmed a. 놀란)
If something alarms you, it makes you afraid or anxious that something unpleasant or dangerous might happen.

hideous^{복습}
[hídiəs]

a. 끔찍한, 오싹한, 흉측한
If you say that someone or something is hideous, you mean that they are very ugly or unattractive.

profit**
[práfit]

n. 이득, 이익; v. 이익을 얻다, 득이 되다
A profit is an amount of money that you gain when you are paid more for something than it cost you to make, get, or do it.

recite*
[risáit]

v. (상세히) 말하다; 열거하다; 암송[낭독]하다
If you recite something such as a list, you say it aloud.

confession*
[kənféʃən]

n. (죄의) 자백, 고백[인정]; 고해, 고백 성사
A confession is a signed statement by someone in which they admit that they have committed a particular crime.

encourage^{복습}
[inkɔ́:ridʒ]

vt. 용기를 북돋우다, 장려하다
If you encourage someone, you give them confidence, hope, or support.

sniff ^{복습}
[snif]

v. 코를 훌쩍이다; 냄새를 맡다, 코를 킁킁거리다; n. 냄새 맡음
When you sniff, you breathe in air through your nose hard enough to make a sound.

worth**
[wəːrθ]

a. ~의 가치가 있는; n. 가치, 값어치
If something is worth a particular amount of money, it can be sold for that amount or is considered to have that value.

remind**
[rimáind]

vt. 생각나게 하다, 상기시키다, 일깨우다
If someone reminds you of a fact or event that you already know about, they say something which makes you think about it.

ease**
[iːz]

v. (고통·고민 등을) 진정[완화]시키다; 살짝 움직이다[옮기다]; n. 편함, 안정
If something unpleasant eases or if you ease it, it is reduced in degree, speed, or intensity.

burden**
[bəːrdn]

n. 짐, 부담; vt. 짐을 지우다, 부담시키다
If you describe a problem or a responsibility as a burden, you mean that it causes someone a lot of difficulty, worry, or hard work.

hind ^{복습}
[haind]

a. 뒤쪽의, 후방의
An animal's hind legs are at the back of its body.

bow ^{복습}
[bau]

① v. 머리를 숙이다, 굽히다 ② n. 활; 곡선
When you bow, you move your head or the top half of your body forward and downward as a formal way of greeting them or showing respect.

reminder
[rimáindəːr]

n. 생각나게 하는 것, 상기시키는 조언
Something that serves as a reminder of another thing makes you think about the other thing.

reverse*
[rivə́ːrs]

n. (정)반대, 역; a. 거꾸로 된, 정반대의; v. (정반대로) 뒤바꾸다, 반전[역전]시키다
(in reverse idiom 반대로, 거꾸로)
If something happens in reverse or goes into reverse, things happen in the opposite way to what usually happens or to what has been happening.

accurate**
[ǽkjurət]

a. 정확한, 틀림없는; 정밀한
Accurate information, measurements, and statistics are correct to a very detailed level.

drag ^{복습}
[dræg]

v. 끌(리)다, 끌고 오다; (발을) 질질 끌다; n. 견인, 끌기; 빨아들이기
If you drag something, you pull it along the ground, often with difficulty.

consider ^{복습}
[kənsídər]

v. 고려하다, 숙고하다
If you consider something, you think about it carefully.

flood**
[flʌd]

v. 가득 차(게 하)다, 쇄도하다, 물밀듯이 밀려들다; 넘치다, 범람하다; n. 홍수; 다수
If light floods a place or floods into it, it suddenly fills it.

blind**
[blaind]

vt. 눈멀게 하다; 가리다, 보이지 않게 하다; a. 눈먼, 장님인
If something blinds you, it makes you unable to see, either for a short time or permanently.

84

1분에 몇 단어를 읽는지 리딩 속도를 측정해보세요.

$$\frac{406 \text{ words}}{\text{reading time (} \quad \text{) sec}} \times 60 = (\quad) \text{ WPM}$$

Build Your Vocabulary

polish*
[páliʃ]

v. 닦다, 윤내다; n. 광택; 세련 (polished a. 광이 나는)
If you polish something, you rub it with a cloth to make it shine.

wink*
[wiŋk]

v. (빛이) 깜박거리다; 윙크하다; n. 윙크
If something winks, it shines with a light which changes from bright to faint.

copper*
[kápər]

n. 구리 (제품), 동; 동전; vt. 구리를 씌우다
Copper is reddish brown metal that is used to make things such as coins and electrical wires.

armor^{복습}
[á:rmər]

n. 갑옷, 철갑; vt. ~에게 갑옷을 입히다
In former times, armor was special metal clothing that soldiers wore for protection in battle.

tapestry*
[tǽpistri]

n. 태피스트리(색색의 실로 수놓은 벽걸이나 실내장식용 비단)
A tapestry is a large piece of heavy cloth with a picture sewn on it using colored threads.

sew*
[sou]

v. (sewed–sewn/sewed) 바느질하다, 꿰매다, 깁다
When you sew something such as clothes, you make them or repair them by joining pieces of cloth together by passing thread through them with a needle.

destine^{복습}
[déstin]

vt. ~할 운명에 있다
If something is destined to happen or if someone is destined to behave in a particular way, that thing seems certain to happen or be done.

bedazzle
[bidǽzl]

v. 강렬한 인상을 주다, 매혹하다
If you are bedazzled by someone or something, you are so amazed and impressed by them that you feel confused.

occur**
[əkə́:r]

vi. 일어나다, 생기다; 생각이 떠오르다
When something occurs, it happens.

delighted^{복습}
[diláitid]

a. 아주 기뻐하여, 즐거워하는
If you are delighted, you are extremely pleased and excited about something.

spin^{복습}
[spin]

v. 돌다, 회전시키다; (실을) 잣다, (이야기를) 지어내다; n. 회전
If something spins or if you spin it, it turns quickly around a central point.

dizzy*
[dízi]

a. 현기증 나는, 아찔한; vt. 어지럽게 하다 (dizzily ad. 현기증이 나게, 어지럽게)
If you feel dizzy, you feel as if everything is spinning round and being unable to balance.

torture^{복습}
[tɔ́ːrʧər]

vt. 고문하다, 고통을 주다; n. 고문, 고뇌
To torture someone means to cause them to suffer mental pain or anxiety.

waltz
[wɔːlts]

v. 춤추듯이 걷다; 왈츠를 추다; n. 왈츠(두 사람이 추는 3박자의 우아한 원무)
If you say that someone waltzes somewhere, you mean that they do something in a relaxed and confident way.

banquet*
[bǽŋkwit]

n. 연회; v. 연회를 베풀어 대접하다
A banquet is a grand formal dinner.

noble*
[noubl]

a. 귀족의; 고결한, 숭고한
Noble means belonging to a high social class and having a title.

juggle*
[dʒʌgl]

v. 저글링 하다, 공중 던지기하다; 곡예를 하다 (juggler n. 저글링 하는 사람)
If you juggle, you entertain people by throwing things into the air, catching each one and throwing it up again so that there are several of them in the air at the same time.

minstrel
[mínstrəl]

n. (중세의) 음악가[음유 시인]
In medieval times, a minstrel was a singer and musician who traveled around and entertained noble families.

miserable*
[mízərəbl]

a. 비참한, 초라한, 불쌍한
If you are miserable, you are very unhappy.

jailer^{복습}
[dʒéilər]

n. 교도관, 간수
A jailer is a person who is in charge of a jail and the prisoners in it.

consign
[kənsáin]

v. 위탁하다, 넘기다, 맡기다; 충당하다, 할당하다
To consign something or someone to a place where they will be forgotten about, or to an unpleasant situationor place, means to put them there.

domain^{복습}
[douméin]

n. 영역, 영토
A domain is a particular field of thought, activity, or interest, especially one over which someone has control, influence, or rights.

clink
[kliŋk]

v. 쨍그랑[짤랑] 하는 소리를 내다; n. 쨍그랑, 짤랑
If objects clink or if you clink them, they touch each other and make a short, light sound.

enchant*
[inʧǽnt]

vt. 매혹하다; 마법을 걸다
If you are enchanted by someone or something, they cause you to have feelings of great delight or pleasure.

glitter*
[glítər]

vi. 반짝반짝 빛나다, 반짝이다; n. 반짝이는 빛
If something glitters, light comes from or is reflected off different parts of it.

jingle
[dʒiŋgl]

v. 짤랑짤랑 소리를 내다; n. 딸랑딸랑 울리는 소리 (jingle bell n. 징글벨, 방울)
When something jingles or when you jingle it, it makes a gentle ringing noise, like small bells.

86

string**
[striŋ]

n. (악기의) 현[줄]; 끈, 실; v. 묶다, 매달다
The strings on a musical instrument such as a violin or guitar are the thin pieces of wire or nylon stretched across it that make sounds when the instrument is played.

gown*
[gaun]

n. 특별한 경우에 입는 여성의) 드레스; (판사의) 법복; 가운
A gown is a dress, usually a long dress, which women wear on formal occasions.

sequin
[síːkwin]

n. 장식용 번쩍이는 작은 원형 금속 조각
Sequins are small, shiny discs that are sewn on clothes to decorate them.

glimmer^{복습}
[glímər]

vi. 희미하게 빛나다, 깜빡이다; n. 희미한 빛
If something glimmers, it produces or reflects a faint, gentle, often unsteady light.

glow^{복습}
[glou]

vi. 빛을 내다, 빛나다; n. 빛, 밝음
If something glows, it produces a dull, steady light.

extraordinary^{복습}
[ikstrɔ́ːrdənèri]

a. 놀라운, 비상한
If you describe something as extraordinary, you mean that it is very unusual or surprising.

angle**
[ǽŋgl]

n. 각도, 관점; 귀퉁이; vt. (어떤 각도로) 기울이다, 굽다, 움직이다
(at an angle idiom 어떤 각도로, 비스듬이)
If something is at an angle, it is leaning in a particular direction so that it is not straight, horizontal, or vertical.

march***
[maːrʧ]

① v. 당당하게 걷다, 행진하다; n. 행진, 행군 ② n. 3월
If you say that someone marches somewhere, you mean that they walk there quickly and in a determined way, for example because they are angry.

in time^{복습}

idiom 박자를 맞추어; 제시간에, 늦지 않게; 이윽고, 장차
If you play, sing, or dance to music in time, you do it at the right speed.

1분에 몇 단어를 읽는지 리딩 속도를 측정해보세요.

$$\frac{350 \text{ words}}{\text{reading time ( ) sec}} \times 60 = (\quad) \text{ WPM}$$

Build Your Vocabulary

banquet ^{복습}
[bǽŋkwit]

n. 연회; v. 연회를 베풀어 대접하다
A banquet is a grand formal dinner.

ornate
[ɔ:rnéit]

a. 화려하게 장식한, 잘 꾸민
An ornate building, piece of furniture, or object is decorated with complicated patterns or shapes.

chandelier
[ʃændəlíər]

n. 샹들리에(천장에서 내리 드리운 호화로운 장식등)
A chandelier is a large, decorative frame which holds light bulbs or candles and hangs from the ceiling.

rhythm ^{복습}
[ríðm]

n. 리듬, 율동; 박자
A rhythm is a regular series of sounds or movements.

minstrel ^{복습}
[mínstrəl]

n. (중세의) 음악가[음유 시인]
In medieval times, a minstrel was a singer and musician who traveled around and entertained noble families.

sway ^{복습}
[swei]

v. 흔들(리)다, 움직이다; 동요하다; 설득하다; n. 동요
When people or things sway, they lean or swing slowly from one side to the other.

twinkle *
[twíŋkl]

v. 반짝거리다, 빛나(게 하)다; (눈을) 깜박거리다; n. 반짝거림
If a star or a light twinkles, it shines with an unsteady light which rapidly and constantly changes from bright to faint.

beckon
[békən]

v. 매력적으로 보이다; 손짓하다, 부르다
If something beckons, it is so attractive to someone that they feel they must become involved in it.

glory *
[glɔ́:ri]

n. 장관, 찬란함; 영광, 영예; vi. 기뻐하다, 자랑으로 여기다
The glory of something is its great beauty or impressive nature.

juggle ^{복습}
[dʒʌ́gl]

v. 저글링 하다, 공중 던지기하다; 곡예를 하다
If you juggle, you entertain people by throwing things into the air, catching each one and throwing it up again so that there are several of them in the air at the same time.

fling ^{복습}
[fliŋ]

vt. (flung–flung) 내던지다; 내밀다, 던지다; n. 내던지기, 돌진
If you fling yourself somewhere, you move or jump there suddenly and with a lot of force.

branch **
[bræntʃ]

n. 가지; 지점; 분파; v. 가지를 내다
A branch of a subject is a part or type of it.

88

paw ^{복습}
[pɔ:]

n. (갈고리 발톱이 있는 동물의) 발; v. 앞발로 차다
The paws of an animal such as a cat, dog, or bear are its feet, which have claws for gripping things and soft pads for walking on.

swing ^{복습}
[swiŋ]

v. (swung–swung) 휘두르다; (한 점을 축으로 하여) 빙 돌다, 휙 움직이다; n. 휘두르기, 스윙; 흔들기
If something swings in a particular direction or if you swing it in that direction, it moves in that direction with a smooth, curving movement.

admire ^{복습}
[ædmáiər]

v. 감탄하다, 칭찬하다
If you admire someone or something, you like and respect them very much.

spectacle *
[spéktəkl]

n. 광경, 장관; 안경
A spectacle is a strange or interesting sight.

unbelievable ^{복습}
[ʌnbilí:vəbl]

a. 믿을 수 없는, 놀라운
You can use unbelievable to emphasize that you think something is very bad or shocking.

unfortunate *
[ʌnfɔ́:rʧənət]

a. 불운한, 불행한 (unfortunately ad. 불행하게도, 유감스럽게도)
If you describe someone as unfortunate, you mean that something unpleasant or unlucky has happened to them.

spot ^{복습}
[spat]

vt. 발견하다, 분별하다; n. 반점, 얼룩; 장소, 지점
If you spot something or someone, you notice them.

note ***
[nout]

v. (중요하거나 흥미로운 것을) 언급하다; 주의하다, 주목하다; 적다; n. 메모
If you note something, you mention it in order to draw people's attention to it.

strum ^{복습}
[strʌm]

v. (현악기를) 가볍게 퉁기다, 연주하다; n. 가볍게 타기
If you strum a stringed instrument such as a guitar, you play it by moving your fingers backward and forward across the strings.

jingle ^{복습}
[dʒiŋgl]

v. 짤랑짤랑 소리를 내다; n. 딸랑딸랑 울리는 소리
When something jingles or when you jingle it, it makes a gentle ringing noise, like small bells.

midst *
[midst]

n. 한복판, 중앙, 한가운데
If someone or something is in the midst of a group of people or things, they are among them or surrounded by them.

merry **
[méri]

a. 웃고 즐기는, 왁자지껄한; 명랑한, 유쾌한 (merriment n. 흥겹게 떠듦)
A merry party is festively joyous and happy.

aware ^{복습}
[əwéər]

a. 알고 있는, 의식하고 있는, 알아차린
If you are aware of something, you know about it.

immediately ^{복습}
[imí:diətli]

ad. 곧, 바로, 즉시
If something happens immediately, it happens without any delay.

extreme ^{복습}
[ikstrí:m]

a. 지나친, 과도한; 극단의, 극도의 (extremely ad. 극도로, 매우)
Extreme means very great in degree or intensity.

distasteful
[distéistfəl]

a. 불쾌한, 싫은
If something is distasteful to you, you think it is unpleasant, disgusting, or immoral.

syllable*
[síləbl]

n. 음절, 한마디; v. 음절을 발음하다
A syllable is a part of a word that contains a single vowel sound and that is pronounced as a unit.

curse*
[kəːrs]

n. 저주(의 말), 악담; vt. 저주하다, 욕설을 퍼붓다
If you say that there is a curse on someone, you mean that there seems to be a supernatural power causing unpleasant things to happen to them.

insult복습
[insʌlt]

n. 모욕(적인 말·행동); vt. 모욕하다, 창피주다
An insult is a rude remark, or something a person says or does which insults you.

revelation
[rèvəléiʃən]

n. 뜻밖의 사실; 폭로, 적발, 누설
A revelation is a surprising or interesting fact that is made known to people.

grip
[grip]

n. 움켜짐, 꽉 붙잡음; 손잡이; v. 꽉 잡다, 움켜잡다
A grip is a firm, strong hold on something.

1분에 몇 단어를 읽는지 리딩 속도를 측정해보세요.

$$\frac{579 \text{ words}}{\text{reading time (}\qquad\text{) sec}} \times 60 = (\qquad) \text{ WPM}$$

Build Your Vocabulary

serve ^{복습}
[sə:rv]

v. 제공하다, 시중 들다; 섬기다, 복무하다; n. 서브
When you serve food and drink, you give people food and drink.

admire ^{복습}
[ædmáiər]

v. 감탄하다, 칭찬하다 (admiration n. 감탄, 칭찬)
If you admire someone or something, you like and respect them very much.

palate
[pǽlət]

n. (좋은 음식·술을 알아보는) 미각[감식력]; 감상력, 심미안
You can refer to someone's palate as a way of talking about their ability to judge good food or drink.

concoct
[kankákt]

vt. (수프·음료 등을) 혼합하여 만들다; (이야기·변명 등을) 지어내다
If you concoct something, especially something unusual, you make it by mixing several things together.

mere ^{**}
[miər]

a. 단지 ~에 불과한; 단순한
You use mere to emphasize how unimportant or inadequate something is, in comparison to the general situation you are describing.

particular ^{복습}
[pərtíkjələr]

a. 특정한, 특별한, 특유의
You use particular to emphasize that you are talking about one thing or one kind of thing rather than other similar ones.

outdo
[àutdu]

vt. (outdid–outdone) ~보다 뛰어나다, 능가하다
(outdo oneself phrasal v. 지금까지보다 잘 하다)
If you outdo someone, you are a lot more successful than they are at a particular activity.

masterwork
[mǽstərwə̀:rk]

n. 명인의 솜씨, 일품; 걸작, 명작
If you describe something such as a book or a painting as a masterwork, you think it is extremely good or the best that someone has produced.

delicate ^{**}
[délikət]

a. (음식이) 맛있는, 담백하고 맛좋은; 섬세한, 고운; 예민한, 민감한
Something that is delicate has a color, taste, or smell which is pleasant and not strong or intense.

mingle [*]
[míŋgl]

v. 섞(이)다, 혼합하다; 어울리다, 교제하다
If things such as sounds, smells, or feelings mingle, they become mixed together but are usually still recognizable.

surface ^{**}
[sə́:rfis]

v. 떠오르(게 하)다; 표면화하다, 겉으로 드러나다; n. 표면, 수면; 외관, 겉보기
If someone or something under water surfaces, they come up to the surface of the water.

capacious
[kəpéiʃəs]

a. (용량이) 큰, 많이 들어가는; 넓은, 널찍한
Something that is capacious has a lot of space to put things in.

appreciate^{복습}
[əpríːʃièit]

vt. 고맙게 생각하다; 평가하다, 감상하다 (appreciative a. 감사하는)
If you appreciate something that someone has done for you or is going to do for you, you are grateful for it.

sip[*]
[sip]

n. 한 모금; vt. (음료를) 홀짝거리다, 조금씩 마시다
A sip is a small amount of drink that you take into your mouth.

distract[*]
[distrǽkt]

vt. (마음·주의를) 흐트러뜨리다, 딴 데로 돌리다 (distracted a. 산만해진)
If you are distracted, you are not concentrating on something because you are worried or are thinking about something else.

miserable^{복습}
[mízərəbl]

a. 비참한, 초라한, 불쌍한 (misery n. 비참, 불행)
If you are miserable, you are very unhappy.

exist^{복습}
[igzíst]

v. 존재하다, 실재하다 (existence n. 존재, 생존)
If something exists, it is present in the world as a real thing.

delightful^{복습}
[diláitfəl]

a. 기쁨을 주는, 정말 기분 좋은
If you describe something or someone as delightful, you mean they are very pleasant.

chandelier^{복습}
[ʃ̀ændəlíər]

n. 샹들리에(천장에서 내리 드리운 호화로운 장식등)
A chandelier is a large, decorative frame which holds light bulbs or candles and hangs from the ceiling.

juggle^{복습}
[dʒʌgl]

v. 저글링 하다, 공중 던지기하다; 곡예를 하다 (juggler n. 저글링 하는 사람)
If you juggle, you entertain people by throwing things into the air, catching each one and throwing it up again so that there are several of them in the air at the same time.

noble^{복습}
[noubl]

a. 귀족의; 고결한, 숭고한
Noble means belonging to a high social class and having a title.

spirit^{**}
[spírit]

n. 태도, 자세; 정신, 영혼
The spirit in which you do something is the attitude you have when you are doing it.

utter[*]
[ʌ́tər]

① v. 발언하다, 말하다 ② a. 완전한, 전적인, 절대적인
If someone utters sounds or words, they say them.

unsavory
[ʌnséivəri]

a. 불미스러운; 맛없는, 불쾌한
If you describe a person, place, or thing as unsavory, you mean that you find them unpleasant or morally unacceptable.

creature^{**}
[kríːtʃər]

n. 생물, 창조물
You can refer to any living thing that is not a plant as a creature, especially when it is of an unknown or unfamiliar kind.

nasty[*]
[nǽsti]

a. 못된, 고약한; 추잡한, 더러운
If you describe a person or their behavior as nasty, you mean that they behave in an unkind and unpleasant way.

beast[*]
[biːst]

n. 야수, 짐승; 짐승 같은 인간
You can refer to an animal as a beast, especially if it is a large, dangerous, or unusual one.

92

cling ^{복습}
[kliŋ]

vi. 달라붙다, 매달리다
If you cling to someone or something, you hold onto them tightly.

whisker ^{복습}
[wískər]

n. (고양이·쥐 등의) 수염; 구레나룻
The whiskers of an animal such as a cat or a mouse are the long stiff hairs that grow near its mouth.

pardon ^{복습}
[pa:rdn]

n. 용서, 관용; vt. 용서하다; int. 뭐라구요(상대방의 말을 되물을 때 하는 말)
You say 'I beg your pardon' as a way of apologizing for accidentally doing something wrong, such as disturbing someone or making a mistake.

fling ^{복습}
[fliŋ]

vt. (flung–flung) 내던지다; 내밀다, 던지다; n. 내던지기, 돌진
If you fling something somewhere, you throw it there using a lot of force.

incredible ^{복습}
[inkrédəbl]

a. 놀라운, 믿어지지 않는
You use incredible to emphasize the degree, amount, or intensity of something.

worthy*
[wə́:rði]

a. ~에 어울리는, ~을 받을 만한; 훌륭한, 괜찮은
If a person or thing is worthy of something, they deserve it because they have the qualities or abilities required.

neigh
[nei]

n. (말의) 울음; vi. (말이) 울다
When a horse neighs, it makes a loud sound with its mouth.

squeal
[skwi:l]

n. 꽥꽥거리는 소리; v. 꺅꺅거리다, 비명을 지르다
If someone or something squeals, they make a long, high-pitched sound.

overly
[óuvərli]

ad. 지나치게, 너무
Overly means more than is normal, necessary, or reasonable.

obvious ^{복습}
[ábviəs]

a. 명백한, 분명한
If something is obvious, it is easy to see or understand.

clutch ^{복습}
[klʌʧ]

v. 부여잡다, 꽉 잡다, 붙들다; n. 붙잡음, 움켜쥠
If you clutch at something or clutch something, you hold it tightly, usually because you are afraid or anxious.

royal**
[rɔ́iəl]

a. 왕의, 왕위의; 위엄 있는
Royal is used to indicate that something is connected with a king, queen, or emperor, or their family.

thump
[θʌmp]

n. 탁[쿵] 하는 소리; 때림, 세게 쥐어박음; v. 탁 치다, 부딪치다
A thump is a loud, dull sound by hitting something.

explode ^{복습}
[iksplóud]

v. 폭발하다, 격발하다; 폭발시키다
If an object such as a bomb explodes or if someone or something explodes it, it bursts loudly and with great force, often causing damage or injury.

thunder ^{복습}
[θʌ́ndər]

v. 소리 지르다, 외치다; 우레가 울리다; 우르릉거리며 질주하다; n. 천둥, 우레
If you thunder something, you say it loudly and forcefully, especially because you are angry.

rescue^{복습}
[réskju:]

vt. 구조하다, 구출하다; n. 구출, 구원
If you rescue someone, you get them out of a dangerous or unpleasant situation.

circumstance^{복습}
[sə́:rkəmstæns]

n. 상황, 환경, 사정
The circumstances of a particular situation are the conditions which affect what happens.

crawl^{복습}
[krɔ:l]

vi. 기어가다, 느릿느릿 가다; 우글거리다, 들끓다; n. 서행; 기어감
When you crawl, you move forward on your hands and knees.

tablecloth^{복습}
[téiblklɔ:θ]

n. 식탁보, 테이블보
A tablecloth is a cloth used to cover a table.

dungeon^{복습}
[dʌ́ndʒən]

n. 지하 감옥; vt. 지하 감옥에 가두다
A dungeon is a dark underground prison in a castle.

glare*
[glɛər]

v. 노려보다; 번쩍번쩍 빛나다; n. 노려봄; 번쩍이는 빛
If you glare at someone, you look at them with an angry expression on your face.

disgust^{복습}
[disgʌ́st]

n. 싫음, 혐오감; vt. 역겹게 하다, 넌더리나게 하다
Disgust is a feeling of very strong dislike or disapproval.

94

1분에 몇 단어를 읽는지 리딩 속도를 측정해보세요.

$$\frac{239 \text{ words}}{\text{reading time ( ) sec}} \times 60 = (\qquad) \text{ WPM}$$

Build Your Vocabulary

bend^{복습}
[bend]

v. (bent–bent) 구부리다, 돌리다; 구부러지다, 휘다; n. 커브, 굽음
When you bend a part of your body such as your arm or leg, or when it bends, you change its position so that it is no longer straight.

encounter^{복습}
[inkáuntər]

v. 만나다, 마주치다; n. 마주침
If you encounter someone, you meet them, usually unexpectedly.

royal^{복습}
[rɔ́iəl]

a. 왕의, 왕위의; 위엄 있는
Royal is used to indicate that something is connected with a king, queen, or emperor, or their family.

revenge*
[rivéndʒ]

n. 복수, 보복; vt. 복수하다, 원수를 갚다
Revenge involves hurting or punishing someone who has hurt or harmed you.

somehow**
[sʌ́mhàu]

ad. 어떻게든지 하여, 어쨌든; 어쩐지, 아무래도
You use somehow to say that you do not know or cannot say how something was done or will be done.

mend***
[mend]

v. 고치다, 회복하다, 개선하다; n. 수선, 개량
If you mend something that is broken or not working, you repair it, so that it works properly or can be used.

heal*
[hi:l]

v. (상처·아픔·고장 등을) 낫게 하다, 치료하다
When something heals it, it becomes healthy and normal again.

crooked
[krúkid]

a. 비뚤어진, 구부러진; 부정직한
If you describe something as crooked, especially something that is usually straight, you mean that it is bent or twisted.

lopsided
[lápsáidid]

a. 한쪽으로 기운
Something that is lopsided is uneven because one side is lower or heavier than the other.

sew^{복습}
[sou]

v. (sewed–sewn/sewed) 바느질하다, 꿰매다, 깁다
When you sew something such as clothes, you make them or repair them by joining pieces of cloth together by passing thread through them with a needle.

careless**
[kɛ́ərlis]

a. 부주의한, 무관심한, 개의치 않는
If you are careless, you do not pay enough attention to what you are doing, and so you make mistakes, or cause harm or damage.

craftsman
[krǽftsmən]

n. 장인, 숙련공, 공예가
A craftsman is a man who makes things skillfully with his hands.

fate^{복습}
[feit]

n. 운명, 숙명
A person's or thing's fate is what happens to them.

alas^{복습}
[əlǽs]

int. (슬픔·걱정을 나타내어) 아아, 슬프도다!, 불쌍한지고!
Alas is used to express sadness or regret.

mutter^{복습}
[mʌ́tər]

v. 중얼거리다, 불평하다; n. 중얼거림, 불평
If you mutter, you speak very quietly so that you cannot easily be heard, often because you are complaining about something.

1분에 몇 단어를 읽는지 리딩 속도를 측정해보세요.

$$\frac{851 \text{ words}}{\text{reading time ( ) sec}} \times 60 = (\quad) \text{ WPM}$$

Build Your Vocabulary

dire
[daiər]

a. 끔찍한, 불길한; 절박한, 극심한
Dire is used to emphasize how serious or terrible a situation or event is.

consequence[*]
[kánsəkwèns]

n. 결과, 결말; 중요성, 중대함
The consequences of something are the results or effects of it.

gnaw
[nɔː]

v. 갉아먹다, 물어뜯다; 괴롭히다
If people or animals gnaw something or gnaw at it, they bite it repeatedly.

jailer[복습]
[dʒéilər]

n. 교도관, 간수
A jailer is a person who is in charge of a jail and the prisoners in it.

match[복습]
[mætʃ]

① n. 성냥 ② vt. ~에 필적하다, 대등하다; 조화하다, 어울리다; n. 상대, 경기
A match is a small wooden stick with a substance on one end that produces a flame when you rub it along the rough side of a matchbox.

afire
[əfáiər]

ad. 불타서; (감정이) 격하여, 달아올라
(set afire idiom ~을 불태우다, 자극하다)
If something is afire or is set afire, it is on fire or looks as if it is on fire.

journey[**]
[dʒə́ːrni]

vi. 여행하다; n. 여정, 여행
If you journey somewhere, you travel there.

seek[복습]
[siːk]

v. 찾다, 추구하다; 얻으려 하다
When someone seeks something, they try to obtain it.

banquet[복습]
[bǽŋkwit]

n. 연회; v. 연회를 베풀어 대접하다
A banquet is a grand formal dinner.

indulge[복습]
[indʌ́ldʒ]

v. 제멋대로 하게 하다, 맘껏 하다; (욕망·정열 따위를) 만족시키다, 충족시키다
If you indulge someone, you let them have or do what they want, even if this is not good for them.

allow[복습]
[əláu]

v. 허락하다, ~하게 두다; 인정하다
If you allow something to happen, you do not prevent it.

meditation[*]
[mèdətéiʃən]

n. 명상, 묵상
Meditation is the act of remaining in a silent and calm state for a period of time, as part of a religious training.

outlaw
[áutlɔ:]

vt. 불법화하다, 금지하다; n. 범법자
When something is outlawed, it is made illegal.

instrument**
[ínstrəmənt]

n. 기구, 도구; 악기
An instrument is a tool or device that is used to do a particular task, especially a scientific task.

kettle복습
[ketl]

n. 솥, 냄비; 주전자
A kettle is a metal pot for boiling or cooking things in.

pile복습
[pail]

v. 쌓아 올리다, 쌓(이)다; n. 쌓아 올린 더미; 다수
If you pile things somewhere, you put them there so that they form a pile.

dazzle*
[dǽzl]

v. 눈부시게 하다; 감탄하게 하다, 현혹시키다; n. 눈부심
If a bright light dazzles you, it makes you unable to see properly for a short time.

tortuous
[tɔ́:rtʃuəs]

a. (강·길이) 구불구불한; 길고 복잡한, 우여곡절이 많은
A tortuous road is full of bends and twists.

maze복습
[meiz]

n. 미로, 미궁; vt. 당혹하게 하다
A maze is a complex system of passages or paths between walls or hedges and is designed to confuse people who try to find their way through it, often as a form of amusement.

desperate복습
[déspərət]

a. 절망적인, 자포자기의; 필사적인 (desperation n. 절망)
A desperate situation is very difficult, serious, or dangerous.

declare***
[diklέər]

v. 선언하다; 단언하다
If you declare something, you state officially and formally that it exists or is the case.

illegal*
[ilí:gəl]

a. 불법의, 비합법적인
If something is illegal, the law says that it is not allowed.

ridiculous복습
[ridíkjuləs]

a. 터무니없는; 웃기는, 우스꽝스러운
If you say that something or someone is ridiculous, you mean that they are very foolish.

official*
[əfíʃəl]

a. 공식적인, 공인된; 공무상의; n. 공무원, 관료 (officially ad. 공식으로)
Official means approved by the government or by someone in authority.

decree복습
[dikrí:]

v. (법령에 의하여) 명령하다, 포고하다; n. 명령, 포고
If someone in authority decrees that something must happen, they decide or state this officially.

soothe*
[su:ð]

v. 달래다, 진정시키다
If you soothe someone who is angry or upset, you make them feel calmer.

particular복습
[pərtíkjələr]

a. 특정한, 특별한, 특유의 (in particular idiom 특히)
You use particular to emphasize that you are talking about one thing or one kind of thing rather than other similar ones.

atop복습
[ətáp]

prep. ~의 꼭대기에, 정상에
If something is atop something else, it is on top of it.

98

fashion**
[fǽʃən]

vt. (재료를 써서) 만들다; 적합시키다; n. 패션, 유행하는 물건[사람]; 유행
If you fashion an object or a work of art, you make it.

kingly
[kíŋli]

a. 왕의, 왕다운
Kingly means like a king, or related to the duties of a king.

cape
[keip]

n. 어깨 망토
A cape is a short cloak.

scrap^{복습}
[skræp]

n. 조각, 파편; vt. 부스러기로 만들다, 해체하다
A scrap of something is a very small piece or amount of it.

swing^{복습}
[swiŋ]

v. 휘두르다; (한 점을 축으로 하여) 빙 돌다, 휙 움직이다; n. 휘두르기, 스윙; 흔들기
If something swings in a particular direction or if you swing it in that direction, it moves in that direction with a smooth, curving movement.

locket^{복습}
[lάkit]

n. 로켓(사진 등을 넣어 목걸이에 다는 작은 갑)
A locket is a piece of jewelry containing something such as a picture, which a woman wears on a chain around her neck.

intend***
[inténd]

vt. ~할 작정이다, 의도하다
If you intend to do something, you have decided or planned to do it.

dank
[dæŋk]

a. 기분 나쁘게 눅눅한, 축축한
A dank place, especially an underground place such as a cave, is unpleasantly damp and cold.

cell^{복습}
[sel]

n. 독방, 독실; 작은 방; 세포
A cell is a small room in which a prisoner is locked.

weep^{복습}
[wi:p]

v. 눈물을 흘리다, 울다; 물기를 내뿜다
If someone weeps, they cry.

sniff^{복습}
[snif]

v. 냄새를 맡다, 코를 킁킁거리다; 코를 훌쩍이다; n. 냄새 맡음
If you sniff something or sniff at it, you smell it by sniffing.

crumb^{복습}
[krʌm]

n. 빵 부스러기, 빵가루
Crumbs are tiny pieces that fall from bread, biscuits, or cake when you cut it or eat it.

cock^{복습}
[kak]

v. (귀·꽁지를) 쫑긋 세우다, 위로 치올리다; n. 수탉; 마개
If you cock a part of your body in a particular direction, you lift it or point it in that direction.

gloom*
[glu:m]

n. 어둑어둑함, 어둠; 우울, 침울
The gloom is a state of near darkness.

dusk*
[dʌsk]

n. 땅거미, 해질녘, 황혼
Dusk is the time just before night when the daylight has almost gone but when it is not completely dark.

draw near

idiom 다가오다, 접근하다
If an event or period of time is drawing closer or is drawing nearer, it is approaching.

wagon[*]
[wǽgən]

n. 수레, 짐마차
A wagon is a strong vehicle with four wheels, usually pulled by horses or oxen and used for carrying heavy loads.

stick[복습]
[stik]

① v. (stuck–stuck) 붙이다, 달라붙다; 내밀다; 찔러 넣다; 고수하다
② n. 막대기, 지팡이
If you stick something somewhere, you put it there in a rather casual way.

instrumental[*]
[ìnstrəméntl]

a. 도움이 되는, 수단[도구]이 되는; 악기로 연주되는
Someone or something that is instrumental in a process or event helps to make it happen.

revenge[복습]
[rivéndʒ]

n. 복수, 보복; vt. 복수하다, 원수를 갚다
Revenge involves hurting or punishing someone who has hurt or harmed you.

Book the Third
(Chapter Twenty-four to Chapter Thirty-four)

1. Who was Miggery Sow named after?
   A. Her father's prize winning cow
   B. Her father's prize winning grandfather
   C. Her father's prize winning pig
   D. Her father's prize winning cat

2. Which of the following was NOT included in the items that were traded for Mig?
   A. A tablecloth
   B. A hen
   C. A soup bowl
   D. A handful of cigarettes

3. What was Uncle fond of giving Mig?
   A. A good clout to the hands
   B. A good clout to the eyes
   C. A good clout to the nose
   D. A good clout to the ears

4. According to the narrative, how was Mig in the center of a vicious cycle?
   A. The more she got hit, the less she understood, and the more she got hit.
   B. The more she worked, the more she broke, and the less money she earned.
   C. The more she got hit, the louder she spoke, and the more her voice broke.
   D. The more she worked, the more tired she became, and the more she made mistakes.

5. Which of the following did NOT happen on Mig's seventh birthday?
   A. Uncle gave her a birthday clout.
   B. Uncle gave her a cake.
   C. Mig saw the royal family and knights riding by her house.
   D. Mig told Uncle that she was seven that day.

6. How did Mig respond to the Princess Pea waving at her?
   A. She waved back at her.
   B. She shouted for them to take her to the castle.
   C. She asked for a birthday gift.
   D. She did not wave back and just stood and watched.

7. How did Mig describe seeing royalty to Uncle?
   A. She described them as real heroes, brave and strong.
   B. She described them as human stars, glittering and glowing.
   C. She described them as celebrities, popular and charismatic.
   D. She described them as human flames, energetic and brilliant.

8. How did Uncle react to Mig wanting to be a princess?
   A. He told her that he already thought she was a princess.
   B. He was moved by her dedication and wanted to help her.
   C. He laughed and called it nonsense.
   D. He was surprised and asked her what else she wanted.

9. Why did Mig stand in the field as the sun set in the evenings?

    A. She hoped that the royal family would pass before her again.

    B. She hoped that the royal family would come to rescue her.

    C. She hoped that she could see the seasons change.

    D. She hoped that she could see the lights in the castle far away.

10. Why did the king's soldier take Mig to the castle?

    A. Mig's parents were waiting for her at the castle.

    B. It was illegal to own another person.

    C. Mig asked for a new job as a servant at the castle.

    D. Uncle sold Mig for a tablecloth and hen to the king's soldier.

11. What was Mig's first job in the castle as a servant?

    A. She was sent to deliver a meal to Princess Pea.

    B. She was sent to deliver a meal to Gregory in the dungeon.

    C. She was sent to deliver red thread to the mice.

    D. She was sent to deliver red thread to Princess Pea.

12. Why did the Princess Pea need red thread?

    A. She needed it for a tapestry about her life.

    B. She needed it for a tapestry about Mig's life

    C. She needed it for a tapestry about the castle's long history.

    D. She needed it for the mice to use to send other mice to the dungeon.

13. How did Mig change once she came to the castle?

    A. She studied more and got smarter.

    B. She worked harder and got thinner.

    C. She ate more and grew bigger.

    D. She met more people and became very popular.

14. Why was Mig sent to the dungeon?
    A. She was sent there to help Desprereaux escape.
    B. She was sent there to bring Gregory his meal.
    C. She was sent there to help the king kill rats.
    D. She was sent there to become a prisoner.

15. Which of the following best described how Mig felt in the dungeon?
    A. She was overcome by the foul smells everywhere.
    B. She was nervous due to the frightening sounds around her.
    C. She was afraid of the darkness around her.
    D. She was not afraid at all because she could not hear or smell well.

16. How did Roscuro react to Mig's song about the princess?
    A. He had been waiting to hear it and followed Mig.
    B. He did not hear it and wanted her to repeat it.
    C. He thought that it sounded like a song he used to know.
    D. He thought it was awful and stayed away from Mig.

17. What surprised Mig about how Gregory ate his meal?
    A. He used a fork and knife.
    B. He ate the bones too.
    C. He forgot to wash his hands.
    D. He only ate one bite.

18. How was Gregory involved in Roscuro's plan for revenge?
    A. He wanted Gregory to help him prevent humans from coming to the dungeon.
    B. He wanted Gregory help Mig become friends with Princess Pea.
    C. He wanted to steal Gregory's next meal.
    D. He wanted to bite through Gregory's rope completely.

19. What was unusual about Roscuro in relation to Mig?

   A. Roscuro's voice was pitched so that Mig could hear it clearly.

   B. Roscuro and Mig had the same exact voice.

   C. Roscuro has been born at the same house as Mig.

   D. Mig could not hear Roscuro but could still understand his body language.

20. How did Roscuro offer to help Mig?

   A. He offered to help her become adopted by the king.

   B. He offered to help her leave the castle.

   C. He offered to help her become a princess.

   D. He offered to help her become a castle cook.

$$\frac{435 \text{ words}}{\text{reading time ( ) sec}} \times 60 = (\quad) \text{ WPM}$$

Build Your Vocabulary

stare^{복습}
[stɛər]

v. 응시하다, 뚫어지게 보다
If you stare at someone or something, you look at them for a long time.

runny
[rʌ́ni]

a. (감기 등으로) 콧물[눈물]이 흐르는
If someone has a runny nose or runny eyes, liquid is flowing from their nose or eyes.

matter^{복습}
[mǽtər]

vi. 중요하다; n. 물질, 문제, 일
If you say that something does matter, you mean that it is important to you because it does have an effect on you or on a particular situation.

squeeze^{복습}
[skwiːz]

v. (꼭) 쥐다, 짜다; (억지로) 비집고 들어가다; n. (꼭) 짜기
If you squeeze something, you press it firmly, usually with your hands.

service^{***}
[sə́ːrvis]

n. 고용살이, 근무; 서비스, 시중[접대]; 봉사, 공헌; 사업, 시설
Your services are the things that you do or the skills that you use in your job, which other people find useful and are usually willing to pay you for.

handful^{복습}
[hǽndfùl]

n. 한 움큼, 한 줌; 소량, 소수
A handful of something is the amount of it that you can hold in your hand.

cigarette^{복습}
[sìgərét]

n. 담배
Cigarettes are small tubes of paper containing tobacco which people smoke.

tablecloth^{복습}
[téiblklɔ̀ːθ]

n. 식탁보, 테이블보
A tablecloth is a cloth used to cover a table.

hen^{복습}
[hen]

n. 암탉
A hen is a female chicken. People often keep hens in order to eat them or sell their eggs.

drape^{복습}
[dreip]

vt. 걸치다, 씌우다; 주름을 잡아 예쁘게 덮다; n. (pl.) 덮는 천, 두꺼운 커튼
If you drape a piece of cloth somewhere, you place it there so that it hangs down in a casual and graceful way.

cape^{복습}
[keip]

n. 어깨 망토
A cape is a short cloak.

108

tug ^{복습}
[tʌg]

v. (세게) 당기다, 끌다; 노력[분투]하다; n. 힘껏 당김; 분투, 노력
If you tug something or tug at it, you give it a quick and usually strong pull.

tangle[*]
[tǽŋgl]

v. 엉키다; 얽히게 하다; n. 엉킴; 혼란 (untangle vt. 얽힌 것을 풀다)
If something is tangled or tangles, it becomes twisted together in an untidy way.

billow
[bílou]

vi. (바람에) 부풀어 오르다; 파도가 일다. (파도처럼) 굽이치다; n. 큰 파도
When something made of cloth billows, it swells out and moves slowly in the wind.

consider ^{복습}
[kənsídər]

v. 고려하다, 숙고하다
If you consider something, you think about it carefully.

frighten ^{복습}
[fraitn]

v. 놀라게 하다. 섬뜩하게 하다; 기겁하다 (frightened a. 겁먹은, 무서워하는)
If something or someone frightens you, they cause you to suddenly feel afraid, anxious, or nervous.

duty ^{복습}
[djú:ti]

n. 의무, 임무
If you say that something is your duty, you believe that you ought to do it because it is your responsibility.

Check Your Reading Speed

1분에 몇 단어를 읽는지 리딩 속도를 측정해보세요.

$$\frac{426 \text{ words}}{\text{reading time ( ) sec}} \times 60 = (\qquad) \text{ WPM}$$

Build Your Vocabulary

purchase*
[pə́:rtʃəs]

vt. 사다, 구입하다; n. 구입, 매입, 획득
When you purchase something, you buy it.

tend*
[tend]

① vt. 손질하다, 돌보다 ② vi. (~하는) 경향이 있다; (어느 방향으로) 나아가다
If you tend someone or something, you do what is necessary to keep them in a good condition or to improve their condition.

scrub*
[skrʌb]

v. 북북 문지르다, 비벼서 씻다
If you scrub something, you rub it hard in order to clean it, using a stiff brush and water.

praise***
[preiz]

n. 칭찬, 찬사, 찬양; vt. 칭찬하다
Praise is what you say or write about someone when you are praising them.

unfortunate복습
[ʌnfɔ́:rtʃənət]

a. 불운한, 불행한
If you describe someone as unfortunate, you mean that something unpleasant or unlucky has happened to them.

refer복습
[rifə́:r]

vi. 언급하다, 나타내다
If you refer to a particular subject or person, you talk about them or mention them.

clout
[klaut]

n. (손바닥·주먹으로) 때리기[강타]; vt. (주먹으로) 때리다
If you clout someone, you hit them.

fair복습
[fɛər]

a. 공평한, 공정한; 아름다운, 매력적인; ad. 정확하게, 알맞게
(fairness n. 공평, 공정)
Something or someone that is fair is reasonable, right, and just.

inquire*
[inkwáiər]

v. 묻다, 문의하다
If you inquire about something, you ask for information about it.

filthy복습
[fílθi]

a. 불결한, 더러운
Something that is filthy is very dirty indeed.

punish복습
[pʌ́niʃ]

v. 처벌하다, 벌주다
To punish someone means to make them suffer in some way because they have done something wrong.

alas복습
[əlǽs]

int. (슬픔·걱정을 나타내어) 아아, 슬프도다!, 불쌍한지고!
Alas is used to express sadness or regret.

entire^{복습}
[intáiər]

a. 전체의; 완전한 (entirely ad. 전적으로, 완전히)
You use entire when you want to emphasize that you are referring to the whole of something, for example, the whole of a place, time, or population.

unconcerned
[ʌnkənsɔ́:rnd]

a. 개의치 않는, 무심한; 관련이 없는
If a person is unconcerned about something, usually something that most people would care about, they are not interested in it or worried about it.

a great deal of^{복습}

idiom 다량의, 많은
If you say that you need or have a great deal of or a good deal of a particular thing, you are emphasizing that you need or have a lot of it.

enthusiasm*
[inθú:ziæzm]

n. 열의, 열광, 열중
Enthusiasm is great eagerness to be involved in a particular activity which you like and enjoy or which you think is important.

absolute^{복습}
[ǽbsəlù:t]

a. 절대적인, 무조건의; 완전한 (absolutely ad. 절대적으로, 무조건)
Absolute means total and complete.

alarm^{복습}
[əlá:rm]

vt. 놀라게 하다; 위급을 알리다; n. 놀람, 불안; 경보 (alarmingly ad. 놀랍게도)
If something alarms you, it makes you afraid or anxious that something unpleasant or dangerous might happen.

frequent*
[frí:kwənt]

a. 자주 일어나는, 빈번한
If something is frequent, it happens often.

scrupulous
[skrú:pjuləs]

a. 용의주도한, 빈틈없는; 양심적인, 지조 있는 (scrupulously ad. 세밀하게)
Scrupulous means thorough, exact, and careful about details.

resemble*
[rizémbl]

vt. ~을 닮다, ~와 공통점이 있다
If one thing or person resembles another, they are similar to each other.

cease*
[si:s]

v. 그만두다, 중지하다
If you cease something, you stop it happening or working.

function*
[fʌ́ŋkʃən]

vi. 작용하다, 기능하다; n. 기능; 역할, 직무
If someone or something functions as a particular thing, they do the work or fulfill the purpose of that thing.

edge^{복습}
[edʒ]

n. (칼 등의) 날; 예리함, 날카로움; 끝, 가장자리, 모서리
If you say that someone or something has an edge, you mean that they have a powerful quality.

blurry
[blə́:ri]

a. 흐릿한, 모호한
A blurry shape is one that has an unclear outline.

make sense^{복습}

idiom 뜻이 통하다, 도리에 맞다
If something makes sense, it has a meaning that you can easily understand.

vicious*
[víʃəs]

a. 지독한, 극심한; 잔인한, 악랄한 (vicious circle n. 악순환)
A vicious circle is a problem or difficult situation that has the effect of creating new problems which then cause the original problem or situation to occur again.

1분에 몇 단어를 읽는지 리딩 속도를 측정해보세요.

$$\frac{520 \text{ words}}{\text{reading time } (\quad) \text{ sec}} \times 60 = (\quad) \text{ WPM}$$

Build Your Vocabulary

celebrate**
[sélǝbrèit]

v. 기념하다, 축하하다 (celebration n. 축하)
If you celebrate, you do something enjoyable because of a special occasion or to mark someone's success.

acknowledge**
[ǝknálidʒ]

vt. 인정하다, 알리다; 감사하다 (acknowledgement n. 인정)
If you acknowledge a fact or a situation, you accept or admit that it is true or that it exists.

clout^{복습}
[klaut]

n. (손바닥·주먹으로) 때리기[강타]; vt. (주먹으로) 때리다
If you clout someone, you hit them.

glitter^{복습}
[glítǝr]

vi. 반짝반짝 빛나다, 반짝이다; n. 반짝이는 빛
If something glitters, light comes from or is reflected off different parts of it.

glow^{복습}
[glou]

vi. 빛을 내다, 빛나다; n. 빛, 밝음
If something glows, it produces a dull, steady light.

horizon**
[hǝráizn]

n. 지평선, 수평선
The horizon is the line in the far distance where the sky seems to meet the land or the sea.

sink^{복습}
[siŋk]

v. 침몰하다, 가라앉히다; (마음 등이) 가라앉다, 낙심하다
If something sinks, it moves slowly downward.

shine^{복습}
[ʃain]

v. (shone-shone) 빛나(게 하)다, 반짝이다; n. 빛, 빛남, 광채
Something that shines is very bright and clear because it is reflecting light.

shade^{복습}
[ʃeid]

vt. 그늘지게 하다; n. (시원한) 그늘; 색조, 음영
If you shade your eyes, you put your hand or an object partly in front of your face in order to prevent a bright light from shining into your eyes.

brilliant^{복습}
[bríljǝnt]

a. 빛나는, 반짝이는; 훌륭한, 멋진
You describe light, or something that reflects light, as brilliant when it shines very brightly.

draw close^{복습}

idiom 다가오다, 접근하다
If an event or period of time is drawing closer or is drawing nearer, it is approaching.

reveal^{복습}
[riví:l]

vt. 드러내다, 폭로하다, 밝히다
If you reveal something that has been out of sight, you uncover it so that people can see it.

royal ^{복습}
[rɔ́iəl]

a. 왕의, 왕위의; 위엄 있는
Royal is used to indicate that something is connected with a king, queen, or emperor, or their family.

surround^{**}
[səráund]

vt. 둘러싸다, 에워싸다; 포위하다
If a person or thing is surrounded by something, that thing is situated all around them.

knight ^{복습}
[nait]

n. (중세의) 기사
In medieval times, a knight was a man of noble birth, who served his king or lord in battle.

armor ^{복습}
[á:rmər]

n. 갑옷, 철갑; vt. ~에게 갑옷을 입히다
In former times, armor was special metal clothing that soldiers wore for protection in battle.

atop ^{복습}
[ətáp]

prep. ~의 꼭대기에, 정상에
If something is atop something else, it is on top of it.

robe[*]
[roub]

n. 예복, 관복; 길고 헐거운 겉옷
A robe is a loose piece of clothing which covers all of your body and reaches the ground.

decorate^{**}
[dékərèit]

vt. 장식하다, 꾸미다 (decorated a. 장식된, 훌륭하게 꾸민)
If you decorate something, you make it more attractive by adding things to it.

sequin ^{복습}
[sí:kwin]

n. 장식용 번쩍이는 작은 원형 금속 조각
Sequins are small, shiny discs that are sewn on clothes to decorate them.

reflect ^{복습}
[riflékt]

v. 비추다, 반사하다; 반영하다, 나타내다
When light, heat or other rays reflect off a surface or when a surface reflects them, they are sent back from the surface and do not pass through it.

breathe^{**}
[bri:ð]

v. 호흡하다, 숨을 쉬다; 냄새를 풍기다[연기를 내뿜다]
When people or animals breathe, they take air into their lungs and let it out again.

dainty
[déinti]

a. 고상한, 우아한; 맛 좋은 (daintily ad. 우아하게)
If you describe a movement, person, or object as dainty, you mean that they are small, delicate, and pretty.

stare ^{복습}
[stɛər]

v. 응시하다, 뚫어지게 보다
If you stare at someone or something, you look at them for a long time.

merry ^{복습}
[méri]

a. 명랑한, 유쾌한; 웃고 즐기는, 왁자지껄한 (merrily a. 명랑하게)
If you describe someone's character or behavior as merry, you mean that they are happy and cheerful.

consequence ^{복습}
[kánsəkwèns]

n. 중요성, 중대함; 결과, 결말
If something or someone is of no consequence, or of little consequence, they are not important or valuable.

awaken[*]
[əwéikən]

v. (= awake) (awakened–awakened) 깨닫(게 하)다, 알아채다; (잠에서) 깨(우)다
To awaken a feeling in a person means to cause them to start having this feeling.

slumber
[slʌ́mbər]

v. 잠시 졸다, 잠자다; n. 선잠
To slumber means to be asleep.

interior[**]
[intíəriər]

n. 안쪽, 내부; 인테리어, 실내 장식; a. 내부의, 안쪽의
The interior of something is the inside part of it.

spark[*]
[spaːrk]

v. 불꽃이 튀다, 점화하다; n. 불꽃, 스파크
If one thing sparks another, the first thing causes the second thing to start happening.

brilliance[복습]
[bríljəns]

n. 환한 빛, 광명, 광택
Brilliance is great brightness of light or color.

ridiculous[복습]
[ridíkjuləs]

a. 터무니없는; 웃기는, 우스꽝스러운
If you say that something or someone is ridiculous, you mean that they are very foolish.

ache[*]
[eik]

vi. 쑤시다, 아프다; n. 아픔, 쑤심
If you ache or a part of your body aches, you feel a steady, fairly strong pain.

bloom[*]
[bluːm]

v. 꽃이 피다, 개화하다; 번영시키다; n. 꽃
When a plant or tree blooms, it produces flowers. When a flower blooms, it opens.

opposite[복습]
[ápəzit]

n. 정반대의 일[것]; a. 반대편의, 맞은편의; 정반대의; ad. 정반대의 위치에
The opposite of someone or something is the person or thing that is most different from them.

1분에 몇 단어를 읽는지 리딩 속도를 측정해보세요.

$$\frac{350 \text{ words}}{\text{reading time (} \quad \text{) sec}} \times 60 = (\quad) \text{ WPM}$$

Build Your Vocabulary

hut*
[hʌt]

n. 오두막; vi. 오두막에 묵다
A hut is a small house with only one or two rooms, especially one which is made of wood, mud, grass, or stones.

tippy-toe
[típi-tòu]

vi. 발끝으로 살금살금 걷다; a. 살금살금 하는
If you tippy-toe somewhere, you walk there very quietly without putting your heels on the floor when you walk.

dumb*
[dʌm]

a. (구어) 멍청한, 우둔한; 벙어리의, 말을 하지 않는
If you call a person dumb, you mean that they are stupid or foolish.

worth복습
[wɔːrθ]

a. ~의 가치가 있는; n. 가치, 값어치
If something is worth a particular amount of money, it can be sold for that amount or is considered to have that value.

enormous*
[inɔ́ːrməs]

a. 엄청난, 거대한, 막대한
You can use enormous to emphasize the great degree or extent of something.

hen복습
[hen]

n. 암탉
A hen is a female chicken. People often keep hens in order to eat them or sell their eggs.

tablecloth복습
[téiblklɔ̀ːθ]

n. 식탁보, 테이블보
A tablecloth is a cloth used to cover a table.

lay복습
[lei]

v. 알을 낳다; 놓다, 눕히다
When a female bird lays an egg, it produces an egg by pushing it out of its body.

like nobody's business

idiom 굉장히, 훌륭히, 멋지게
Like nobody's business means very fast, very much, or very hard.

kettle복습
[ketl]

n. 솥, 냄비; 주전자
A kettle is a metal pot for boiling or cooking things in.

nonsense**
[nánsens]

n. 허튼소리; 바보 같은 짓; a. 어리석은, 무의미한
If you say that something spoken or written is nonsense, you mean that you consider it to be untrue or silly.

1분에 몇 단어를 읽는지 리딩 속도를 측정해보세요.

$$\frac{850 \text{ words}}{\text{reading time (\quad) sec}} \times 60 = (\qquad) \text{ WPM}$$

Build Your Vocabulary

scrub^{복습}
[skrʌb]

v. 북북 문지르다, 비벼서 씻다
If you scrub something, you rub it hard in order to clean it, using a stiff brush and water.

tend^{복습}
[tend]

① vt. 손질하다, 돌보다 ② vi. (~하는) 경향이 있다; (어느 방향으로) 나아가다
If you tend someone or something, you do what is necessary to keep them in a good condition or to improve their condition.

hut^{복습}
[hʌt]

n. 오두막; vi. 오두막에 묵다
A hut is a small house with only one or two rooms, especially one which is made of wood, mud, grass, or stones.

innumerable*
[injú:mərəbl]

a. 셀 수 없는, 무수한
Innumerable means very many, or too many to be counted.

uncountable
[ʌnkáuntəbl]

a. 셀 수 없는
Uncountable menas too many to be counted.

extreme^{복습}
[ikstrí:m]

a. 지나친, 과도한; 극단의, 극도의 (extremely ad. 극도로, 매우)
Extreme means very great in degree or intensity.

pony*
[póuni]

n. 조랑말, 작은 말
A pony is a type of small horse.

tippy-toe^{복습}
[típi-tòu]

vi. 발끝으로 살금살금 걷다; a. 살금살금 하는
If you tippy-toe somewhere, you walk there very quietly without putting your heels on the floor when you walk.

lodge*
[ladʒ]

v. 박히다, 꽂히다; 숙박하다, 묵다; n. 오두막
If an object lodges somewhere, it becomes stuck there.

firm***
[fə:rm]

① a. 굳은, 단단한; 견고한 (firmly ad. 굳게) ② n. 회사
A firm decision or opinion is definite and unlikely to change.

grant^{복습}
[grænt]

vt. 주다, 수여하다; 승인하다; n. 허가, 인가
If someone in authority grants you something, or if something is granted to you, you are allowed to have it.

roundabout
[ráundəbàut]

a. 간접의, 완곡한; 에움길의, 빙 도는; n. 완곡한[간접적인] 방법; 에움길
If you do or say something in a roundabout way, you do not do or say it in a simple, clear, and direct way.

outlaw^{복습}
[áutlɔ:]

vt. 불법화하다, 금지하다; n. 범법자
When something is outlawed, it is made illegal.

grim[*]
[grim]

a. 암울한; 엄숙한, 단호한
A situation or piece of information that is grim is unpleasant, depressing, and difficult to accept.

announce[복습]
[ənáuns]

vt. 알리다, 공고하다, 전하다
If you announce something, you tell people about it publicly or officially.

consume[*]
[kənsúːm]

v. 소비하다, 소모하다; ~의 마음을 빼앗다, 사로잡다
If you consume something, you eat or drink it.

loyal[**]
[lɔ́iəl]

a. 충성스러운, 성실한, 충실한
Someone who is loyal remains firm in their friendship or support for a person or thing.

servant[*]
[sə́ːrvənt]

n. 하인, 종; 부하
A servant is someone who is employed to work at another person's home.

nevertheless[*]
[nèvərðəlés]

ad. 그럼에도 불구하고
You use nevertheless when saying something that contrasts with what has just been said.

afford[**]
[əfɔ́ːrd]

vt. ~할 여유가 있다; 주다, 공급하다
If you cannot afford something, you do not have enough money to pay for it.

shrug[*]
[ʃrʌg]

v. (어깨를) 으쓱하다; n. (양 손바닥을 내보이면서 어깨를) 으쓱하기
If you shrug, you raise your shoulders to show that you are not interested in something or that you do not know or care about something.

duty[복습]
[djúːti]

n. 의무, 임무
If you say that something is your duty, you believe that you ought to do it because it is your responsibility.

hand over

phrasal v. 건네주다, 넘겨주다
If you hand something over to someone, you pass it to them.

grab[복습]
[græb]

v. 움켜쥐다, 부여잡다; n. 부여잡기
If you grab something such as food, drink, or sleep, you manage to get some quickly.

beard[*]
[biərd]

n. (턱)수염
A man's beard is the hair that grows on his chin and cheeks.

let go of[복습]

idiom (쥐고 있던 것을) 놓다, ~에서 손을 놓다
To let go of someone or something means to stop holding them.

unbelievable[복습]
[ʌnbilíːvəbl]

a. 믿을 수 없는, 놀라운
You can use unbelievable to emphasize that you think something is very bad or shocking.

possess[복습]
[pəzés]

vt. 소유하다, 가지고 있다; 지배하다 (possession n. 소유)
If you possess something, you have it or own it.

fair and square
[idiom] 정직하게, 정정당당하게
If you say that someone won a competition fair and square, you mean that they won honestly and without cheating.

hen ^{복습}
[hen]
n. 암탉
A hen is a female chicken. People often keep hens in order to eat them or sell their eggs.

handful ^{복습}
[hǽndfùl]
n. 한 움큼, 한 줌; 소량, 소수
A handful of something is the amount of it that you can hold in your hand.

cigarette ^{복습}
[sìɡərét]
n. 담배
Cigarettes are small tubes of paper containing tobacco which people smoke.

imprison*
[imprízn]
vt. 투옥하다, 감금하다
If someone is imprisoned, they are locked up or kept somewhere, usually in prison as a punishment for a crime or for political opposition.

dungeon ^{복습}
[dʌ́ndʒən]
n. 지하 감옥; vt. 지하 감옥에 가두다
A dungeon is a dark underground prison in a castle.

wagon ^{복습}
[wǽɡən]
n. 수레, 짐마차
A wagon is a strong vehicle with four wheels, usually pulled by horses or oxen and used for carrying heavy loads.

confuse**
[kənfjúːz]
v. 어리둥절하게 하다, 혼동하다 (confusion n. 당황)
To confuse someone means to make it difficult for them to know exactly what is happening or what to do.

paddle*
[pædl]
v. 노를 젓다, 물을 젓다; n. 라켓; 노, 패들
If you paddle a boat, you move it through water using a paddle.

cluck
[klʌk]
v. (혀를) 쯧쯧 차다;(닭이) 꼬꼬 울다; n. 꼬꼬댁 우는 소리
If you cluck, you make short, low noise with your tongue.

tap ^{복습}
[tæp]
① v. 가볍게 두드리다; n. 가볍게 두드리기 ② n. 주둥이, (수도 등의) 꼭지
If you tap something, you hit it with a quick light blow or a series of quick light blows.

rein*
[rein]
n. 고삐; 통제 수단, 제어; v. 고삐로 조종하다
Reins are the thin leather straps attached round a horse's neck which are used to control the horse.

slave*
[sleiv]
n. 노예; v. 노예처럼[고되게] 일하다
A slave is someone who is the property of another person and has to work for that person.

deaf*
[def]
a. 귀가 먹은, 청각 장애가 있는
Someone who is deaf is unable to hear anything or is unable to hear very well.

118

1분에 몇 단어를 읽는지 리딩 속도를 측정해보세요.

$$\frac{933 \text{ words}}{\text{reading time (}\quad\text{) sec}} \times 60 = (\qquad) \text{ WPM}$$

Build Your Vocabulary

servant^{복습}
[sə́:rvənt]

n. 하인, 종; 부하
A servant is someone who is employed to work at another person's home.

spool^{복습}
[spu:l]

n. (실·전선·필름 등을 감는) 릴, 얼레
A spool is a round object onto which thread, tape, or film can be wound, especially before it is put into a machine.

thread^{복습}
[θred]

n. 실, 바느질 실; vt. 실을 꿰다
A thread is a long very thin piece of a material such as cotton, nylon, or silk, especially one that is used in sewing.

serve^{복습}
[sə:rv]

v. 시중 들다, 제공하다; 섬기다, 복무하다; n. 서브
If you serve your country, an organization, or a person, you do useful work for them.

dour
[duər]

a. 음울한, 뚱한, 시무룩한
If you describe someone as dour, you mean that they are very serious and unfriendly.

royalty^{복습}
[rɔ́iəlti]

n. 왕족, 왕위; 특허권 사용료
The members of royal families are sometimes referred to as royalty.

curtsy
[kə́:rtsi]

vi. (왼발을 빼고 무릎을 굽혀 몸을 약간 숙여) 절하다; n. 절, 인사
If a woman or a girl curtsies, she lowers her body briefly, bending her knees and sometimes holding her skirt with both hands, as a way of showing respect for an important person.

personal^{복습}
[pə́rsənl]

a. 개인의, 사사로운; 몸소 하는; 인격의, 성격의
A personal opinion, quality, or thing belongs or relates to one particular person rather than to other people.

crisis[*]
[krɑ́isis]

n. 위기, 최악의 고비
A crisis is a situation in which something or someone is affected by one or more very serious problems.

confidence^{**}
[kánfədəns]

n. 자신, 확신
If you have confidence, you feel sure about your abilities, qualities, or ideas.

clutch^{복습}
[klʌʧ]

v. 부여잡다, 꽉 잡다, 붙들다; n. 붙잡음, 움켜쥠
If you clutch at something or clutch something, you hold it tightly, usually because you are afraid or anxious.

mutter 복습
[mʌ́tər]

v. 중얼거리다, 불평하다; n. 중얼거림, 불평
If you mutter, you speak very quietly so that you cannot easily be heard, often because you are complaining about something.

fling 복습
[fliŋ]

vt. (flung–flung) 내던지다; 내밀다, 던지다; n. 내던지기, 돌진
If you fling something somewhere, you throw it there using a lot of force.

stare 복습
[stɛər]

v. 응시하다, 뚫어지게 보다
If you stare at someone or something, you look at them for a long time.

stick 복습
[stik]

① v. (stuck–stuck) 내밀다; 찔러 넣다; 붙이다, 달라붙다; 고수하다
② n. 막대기, 지팡이
If something is sticking out from a surface or object, it extends up or away from it.

rock **
[rak]

① v. 흔들리다, 진동하다 ② n. 바위, 암석
When something rocks or when you rock it, it shakes violently.

thud 복습
[θʌd]

n. 쿵(무거운 물건이 떨어지는 소리); v. 쿵 떨어지다; (심장이) 고동치다, 두근거리다
A thud is a dull sound, such as that a heavy object makes when it hits something soft.

spirit 복습
[spírit]

n. 태도, 자세; 정신, 영혼
The spirit in which you do something is the attitude you have when you are doing it.

get to one's feet 복습

idiom 벌떡 일어서다
If you get or rise to your feet, you stand up.

locate 복습
[lóukeit]

vt. (물건의 위치 등을) 알아내다; 놓다, 두다; (어떤 장소에) 정하다
If you locate something or someone, you find out where they are.

somehow
[sʌ́mhàu]

ad. 어떻게든지 하여, 어쨌든; 어쩐지, 아무래도
You use somehow to say that you do not know or cannot say how something was done or will be done.

squint 복습
[skwint]

v. 눈을 가늘게 뜨고[찡그리고] 보다; n. 사시, 사팔뜨기
If you squint at something, you look at it with your eyes partly closed.

tapestry 복습
[tǽpistri]

n. 태피스트리(색색의 실로 수놓은 벽걸이나 실내장식용 비단)
A tapestry is a large piece of heavy cloth with a picture sewn on it using colored threads.

outlaw 복습
[áutlɔ:]

vt. 불법화하다, 금지하다; n. 범법자
When something is outlawed, it is made illegal.

tremble 복습
[trembl]

v. 떨(리)다, 진동하다, 흔들리다
If you tremble, you shake slightly because you are frightened or cold.

bold *
[bould]

a. 용감한, 대담한; 선명한, 굵은
Someone who is bold is not afraid to do things which involve risk or danger.

sympathy **
[símpəθi]

n. 공감, 연민, 동정심
If you have sympathy with someone's ideas or opinions, you agree with them.

120

nod 복습
[nɔd]

v. 끄덕이다, 끄덕여 표시하다; n. (동의·인사·신호·명령의) 끄덕임
If you nod, you move your head downward and upward to show agreement, understanding, or approval.

roar 복습
[rɔːr]

vi. 고함치다, 으르렁거리다; n. 외치는 소리, 왁자지껄함; 으르렁거리는 소리
If someone roars, they shout something in a very loud voice.

clout 복습
[klaut]

n. (손바닥·주먹으로) 때리기[강타]; vt. (주먹으로) 때리다
If you clout someone, you hit them.

destine 복습
[déstin]

vt. ~할 운명에 있다
If something is destined to happen or if someone is destined to behave in a particular way, that thing seems certain to happen or be done.

abundantly
[əbʌ́ndəntli]

ad. 아주 분명하게; 풍부하게
If something is abundantly clear, it is extremely obvious.

notion *
[nóuʃən]

n. 생각, 개념, 관념
A notion is an idea or belief about something.

ridiculous 복습
[ridíkjuləs]

a. 터무니없는; 웃기는, 우스꽝스러운
If you say that something or someone is ridiculous, you mean that they are very foolish.

1분에 몇 단어를 읽는지 리딩 속도를 측정해보세요.

$$\frac{803 \text{ words}}{\text{reading time (\quad) sec}} \times 60 = (\quad\quad) \text{ WPM}$$

Build Your Vocabulary

plump**
[plʌmp]

a. 포동포동한, 둥그스름한; 속이 가득 찬
You can describe someone or something as plump to indicate that they are rather fat or rounded.

utter^{복습}
[ʌ́tər]

① v. 발언하다, 말하다 ② a. 완전한, 전적인, 절대적인
You use utter to emphasize that something is great in extent, degree, or amount.

disagreeable*
[dìsəgríːəbl]

a. 유쾌하지 못한; 무례한, 무뚝뚝한
Something that is disagreeable is rather unpleasant.

spirit^{복습}
[spírit]

n. 태도, 자세; 정신, 영혼
The spirit in which you do something is the attitude you have when you are doing it.

drawer**
[drɔ́ːər]

n. 서랍; 장롱 (not the sharpest knife in the drawer idiom 똑똑하지 못한)
If you say that someone is not the sharpest knife in the drawer, you mean they are not that intelligent.

slow-witted
[slou-wítid]

a. 이해가 느린, 머리가 둔한
Someone who is slow-witted is slow to understand things.

shortcoming
[ʃɔ́ːrtkʌmiŋ]

n. 결점, 단점
Someone's or something's shortcomings are the faults or weaknesses which they have.

hard-pressed
[haːrd-prest]

a. ~을 하는 데 애를 먹는; (일·돈·시간에) 쪼들리는
If you will be hard-pressed to do something, you will have great difficulty doing it.

succession*
[səkséʃən]

n. 연속, 잇따름; 상속, 계승
A succession of things of the same kind is a number of them that exist or happen one after the other.

gown^{복습}
[gaun]

n. 특별한 경우에 입는 여성의) 드레스; (판사의) 법복; 가운
A gown is a dress, usually a long dress, which women wear on formal occasions.

duchess*
[dʌ́ʧis]

n. 공작부인, 여 공작
A duchess is a woman who has the same rank as a duke, or who is a duke's wife or widow.

seamstress
[síːmstris]

n. 침모, 여자 재봉사
A seamstress is a woman who sews and makes clothes as her job.

sew [복습]
[sou]

v. (sewed–sewn/sewed) 바느질하다, 꿰매다, 깁다
When you sew something such as clothes, you make them or repair them by joining pieces of cloth together by passing thread through them with a needle.

cloak [복습]
[klouk]

n. 소매 없는 외투, 망토; vt. 가리다, 은폐하다
A cloak is a long, loose, sleeveless piece of clothing which people used to wear over their other clothes when they went out.

master [복습]
[mǽstər]

n. 대가, 명인, 정통한 사람; vt. 숙달하다, 터득하다
If you say that someone is a master of a particular activity, you mean that they are extremely skilled at it.

frock
[frak]

n. 드레스
A frock is a woman's or girl's dress.

ruin [복습]
[ruːin]

v. 망치다, 못쓰게 만들다; 몰락하다; n. 폐허; 파멸
To ruin something means to severely harm, damage, or spoil it.

chambermaid
[ʧéimbərmeid]

n. (호텔의) 객실 (여자) 청소부
A chambermaid is a woman who cleans and tidies the bedrooms in a hotel.

delighted [복습]
[diláitid]

a. 아주 기뻐하여, 즐거워하는
If you are delighted, you are extremely pleased and excited about something.

admire [복습]
[ædmáiər]

v. 감탄하다, 칭찬하다
If you admire someone or something, you like and respect them very much.

exclaim***
[ikskléim]

v. 외치다, 소리치다
If you exclaim, you say or shout something suddenly because of surprise, fear and pleasure.

domestic*
[dəméstik]

a. 가정의, 가정적인; 국내의, 자국의
Domestic duties and activities are concerned with the running of a home and family.

chore*
[ʧɔːr]

n. (pl.) (가정의) 잡일, 가사; 자질구레한 일, 허드렛일; 지루한 일
Chores are tasks such as cleaning, washing, and ironing that have to be done regularly at home.

pace*
[peis]

v. 서성거리다; (일의) 속도를 유지하다; n. 속도
If you pace a small area, you keep walking up and down it, because you are anxious or impatient.

mutter [복습]
[mʌ́tər]

v. 중얼거리다, 불평하다; n. 중얼거림, 불평
If you mutter, you speak very quietly so that you cannot easily be heard, often because you are complaining about something.

revenge [복습]
[rivéndʒ]

n. 복수, 보복; vt. 복수하다, 원수를 갚다
Revenge involves hurting or punishing someone who has hurt or harmed you.

consequence [복습]
[kánsəkwèns]

n. 결과, 결말; 중요성, 중대함
The consequences of something are the results or effects of it.

bet*
[bet]

v. 틀림없다, ~라고 확신하다; 걸다, 내기를 하다; n. 내기, 내기돈
You use expressions such as 'I bet', 'I'll bet', and 'you can bet' to indicate that you are sure something is true.

inability*
[inəbíləti]

n. 무능, 무력
If you refer to someone's inability to do something, you are referring to the fact that they are unable to do it.

last resort
[læst rizɔ́:t]

n. 마지막 수단
If you do something as a last resort, you do it because you can find no other way of getting out of a difficult situation or of solving a problem.

reputation*
[repjutéiʃən]

n. 평판, 명성
Something's or someone's reputation is the opinion that people have about how good they are.

eggshell
[égshèl]

n. 달걀 껍질
An eggshell is the hard covering on the outside of an egg.

batter
[bǽtər]

n. 케이크 반죽; 타자; v. 두드리다, 때리다
Batter is a mixture of flour, eggs, and milk that is used in cooking.

scrub 복습
[skrʌb]

v. 북북 문지르다, 비벼서 씻다
If you scrub something, you rub it hard in order to clean it, using a stiff brush and water.

sneeze 복습
[sni:z]

vi. 재채기하다; n. 재채기
When you sneeze, you suddenly take in your breath and then blow it down your nose noisily without being able to stop yourself, for example because you have a cold.

chop*
[tʃap]

n. 잘라낸 조각, (뼈가 붙은) 토막 고기; 절단; vt. 자르다, 잘게 썰다
A chop is a small piece of meat cut from the ribs of a sheep or pig.

good-for-nothing
[gúd-fər-nʌ́θiŋ]

a. 무가치한, 쓸모없는
If you describe someone as good-for-nothing, you think that they are lazy or irresponsible.

encounter 복습
[inkáuntər]

v. 만나다, 마주치다; n. 마주침
If you encounter problems or difficulties, you experience them.

cup 복습
[kʌp]

vt. 손바닥으로 받다[떠내다]; 두 손을 (컵 모양으로) 동그랗게 모아 쥐다; n. 컵, 잔
If you cup something in your hands, you make your hands into a curved dish-like shape and support it or hold it gently.

jailer 복습
[dʒéilər]

n. 교도관, 간수
A jailer is a person who is in charge of a jail and the prisoners in it.

noonday
[nú:ndèi]

a. 정오[한낮]의
Noonday means happening or appearing in the middle part of the day.

foul 복습
[faul]

a. 악취가 나는, (성격·맛 등이) 더러운
If you describe something as foul, you mean it is dirty and smells or tastes unpleasant.

124

odor*
[óudər]

n. (불쾌한) 냄새, 악취
An odor is a particular and distinctive smell.

permeate
[pə́:rmièit]

v. 스며들다, 침투하다, 퍼지다
If something permeates a place, it spreads throughout it.

howl**
[haul]

n. 울부짖음; v. 울다, 울부짖다
If you howl something, you say it in a very loud voice.

issue***
[íʃuː]

v. 내다; 발하다; 발행하다; n. 발행; 논쟁점
If you issue a statement or a warning, you make it known formally or publicly.

weep^{복습}
[wiːp]

v. 눈물을 흘리다, 울다; 물기를 내뿜다
If someone weeps, they cry.

moan**
[moun]

v. 신음하다, 끙끙대다; 투덜대다; n. 신음; 불평
If you moan, you make a low sound, usually because you are unhappy or in pain.

assure^{복습}
[əʃúə:r]

vt. 확신하다, 보증하다
If you assure someone that something is true or will happen, you tell them that it is definitely true or will definitely happen, often in order to make them less worried.

bear***
[bɛər]

① v. 가지고 가다; 참다, 견디다 ② n. 곰
If you bear something somewhere, you carry it there or take it there.

white-faced
[hwáit-fèist]

a. 안색이 창백한
Someone who is white-faced is pale, often as a result of nerves.

chatter^{복습}
[tʃǽtər]

v. (이가 공포·추위로) 딱딱 맞부딪치다; 수다를 떨다, 재잘거리다; n. 재잘거림, 수다
If you chatter, you talk quickly and continuously, usually about things which are not important.

whisper^{복습}
[hwíspə:r]

v. 속삭이다; n. 속삭임; 속삭이는 소리
When you whisper, you say something very quietly.

servant^{복습}
[sə́:rvənt]

n. 하인, 종; 부하
A servant is someone who is employed to work at another person's home.

fate^{복습}
[feit]

n. 운명, 숙명
A person's or thing's fate is what happens to them.

reckon**
[rékən]

vt. ~라고 생각하다; 세다, 계산하다
If you reckon that something is true, you think that it is true.

bungle
[bʌ́ŋgl]

v. ~을 엉망으로[서투르게] 하다
If you bungle something, you fail to do it properly, because you make mistakes or are clumsy.

descend^{복습}
[disénd]

v. 내려가다; (어둠 등이) 내려앉다; 전해지다, 유래하다
If you descend, you move downward from a higher to a lower level.

flicker*
[flíkər]

v. (등불·희망·빛 등이) 깜박이다; n. 깜박임
If a light or flame flickers, it shines unsteadily.

Check Your Reading Speed

1분에 몇 단어를 읽는지 리딩 속도를 측정해보세요.

$$\frac{548 \text{ words}}{\text{reading time ( ) sec}} \times 60 = (\quad) \text{ WPM}$$

Build Your Vocabulary

odor^{복습}
[óudər]

n. (불쾌한) 냄새, 악취
An odor is a particular and distinctive smell.

clout^{복습}
[klaut]

n. (손바닥·주먹으로) 때리기[강타]; vt. (주먹으로) 때리다
If you clout someone, you hit them.

mark^{복습}
[ma:rk]

n. 표적, 목표물; 표시, 부호; v. 표시하다, 나타내다
If something is off the mark, it is inaccurate or incorrect. If it is on the mark, it is accurate or correct.

interrupt**
[ìntərʌ́pt]

v. 중단하다, 가로막다, 저지하다
If you interrupt someone who is speaking, you say or do something that causes them to stop.

olfactory
[alfǽktəri]

a. 후각의
Olfactory means concerned with the sense of smell.

overwhelm**
[òuvərhwélm]

vt. 압도하다, 제압하다; 질리게 하다 (overwhelming a. 압도적인)
If something is overwhelming, it affects you very strongly, and you do not know how to deal with it.

stench
[stentʃ]

n. 불쾌한 냄새, 악취
A stench is a strong and very unpleasant smell.

despair^{복습}
[dispέər]

n. 절망, 자포자기; vi. 절망하다
Despair is the feeling that everything is wrong and that nothing will improve.

discernible
[disə́:rnəbl]

a. 보고 알 수 있는, 인식할 수 있는
If something is discernible, you can see it or recognize that it exists.

twist^{복습}
[twist]

v. 비틀다, 돌리다, 꼬다; n. 뒤틀림; 엉킴; 변화
If you twist something, you turn it so that it moves around in a circular direction.

glitter^{복습}
[glítər]

vi. 반짝반짝 빛나다, 반짝이다; n. 반짝이는 빛 (glittery a. 반짝반짝 하는)
If something glitters, light comes from or is reflected off different parts of it.

bellow^{복습}
[bélou]

v. (우렁찬 소리로) 고함치다, 큰 소리로 울다; n. 울부짖기, 포효
If someone bellows, they shout angrily in a loud, deep voice.

wrap^{복습}
[ræp]

v. 감싸다; 포장하다; n. 싸개, 덮개
If someone wraps their arms, fingers, or legs around something, they put them firmly around it.

ominous ^{복습}
[ámənəs]

a. 불길한, 나쁜 징조의
If you describe something as ominous, you mean that it worries you because it makes you think that something unpleasant is going to happen.

frighten ^{복습}
[fraitn]

v. 놀라게 하다, 섬뜩하게 하다; 기겁하다 (frightening a. 무서운)
If something is frightening, it makes you feel afraid, anxious, or nervous.

snail[*]
[sneil]

n. 달팽이
A snail is a small animal with a long, soft body, no legs, and a spiral-shaped shell.

slither
[slíðər]

n. 주르르 미끄러짐; v. 주르르 미끄러지다, 미끄러지게 하다
If you slither somewhere, you slide along in an uneven way.

ooze[*]
[u:z]

v. 스며 나오다, 새어나오다; n. 스며 나옴
When a thick or sticky liquid oozes from something or when something oozes it, the liquid flows slowly and in small quantities.

moan ^{복습}
[moun]

n. 신음; 불평; v. 신음하다, 끙끙대다; 투덜대다
A moan is a low noise.

drag ^{복습}
[dræg]

v. 끌(리)다, 끌고 오다; (발을) 질질 끌다; n. 견인, 끌기; 빨아들이기
If you drag something, you pull it along the ground, often with difficulty.

muck ^{복습}
[mʌk]

n. 쓰레기, 오물; 거름, 퇴비; vt. 실패하다, 망쳐놓다
Muck is dirt or some other unpleasant substance.

disturb ^{복습}
[distə́:rb]

v. (마음·일 등을) 방해하다, 어지럽히다 (disturbing a. 불안하게 하는)
If you disturb someone, you interrupt what they are doing and upset them.

cling ^{복습}
[kliŋ]

vi. 달라붙다, 매달리다
If you cling to someone or something, you hold onto them tightly.

shed[*]
[ʃed]

v. (shed-shed) (빛을) 비추다; 없애다; 흘리다; n. 보관소, 헛간
To shed light on something means to make it easier to understand, because more information is known about it.

tower ^{복습}
[tauər]

vi. 솟다; (~보다) 뛰어나다; n. 탑
Someone or something that towers over surrounding people or things is a lot taller than they are.

pile ^{복습}
[pail]

n. 쌓아 올린 더미; 다수; v. 쌓아 올리다, 쌓(이)다
A pile of things is a mass of them that is high in the middle and has sloping sides.

kettle ^{복습}
[ketl]

n. 솥, 냄비; 주전자
A kettle is a metal pot for boiling or cooking things in.

boom ^{복습}
[bu:m]

v. (소리가) 울려 퍼지다, 쿵 하는 소리를 내다; n. 쿵 울리는 소리; 인기, 붐
When something such as someone's voice, a cannon, or a big drum booms, it makes a loud, deep sound that lasts for several seconds.

1분에 몇 단어를 읽는지 리딩 속도를 측정해보세요.

$$\frac{500 \text{ words}}{\text{reading time ( ) sec}} \times 60 = (\quad) \text{ WPM}$$

Build Your Vocabulary

reveal ^{복습}
[rivíːl]

vt. 드러내다, 폭로하다, 밝히다
If you reveal something that has been out of sight, you uncover it so that people can see it.

limp
[limp]

v. 다리를 절다, 절뚝거리다; a. 기운이 없는, 축 처진
If a person or animal limps, they walk with difficulty or in an uneven way because one of their legs or feet is hurt.

ankle ^{복습}
[æŋkl]

n. 발목
Your ankle is the joint where your foot joins your leg.

outstretch
[àutstrétʃ]

v. 펴다, 뻗다, 확장하다
When you outstretch, you are stretching or extending beyond.

presume*
[prizúːm]

v. 추정하다, 생각하다
If you presume that something is the case, you think that it is the case, although you are not certain.

overturn*
[òuvərtə́ːrn]

v. 뒤집히다, 뒤집다
If something overturns or if you overturn it, it turns upside down or on its side.

balance ^{복습}
[bǽləns]

v. 균형을 유지하다[잡다]; n. 균형, 평형; 저울; 나머지, 잔여
If you balance something somewhere, or if it balances there, it remains steady and does not fall.

stare ^{복습}
[stɛər]

v. 응시하다, 똥그렇게 보다
If you stare at someone or something, you look at them for a long time.

assume ^{복습}
[əsjúːm]

vt. 추정하다, 가정하다; (역할·임무 등을) 맡다
If you assume that something is true, you imagine that it is true, sometimes wrongly.

illegal ^{복습}
[ilíːgəl]

a. 불법의, 비합법적인
If something is illegal, the law says that it is not allowed.

mutter ^{복습}
[mʌ́tər]

v. 중얼거리다, 불평하다; n. 중얼거림, 불평
If you mutter, you speak very quietly so that you cannot easily be heard, often because you are complaining about something.

chew ^{복습}
[tʃuː]

v. 씹다
If a person or animal chews an object, they bite it with their teeth.

swallow 복습
[swálou]

v. 삼키다, 목구멍으로 넘기다; (초조해서) 마른침을 삼키다
If you swallow something, you cause it to go from your mouth down into your stomach.

ferocious＊
[fəróuʃəs]

a. 잔인한, 지독한, 사나운
A ferocious animal, person, or action is very fierce and violent.

admire 복습
[ædmáiər]

v. 감탄하다, 칭찬하다 (admiringly ad. 감탄하여)
If you admire someone or something, you like and respect them very much.

pronounce＊＊
[prənáuns]

v. 선언[표명]하다; 발음하다 (pronouncement n. 공표, 선언)
If you pronounce something to be true, you state that it is the case.

deliberate＊
[dilíbərət]

a. 느긋한, 신중한; 계획적인; v. 신중히 생각하다
If a movement or action is deliberate, it is done slowly and carefully.

jig
[dʒig]

n. 지그(빠르고 활발한 4분의 3박자의 춤); v. 춤을 추다, 뛰어 돌아다니다
A jig is a lively dance.

fearsome
[fíərsəm]

a. 무시무시한, 오싹한
Fearsome is used to describe things that are frightening, for example because of their large size or extreme nature.

indeed＊＊＊
[indíːd]

ad. 실로, 참으로, 과연, 정말
You use indeed to confirm or agree with something that has just been said.

cease 복습
[siːs]

v. 그만두다, 중지하다
If you cease something, you stop it happening or working.

sneeze 복습
[sniːz]

vi. 재채기하다; n. 재채기
When you sneeze, you suddenly take in your breath and then blow it down your nose noisily without being able to stop yourself, for example because you have a cold.

instruct 복습
[instrʌ́kt]

vt. 지시[명령]하다; 가르치다 (instruction n. 지시; 설명)
If you instruct someone to do something, you formally tell them to do it.

beware＊＊
[biwéər]

vt. 조심하다, 주의하다
If you tell someone to beware of a person or thing, you are warning them that the person or thing may harm them or be dangerous.

nibble 복습
[nibl]

v. 조금씩 물어뜯다, 갉아먹다; n. 조금씩 물어뜯기, 한 입 분량
If you nibble food, you eat it by biting very small pieces of it.

revenge 복습
[rivéndʒ]

n. 복수, 보복; vt. 복수하다, 원수를 갚다
Revenge involves hurting or punishing someone who has hurt or harmed you.

at hand

idiom (시간·거리상으로) 가까이에 (있는)
If something is at hand, it is near in distance or time.

1분에 몇 단어를 읽는지 리딩 속도를 측정해보세요.

$$\frac{647 \text{ words}}{\text{reading time (} \quad \text{) sec}} \times 60 = (\quad) \text{ WPM}$$

Build Your Vocabulary

detain
[ditéin]

vt. 붙들다, 기다리게 하다; 억류[구금]하다
To detain someone means to delay them, for example by talking to them.

beware^{복습}
[biwéər]

vt. 조심하다, 주의하다
If you tell someone to beware of a person or thing, you are warning them that the person or thing may harm them or be dangerous.

cloak^{복습}
[klouk]

n. 소매 없는 외투, 망토; vt. 입고 있다; 가리다, 은폐하다
A cloak is a long, loose, sleeveless piece of clothing which people used to wear over their other clothes when they went out.

panic^{**}
[pǽnik]

v. 공포에 질리다; n. 공포, 공황
If you panic or if someone panics you, you suddenly feel anxious or afraid, and act quickly and without thinking carefully.

trade^{복습}
[treid]

v. 교환하다; 장사하다; n. 교환, 무역; 직업
When people, firms, or countries trade, they buy, sell, or exchange goods or services between themselves.

tragic[*]
[trǽdʒik]

a. 비극의, 비참한
A tragic event or situation is extremely sad, usually because it involves death or suffering.

pardon^{복습}
[pɑ:rdn]

vt. 용서하다; n. 용서, 관용; int. 뭐라구요(상대방의 말을 되물을 때 하는 말)
Some people say 'Pardon me' instead of 'Excuse me' when they want to politely get someone's attention or interrupt them.

consider^{복습}
[kənsídər]

v. 고려하다, 숙고하다
If you consider something, you think about it carefully.

portentous
[pɔ:rténtəs]

a. (특히 불길한) 전조[징후]가 되는
Something that is portentous is important in indicating or affecting future events.

pitch[*]
[piʧ]

v. (소리·음을 특정한 높이로) 내다; 내던지다, 내동댕이치다
If a sound is pitched at a particular level, it is produced at the level indicated.

tortuous^{복습}
[tɔ́:rʧuəs]

a. (강·길이) 구불구불한; 길고 복잡한, 우여곡절이 많은
A tortuous road is full of bends and twists.

utter^{복습}
[ʌ́tər]

① v. 발언하다, 말하다 ② a. 완전한, 전적인, 절대적인
You use utter to emphasize that something is great in extent, degree, or amount.

tragedy^{복습}
[trǽdʒədi]

n. 비극, 비극적인 이야기
A tragedy is an extremely sad event or situation.

acquaintance^{**}
[əkwéintəns]

n. 아는 사람, 지인
An acquaintance is someone who you have met and know slightly, but not well.

triumph^{**}
[tráiəmf]

n. 승리감; 승리, 대성공; vi. 성공하다, 이기다
A triumph is a great success or achievement, often one that has been gained with a lot of skill or effort.

glory[*]
[glɔ́:ri]

n. 영광, 영예; 장관, 찬란함; vi. 기뻐하다, 자랑으로 여기다
Glory is the fame and admiration that you gain by doing something impressive.

inquire^{복습}
[inkwáiər]

v. 묻다, 문의하다
If you inquire about something, you ask for information about it.

ascertain
[æsərtéin]

v. (옳은 정보를) 알아내다[확인하다]
If you ascertain the truth about something, you find out what it is, especially by making a deliberate effort to do so.

aspiration
[æspəréiʃən]

n. 열망, 포부, 염원
Someone's aspirations are their desire to achieve things.

suit^{***}
[su:t]

① v. 적합하다, 어울리다 ② n. 옷 한 벌, 슈트; 소송
If something suits you, it is convenient for you or is the best thing for you in the circumstances.

mouthful[*]
[máuθfùl]

n. 한 입 가득, 한 입
A mouthful of drink or food is the amount that you put or have in your mouth.

serve^{복습}
[sə:rv]

v. 제공하다, 시중 들다; 섬기다, 복무하다; n. 서브
When you serve food and drink, you give people food and drink.

Highness
[háinis]

n. 전하(왕족에 대한 경칭)
Expressions such as 'Your Highness' or 'His Highness' are used to address or refer to a member of the royal family other than a king or queen.

bow^{복습}
[bau]

① v. 머리를 숙이다, 굽히다 ② n. 활; 곡선
When you bow, you move your head or the top half of your body forward and downward as a formal way of greeting them or showing respect.

royal^{복습}
[rɔ́iəl]

a. 왕의, 왕위의; 위엄 있는
Royal is used to indicate that something is connected with a king, queen, or emperor, or their family.

illustrate^{**}
[íləstreit]

vt. (예를 들어) 설명하다; 삽화를 넣다
If you use an example, story, or diagram to illustrate a point, you use it show that what you are saying is true or to make your meaning clearer.

passionate[*]
[pǽʃənit]

a. 열정적인, 열렬한, 격정적인 (passionately ad. 열정적으로)
A passionate person has very strong feelings about something or a strong belief in something.

intent ^{복습}
[intént]

① a. 몰두하는, 여념이 없는 (intently ad. 골똘하게) ② n. 의지, 의향
If you are intent on doing something, you are eager and determined to do it.

disbelief *
[dìsbilíːf]

n. 믿기지 않음, 불신감
Disbelief is not believing that something is true or real.

outrage ^{복습}
[áutreidʒ]

n. 격분, 격노; vt. 격분[격노]하게 만들다
Outrage is an intense feeling of anger and shock.

issue ^{복습}
[íʃuː]

v. 내다; 발하다; 발행하다; n. 발행; 논쟁점
If you issue a statement or a warning, you make it known formally or publicly.

unfold ^{복습}
[ʌnfóuld]

v. 펴다, 펼치다; 열리다
If a situation unfolds, it develops and becomes known or understood.

diabolic
[dàiəbálik]

a. (= diabolical) 악마의[같은], 마성의
Diabolic is used to describe things that people think are caused by or belong to the Devil.

1분에 몇 단어를 읽는지 리딩 속도를 측정해보세요.

$$\frac{585 \text{ words}}{\text{reading time (} \quad \text{) sec}} \times 60 = (\qquad) \text{ WPM}$$

Build Your Vocabulary

whisper^{복습}
[hwíspə:r]

v. 속삭이다; n. 속삭임; 속삭이는 소리
When you whisper, you say something very quietly.

wrap^{복습}
[ræp]

v. 감싸다; 포장하다; n. 싸개, 덮개
If someone wraps their arms, fingers, or legs around something, they put them firmly around it.

relieve^{**}
[rilí:v]

vt. (걱정·고통 등을) 덜다, 안도하게 하다, 완화하다 (relieved a. 안도하는)
If something relieves an unpleasant feeling or situation, it makes it less unpleasant or causes it to disappear completely.

duty^{복습}
[djú:ti]

n. 의무, 임무
If you say that something is your duty, you believe that you ought to do it because it is your responsibility.

tumble^{복습}
[tʌmbl]

v. 굴러 떨어지다, 넘어지다; n. 추락; 폭락
If someone or something tumbles somewhere, they fall there with a rolling or bouncing movement.

plop
[plap]

n. 퐁당 (하는 소리); v. 털썩 주저앉다; 퐁당[툭] 하고 떨어지다
A plop is a soft, gentle sound, like the sound made by something dropping into water without disturbing the surface much.

measure^{**}
[méʒər]

vt. 재다, 계량하다; n. 치수, 분량; (pl.) 수단, 방책
If you measure a quantity that can be expressed in numbers, such as the length of something, you discover it using a particular instrument or device, for example a ruler.

bend^{복습}
[bend]

v. (bent–bent) 구부리다, 돌리다; 구부러지다, 휘다; n. 커브, 굽음
When you bend a part of your body such as your arm or leg, or when it bends, you change its position so that it is no longer straight.

sink^{복습}
[siŋk]

v. 가라앉히다, 침몰하다; (마음 등이) 가라앉다, 낙심하다 (sinking a. 가라앉는)
If something sinks, it disappears below the surface of a mass of water.

stick^{복습}
[stik]

① v. (stuck–stuck) 내밀다; 찔러 넣다; 붙이다, 달라붙다; 고수하다
② n. 막대기, 지팡이
If you stick something somewhere, you put it there in a rather casual way.

gasp^{복습}
[gæsp]

v. 숨이 턱 막히다, 헉 하고 숨을 쉬다; n. (숨이 막히는 듯) 헉 하는 소리를 냄
When you gasp, you take a short quick breath through your mouth, especially when you are surprised, shocked, or in pain.

cough 복습
[kɔːf]

v. 기침하다; n. 기침
When you cough, you force air out of your throat with a sudden, harsh noise. You often cough when you are ill, or when you are nervous or want to attract someone's attention.

blink 복습
[bliŋk]

v. 눈을 깜박거리다; (등불·별 등이) 깜박이다; n. 깜박거림
When you blink or when you blink your eyes, you shut your eyes and very quickly open them again.

weep 복습
[wiːp]

v. (wept–wept) 눈물을 흘리다, 울다; 물기를 내뿜다
If someone weeps, they cry.

rescue 복습
[réskjuː]

n. 구출, 구원; vt. 구조하다, 구출하다
Rescue is help which gets someone out of a dangerous or unpleasant situation.

slick
[slik]

a. 미끄러운, 매끈거리는; 능숙한, 교묘한
Something is slick is slippery especially from being covered with ice, water or oil.

loosen*
[luːsn]

v. 풀다, 느슨해지다
If you loosen something that is stretched across something else, you make it less stretched or tight.

grip 복습
[grip]

n. 움켜쥠, 꽉 붙잡음; 손잡이; v. 꽉 잡다, 움켜잡다
A grip is a firm, strong hold on something.

bundle***
[bʌndl]

n. 묶음, 꾸러미; vt. (짐을) 꾸리다, 묶다
A bundle of things is a number of them that are tied together or wrapped in a cloth or bag so that they can be carried or stored.

fur 복습
[fəːr]

n. 부드러운 털; 모피
Fur is the thick and usually soft hair that grows on the bodies of many mammals.

philosophy*
[filásəfi]

n. 철학
Philosophy is the study or creation of theories about basic things such as the nature of existence, knowledge, and thought, or about how people should live.

miraculous
[mirǽkjələs]

a. 기적적인, 초자연적인; 놀랄 만한
If you describe a good event as miraculous, you mean that it is very surprising and unexpected.

loom*
[luːm]

vi. 어렴풋이 나타나다, 흐릿하게 보이다
If something looms over you, it appears as a large or unclear shape, often in a frightening way.

skedaddle
[skidǽdl]

vi. (특히 누구를 피하여) 서둘러 가 버리다; 떠나다
If you skedaddle, you run off hastily.

concern 복습
[kənsə́ːrn]

vt. 걱정하다, 염려하다; ~에 관계하다; n. 염려; 관심 (concerned a. 걱정하는)
If something concerns you, it worries you.

blind***
[blaind]

vt. 눈멀게 하다; 가리다, 보이지 않게 하다; a. 눈먼, 장님인
If something blinds you, it makes you unable to see, either for a short time or permanently.

134

intense[**]
[inténs]

a. 강렬한, 격렬한, 심한
Intense is used to describe something that is very great or extreme in strength or degree.

hindquarters
[háindkwɔ́:rtərz]

n. (짐승의 두 뒷다리를 포함하는) 후반신
The hindquarters of a four-legged animal are its back part, including its two back legs.

leap[복습]
[li:p]

v. (leapt/leaped–leapt/leaped) 껑충 뛰다, 뛰어넘다; (심장이) 뛰다, 고동치다;
n. 뜀, 도약
If you leap, you jump high in the air or jump a long distance.

scurry[복습]
[skɔ́:ri]

vi. 종종걸음으로 달리다, 급히 가다
When people or small animals scurry somewhere, they move there quickly and hurriedly, especially because they are frightened.

zigzag[**]
[zígzæg]

v. 지그재그(Z자 꼴)로 나아가다; a. 지그재그의, Z자형의
If you zigzag, you move forward by going at an angle first to one side then to the other.

crack[**]
[kræk]

n. 작은 틈새; 금, 깨진 틈; 날카로운 소리; v. 갈라지다, 금이 가다; 깨지다, 부서지다
A crack is a very narrow gap between two things, or between two parts of a thing.

pantry
[pǽntri]

n. 식료품 저장실
A pantry is a small room or large cupboard in a house, usually near the kitchen, where food is kept.

brace[*]
[breis]

v. 대비하다; 버팀대로 받치다; n. 버팀대
If you brace yourself for something unpleasant or difficult, you prepare yourself for it.

advance[***]
[ædvǽns]

v. (공격하거나 위협하기 위해) 다가가다, 진격하다; 증진되다[진전을 보다]
To advance means to move forward, often in order to attack someone.

intend[복습]
[inténd]

vt. ~할 작정이다, 의도하다
If you intend to do something, you have decided or planned to do it.

clout[복습]
[klaut]

n. (손바닥·주먹으로) 때리기[강타]; vt. (주먹으로) 때리다
If you clout someone, you hit them.

Book the Fourth
(Chapter Thirty-five to Chapter Fifty-two) & Coda

1. How did Despereaux escape from the dungeon?
   A. Gregory wrapped him in a napkin on the tray.
   B. Gregory put him in Mig's apron pocket.
   C. Gregory carried him to the door and let him out.
   D. Gregory showed him a secret tunnel made by mice.

2. Which of the following did NOT happen to Despereaux in the kitchen?
   A. He fell into a cup full of oil.
   B. Mig dropped him to the floor.
   C. Mig cut off his tail with a knife.
   D. Mig dropped him into a bag of flour.

3. Which of the following was NOT a reason for why Despereaux wept in the pantry?
   A. He cried because of the pain in his tail.
   B. He cried because he missed his siblings.
   C. He cried because he was out of the dungeon.
   D. He cried because he had been sent to death but still lived.

4. Who was under the armor in Despereaux's dream?

    A. The king's soldier that brought Mig to the castle

    B. The handsome prince from the story he had read

    C. Nobody, it was empty

    D. An older, bigger version of Despereaux

5. What two things did Mig carry in her apron pockets?

    A. A candle and a sewing needle

    B. A soup spoon and matches

    C. A kitchen knife and Roscuro

    D. A kitchen knife and red thread

6. What part of Roscuro's plan did he not tell Mig?

    A. He planned to take the princess to the dungeon and keep her there forever.

    B. He planned to take the princess outside of the castle and force her to run away.

    C. He planned to keep Mig in the dungeon and leave the princess alone.

    D. He planned to be a king among the rats and humans.

7. What was Princess Pea dreaming of when Mig arrived in her bedroom?

    A. Her father hunting rats

    B. Her mother offering her soup

    C. Roscuro landing in the queen's soup

    D. Despereaux coming to save her

8. How did Princess Pea react when asked if she knew Roscuro?

A. She could not remember him and thought this was their first time meeting.

B. She thought that Roscuro was related to Despereaux.

C. She remembered him as the rat that had fallen in her mother's soup and told him that.

D. She remembered him as the rat that had fallen in her mother's soup but did not tell him that.

9. How was Princess Pea empathetic toward Mig?

A. She pitied Mig for having lost both her parents.

B. She pitied Mig for not being beautiful and smart.

C. She pitied Mig for desperately wanting to be a princess.

D. She pitied Mig for desperately wanting to be rich.

10. Which of the following was NOT one of the parts of Princess Pea's heart?

A. Hatred for the rat responsible for her mother's death

B. Empathy for Mig as they went to the dungeon

C. Deep sorrow for her dead mother

D. Hope for Despereaux as she expected to be saved by him

11. How do people in the castle think that Gregory died?

A. His rope was broken causing him to get lost and frightened to death.

B. A rat poisoned his food and Gregory got sick and died.

C. He plotted to kidnap the princess and was executed by the king.

D. He died peacefully of old age naturally in the dungeon.

12. Who did Despereaux try to find first after he learned about Roscuro's plan involving the princess?
    A. He tried to find Roscuro.
    B. He tried to find his family.
    C. He tried to find the threadmaster.
    D. He tried to find the king.

13. How had Lester changed in the short time Despereaux was away?
    A. He looked stronger and had more muscles.
    B. He looked older and had gray fur.
    C. He looked younger and had dyed fur.
    D. He looked tired and had dark circles under his eyes.

14. Why was Lester crying after Despereaux left again?
    A. He was crying because he was afraid of ghosts.
    B. He was crying because he forgot to tell Despereaux he was sorry.
    C. He was crying because he had been forgiven by Despereaux.
    D. He was crying because he had destroyed his favorite drum.

15. What was the king doing when Despereaux found him?
    A. The king was playing a song on the guitar.
    B. The king was sewing Princess Pea's tapestry.
    C. The king was crying for Princess Pea.
    D. The king was making a plan to save Princess Pea.

16. How did the king react when Despereaux said he knew where the princess had been taken?
    A. He begged Despereaux to save Princess Pea.
    B. He called Despereaux a liar and refused to listen to him.
    C. He was surprised that a mouse would be so brave.
    D. He trusted Despereaux and offered his soldier's to help him.

17. Why did Despereaux go to the threadmaster?
    A. He needed the thread to tie up the rats as prisoners.
    B. He needed the thread to help him climb down into the dungeon.
    C. He needed the thread to trade with the rats for Princess Pea.
    D. He needed the thread to help him find his way out of the dungeon.

18. What did the threadmaster offer Despereaux to use for protection in the dungeon?
    A. A needle
    B. A soup spoon
    C. A thimble
    D. A match

19. Which of the following is NOT true about Despereaux and the thread?
    A. The spool of thread weighed almost as much as he did.
    B. Part of the thread had been tied to hold the needle at his waist.
    C. He had to push it a long way into the kitchen and through the dungeon.
    D. He moved the spool easily by rolling inside of it.

20. Why did Despereaux have to go in the kitchen?
    A. He had to go through the kitchen to get to the dungeon door.
    B. He wanted to ask Cook for a knife to fight the rats.
    C. He was hungry and needed food before he went to the dungeon.
    D. He needed to coat himself with flour to look like a ghost to the rats.

21. How did smelling the soup make Despereaux feel?
    A. He thought it was awful and felt weaker and sicker.
    B. He thought it was wonderful and felt stronger and braver.
    C. He thought it was great but felt it had a little too much garlic.
    D. He thought it was strong and felt that rats would smell it easily.

22. How did Cook react to Despereaux in her kitchen on his way to the dungeon and why?
    A. She tried to kill him with a kitchen knife because she hated all rodents.
    B. She tried to kill him with a kitchen knife because he saw her illegally making soup.
    C. She laughed because she thought he looked funny.
    D. She laughed because she would not be punished for illegally making soup.

23. What did Cook offer Despereaux before he went to the dungeon?
    A. She offered him a saucer of the soup she was making.
    B. She offered him a job in the kitchen as a soup taster.
    C. She offered to help him fight the rats in the dungeon to save Princess Pea.
    D. She offered him a fork as a better weapon than a needle.

24. How did Despereaux feel about Cook's soup?
    A. He felt that it had too much garlic.
    B. He felt that it did not have enough chicken.
    C. He felt that it was perfect without adding anything more.
    D. He felt it was so good that he asked for a second helping.

25. What story did Despereaux tell himself in the dungeon in order to be strong?
    A. He told himself the story of the knight he had read in the library.
    B. He told himself a story about himself saving Princess Pea.
    C. He told himself a story that his mother had told him as a baby mouse.
    D. He told himself a story about Mig helping him save Princess Pea.

26. What happened to the spool of red thread?
    A. It fell down the dungeon stairs ahead of Despereaux.
    B. It fell apart in the kitchen before Despereaux arrived at the dungeon.
    C. It had turned black from all of the dirt on the castle's floor.
    D. It had been forgotten in the kitchen after Despereaux had soup.

27. What did Despereaux tell himself at the steps of the dungeon?
    A. He told himself to go back and bring more mice with him.
    B. He told himself to go back and bring Cook with him.
    C. He told himself that he had a choice to go back home.
    D. He told himself that he had no choice but to go forward.

28. Why did Botticelli offer to bring Despereaux to the princess?
    A. He wanted to sincerely help Despereaux find the princess.
    B. He wanted to make Despereaux suffer before eating him.
    C. He wanted to see Despereaux rescue the princess and leave the dungeon safely.
    D. He wanted to get revenge on Roscuro for not inviting him to the castle banquet.

29. Why did Despereaux close his eyes as Botticelli led him deeper?
    A. The floor was covered with skeletons as they went deeper.
    B. The air around him hurt his eyes as they went deeper.
    C. It became too dark for Despereaux to see at all.
    D. He wanted to hear the sounds around him clearly.

30. How did Botticelli react to the other rats following him and Despereaux?
    A. He told them to wait until after he had brought him to the princess.
    B. He told them to help him find the princess.
    C. He told them to go away because Despereaux was his treasure.
    D. He told them that he would share Despereaux with them.

31. According to Roscuro, how did Mig look when wearing the crown?
    A. He said she looked beautiful and was just like Princess Pea.
    B. He said she looked ridiculous and would never look like a princess.
    C. He said she looked serious and needed to relax more.
    D. He said she looked embarrassed and should be more confident.

32. What question did Princess Pea ask Mig that she had never been asked before?
    A. She asked Mig what she wanted.
    B. She asked Mig who she loved.
    C. She asked Mig what was her full name.
    D. She asked Mig what they should do to escape.

33. According to the narrator, nothing is sweeter in this world than what?
    A. Someone you love singing you a song
    B. Someone you love coming to save you
    C. Someone you love fighting for you
    D. Someone you love calling your name

34. How did Mig intend to use the kitchen knife and what actually happened?
    A. She intended to cut off Roscuro's head but cut off his tail.
    B. She intended to cut off Roscuro's tail but cut off his head.
    C. She intended to cut off Roscuro's head but cut off Despereaux's tail.
    D. She intended to cut off Roscuro's tail but completely missed.

35. What happened that made Roscuro suddenly start to cry?
    A. He cried because he was going to be killed by a mouse.
    B. He cried because the pain from losing his tail was too harsh.
    C. He cried because he smelled the soup on Despereaux.
    D. He cried because he smelled the tears on Despereaux.

36. What did Princess Pea offer Roscuro and why?
    A. She offered to not kill him herself because the other rats would kill him.
    B. She offered him soup in the banquet hall because she wanted to save her own heart.
    C. She offered him Despereaux because she wanted to save herself.
    D. She offered him her crown because he wanted to have something beautiful.

37. How did Roscuro shed light into another life?
    A. He helped free all of the prisoners in the dungeon.
    B. He helped Despereaux marry Princess Pea.
    C. He reunited Mig with her father, who treated her like a princess from then on.
    D. He let Mig visit her father who remained a prisoner in the dungeon.

38. What happened to Princess Pea and Despereaux in the end of the story?

   A. They were married and lived happily ever after.

   B. Princess Pea became queen and Despereaux left the castle.

   C. Princess Pea kept Despereaux as pet mouse in a cage.

   D. They were friends and had many adventures together.

Check Your Reading Speed

1분에 몇 단어를 읽는지 | 리딩 속도를 측정해보세요.

$$\frac{428 \text{ words}}{\text{reading time (} \quad \text{) sec}} \times 60 = (\quad) \text{ WPM}$$

Build Your Vocabulary

ponder*
[pándər]

v. 숙고하다, 깊이 생각하다
If you ponder something, you think about it carefully.

reverse^{복습}
[rivə́:rs]

n. (정)반대, 역; a. 거꾸로 된, 정반대의; v. (정반대로) 뒤바꾸다, 반전[역전]시키다
If you say that one thing is the reverse of another, you are emphasizing that the first thing is the complete opposite of the second thing.

flour**
[flauər]

n. 밀가루; 분말, 가루
Flour is a white or brown powder that is made by grinding grain, which is used to make bread, cakes, and pastry.

atop^{복습}
[ətáp]

prep. ~의 꼭대기에, 정상에
If something is atop something else, it is on top of it.

pantry^{복습}
[pǽntri]

n. 식료품 저장실
A pantry is a small room or large cupboard in a house, usually near the kitchen, where food is kept.

hindquarters^{복습}
[háindkwɔ́:rtərz]

n. (짐승의 두 뒷다리를 포함하는) 후반신
The hindquarters of a four-legged animal are its back part, including its two back legs.

intense^{복습}
[inténs]

a. 강렬한, 격렬한, 심한
Intense is used to describe something that is very great or extreme in strength or degree.

dungeon^{복습}
[dʌ́ndʒən]

n. 지하 감옥; vt. 지하 감옥에 가두다
A dungeon is a dark underground prison in a castle.

recall^{복습}
[rikɔ́:l]

vt. 생각해내다, 상기하다; 소환하다; n. 회상, 상기
When you recall something, you remember it and tell others about it.

in time^{복습}

idiom 제시간에, 늦지 않게; 이윽고, 장차; 박자를 맞추어
In time means early enough or not late.

fate^{복습}
[feit]

n. 운명, 숙명
A person's or thing's fate is what happens to them.

gratitude**
[grǽtətjùːd]

n. 감사, 고마움
gratitude is the state of feeling grateful.

146

exhaust^{복습}
[igzɔ́:st]

vt. 기진맥진하게 만들다; 다 써 버리다, 고갈시키다 (exhaustion n. 탈진, 기진맥진)
If something exhausts you, it makes you so tired, either physically or mentally, that you have no energy left.

despair^{복습}
[dispέər]

n. 절망, 자포자기; vi. 절망하다
Despair is the feeling that everything is wrong and that nothing will improve.

beloved^{복습}
[bilʌ́vd]

a. 가장 사랑하는, 소중한
A beloved person, thing, or place is one that you feel great affection for.

sack[*]
[sæk]

n. 부대, 자루; (쇼핑 물건을 담는 크고 튼튼한 종이) 봉지; vt. 자루에 넣다
Sacks are used to carry or store things such as vegetables or coal.

stain^{복습}
[stein]

v. 착색[염색]하다; 더러워지다, 얼룩지게 하다; n. 얼룩, 오점
If a liquid stains something, the thing becomes colored or marked by the liquid.

brilliant^{복습}
[bríljənt]

a. 빛나는, 반짝이는; 훌륭한, 멋진
You describe light, or something that reflects light, as brilliant when it shines very brightly.

glorious[*]
[glɔ́:riəs]

a. 영광스러운, 찬란한, 훌륭한
Something that is glorious is very beautiful and impressive.

knight^{복습}
[nait]

n. (중세의) 기사
In medieval times, a knight was a man of noble birth, who served his king or lord in battle.

swing^{복습}
[swiŋ]

v. 휘두르다; (한 점을 축으로 하여) 빙 돌다, 휙 움직이다; n. 휘두르기, 스윙; 흔들기
If something swings in a particular direction or if you swing it in that direction, it moves in that direction with a smooth, curving movement.

phrase^{복습}
[freiz]

n. 구절; 관용구
A phrase is a short group of words that people often use as a way of saying something.

beat^{복습}
[bi:t]

v. 치다, 두드리다; 패배시키다, 이기다; n. [음악] 박자, 고동
If you beat a drum or similar instrument, you hit it in order to make a sound.

hood^{복습}
[hud]

n. 복면; 두건; 자동차 보닛, 덮개
A hood is a piece of clothing pulled down over a person's face in order to make others difficult to recognize it.

murmur^{복습}
[mə́:rmə:r]

v. 중얼거리다; 투덜거리다; n. 중얼거림
If you murmur something, you say it very quietly, so that not many people can hear what you are saying.

reveal^{복습}
[rivíːl]

vt. 드러내다, 폭로하다, 밝히다
If you reveal something that has been out of sight, you uncover it so that people can see it.

Check Your Reading Speed

1분에 몇 단어를 읽는지 | 리딩 속도를 측정해보세요.

$$\frac{803 \text{ words}}{\text{reading time ( ) sec}} \times 60 = (\quad) \text{ WPM}$$

Build Your Vocabulary

unfold ^{복습}
[ʌ̀nfóuld]

v. 펴다, 펼치다; 열리다
If a situation unfolds, it develops and becomes known or understood.

cruelty*
[krú:əlti]

n. 잔학함, 잔인한 행위
Cruelty is behavior that deliberately causes pain or distress to people or animals.

once and for all

idiom 최종적으로, 완전히
If something happens once and for all, it happens completely or finally.

chew ^{복습}
[tʃu:]

v. 씹다
If a person or animal chews an object, they bite it with their teeth.

jailer ^{복습}
[dʒéilər]

n. 교도관, 간수
A jailer is a person who is in charge of a jail and the prisoners in it.

maze ^{복습}
[meiz]

n. 미로, 미궁; vt. 당혹하게 하다
A maze is a complex system of passages or paths between walls or hedges and is designed to confuse people who try to find their way through it, often as a form of amusement.

serve ^{복습}
[sə:rv]

v. 제공하다, 시중 들다; 섬기다, 복무하다; n. 서브
When you serve food and drink, you give people food and drink.

apron**
[éiprən]

n. 앞치마, 에이프런
An apron is a piece of clothing that you put on over the front of your normal clothes and tie round your waist, especially when you are cooking.

ominous ^{복습}
[ámənəs]

a. 불길한, 나쁜 징조의
If you describe something as ominous, you mean that it worries you because it makes you think that something unpleasant is going to happen.

encounter ^{복습}
[inkáuntər]

v. 만나다, 마주치다; n. 마주침
If you encounter someone, you meet them, usually unexpectedly.

cloak ^{복습}
[klouk]

n. 소매 없는 외투, 망토; vt. 입고 있다, 가리다, 은폐하다
A cloak is a long, loose, sleeveless piece of clothing which people used to wear over their other clothes when they went out.

glorious ^{복습}
[glɔ́:riəs]

a. 영광스러운, 찬란한, 훌륭한
Something that is glorious is very beautiful and impressive.

148

covert
[kóuvərt]

a. 비밀의, 은밀한
Covert activities or situations are secret or hidden.

institute＊
[ínstətjùːt]

vt. (제도·습관을) 시작하다, 만들다, 설치하다; n. 협회, 학회; 연구소
If you institute a system, rule, or course of action, you start it.

immediately복습
[imíːdiətli]

ad. 곧, 바로, 즉시
If something happens immediately, it happens without any delay.

tap복습
[tæp]

① v. 가볍게 두드리다; n. 가볍게 두드리기 ② n. 주둥이, (수도 등의) 꼭지
If you tap something, you hit it with a quick light blow or a series of quick light blows.

comfort복습
[kʌ́mfərt]

vt. 위로[위안]하다; n. 위로, 위안 (comforting a. 위로가 되는)
If you comfort someone, you make them feel less worried, unhappy, or upset, for example by saying kind things to them.

snooze
[snuːz]

v. 꾸벅꾸벅 졸다
If you snooze, you sleep lightly for a short period of time.

snore＊
[snɔːr]

v. 코를 골다
When someone who is asleep snores, they make a loud noise each time they breathe.

divine＊＊
[diváin]

a. 신의, 신성한; 비범한, 아주 멋진
You use divine to describe something that is provided by or relates to a god or goddess.

comeuppance
[kʌmʌ́pəns]

n. 마땅한 벌
If you say that someone has got their comeuppance, you approve of the fact that they have been punished or have suffered for something wrong that they have done.

phrase복습
[freiz]

n. 구절; 관용구
A phrase is a short group of words that people often use as a way of saying something.

journey복습
[dʒə́ːrni]

n. 여정, 여행; vi. 여행하다
When you make a journey, you travel from one place to another.

understatement
[ʌ̀ndərstéitmənt]

n. 절제된 표현; 절제
If you say that a statement is an understatement, you mean that it does not fully express the extent to which something is true.

indeed복습
[indíːd]

ad. 실로, 참으로, 과연, 정말
You use indeed to confirm or agree with something that has just been said.

switch＊
[switʃ]

v. 전환하다, 바꾸다; n. 스위치
If you switch to something different, for example to a different system, task, or subject of conversation, you change to it from what you were doing or saying before.

ridiculous복습
[ridíkjuləs]

a. 터무니없는; 웃기는, 우스꽝스러운
If you say that something or someone is ridiculous, you mean that they are very foolish.

blind^{복습}
[blaind]

a. 눈먼. 장님인; vt. 눈멀게 하다; 가리다. 보이지 않게 하다
A blind minute is used for short periods of time when one is not paying careful attention, especially when something is switched for something else.

drawer^{복습}
[drɔ́:ər]

n. 서랍; 장롱 (not the sharpest knife in the drawer idiom 똑똑하지 못한)
If you say that someone is not the sharpest knife in the drawer, you mean they are not intelligent.

desperate^{복습}
[déspərət]

a. 필사적인; 절망적인. 자포자기의 (desperately ad. 필사적으로)
If you are desperate for something or desperate to do something, you want or need it very much indeed.

ounce[*]
[auns]

n. 온스(무게 단위. 1/16파운드. 28.35그램)
An ounce is a unit of weight used in Britain and the USA. There are sixteen ounces in a pound and one ounce is equal to 28.35 grams.

intend^{복습}
[inténd]

vt. ~할 작정이다. 의도하다
If you intend to do something, you have decided or planned to do it.

glitter^{복습}
[glítər]

vi. 반짝반짝 빛나다. 반짝이다; n. 반짝이는 빛
If something glitters, light comes from or is reflected off different parts of it.

glow^{복습}
[glou]

vi. 빛을 내다. 빛나다; n. 빛. 밝음
If something glows, it produces a dull, steady light.

150

$$\frac{1,055 \text{ words}}{\text{reading time ( ) sec}} \times 60 = (\qquad) \text{ WPM}$$

Build Your Vocabulary

sip ^{복습}
[sip]

vt. (음료를) 홀짝거리다, 조금씩 마시다; n. 한 모금
If you sip a drink or sip at it, you drink by taking just a small amount at a time.

command ^{복습}
[kəmǽnd]

v. 명령하다, 지휘하다, 지배하다; n. 명령, 지휘
If someone in authority commands you to do something, they tell you that you must do it.

annoy ^{**}
[ənɔ́i]

v. 성가시게 굴다, 괴롭히다; 불쾌하다 (annoyed a. 짜증이 난)
If someone or something annoys you, it makes you fairly angry and impatient.

note ^{복습}
[nout]

v. (중요하거나 흥미로운 것을) 언급하다; 주의하다, 주목하다; 적다; n. 메모
If you note something, you mention it in order to draw people's attention to it.

Highness ^{복습}
[háinis]

n. 전하(왕족에 대한 경칭)
Expressions such as 'Your Highness' or 'His Highness' are used to address or refer to a member of the royal family other than a king or queen.

crawl ^{복습}
[krɔ:l]

vi. 기어가다, 느릿느릿 가다; 우글거리다; 들끓다; n. 서행; 기어감
When you crawl, you move forward on your hands and knees.

situate
[sítʃuèit]

v. (어떤 위치에) 두다, 위치시키다
If something is situated in a particular place or position, it is in that place or position.

lay ^{복습}
[lei]

v. (laid-laid) 놓다, 눕히다; 알을 낳다
If you lay something somewhere, you put it there in a careful, gentle, or neat way.

balance ^{복습}
[bǽləns]

v. 균형을 유지하다[잡다]; n. 균형, 평형; 저울; 나머지, 잔여
If you balance something somewhere, or if it balances there, it remains steady and does not fall.

mouthful ^{복습}
[máuθfùl]

n. 한 입 가득, 한 입
A mouthful of drink or food is the amount that you put or have in your mouth.

hideous ^{복습}
[hídiəs]

a. 끔찍한, 오싹한, 흉측한
If you say that someone or something is hideous, you mean that they are very ugly or unattractive.

possess ^{복습}
[pəzés]

vt. 소유하다, 가지고 있다; 지배하다 (possession n. 소유)
If you possess something, you have it or own it.

threaten^{**}
[θretn]

v. 위협하다, 협박하다; 조짐을 보이다
If something or someone threatens a person or thing, they are likely to harm that person or thing.

royalty ^{복습}
[rɔ́iəlti]

n. 왕족, 왕위; 특허권 사용료
The members of royal families are sometimes referred to as royalty.

bleed[*]
[bli:d]

v. 피가 나다, 출혈하다
When you bleed, you lose blood from your body as a result of injury or illness.

assume ^{복습}
[əsjú:m]

vt. 추정하다, 가정하다; (역할·임무 등을) 맡다
If you assume that something is true, you imagine that it is true, sometimes wrongly.

glint[*]
[glint]

v. 반짝이다, 빛나다; n. 반짝임, 섬광
If something glints, it produces or reflects a quick flash of light.

persuasion[*]
[pərswéiʒən]

n. 설득, 납득; 설득력
Persuasion is the act of persuading someone to do something or to believe that something is true.

individual^{**}
[indəvídʒuəl]

n. 개인; a. 개개의; 개인의
An individual is a person.

address^{***}
[ədrés]

v. ~에게 말을 걸다; 연설하다; n. 연설; 주소
If you address someone or address a remark to them, you say something to them.

in charge

idiom ~을 맡고 있는, 담당의
If you have charge of or are in charge of something or someone, you have responsibility for them.

skip^{**}
[skip]

v. 뛰어다니다, 깡충깡충 뛰다; 건너뛰다, 생략하다
If you skip along, you move almost as if you are dancing, with a series of little jumps from one foot to the other.

concentrate ^{복습}
[kánsəntrèit]

v. 집중하다, 전념하다
If you concentrate on something, you give all your attention to it.

contain^{***}
[kəntéin]

vt. 억누르다, 참다; 포함하다, 담고 있다
If you cannot contain a feeling such as excitement or anger, or if you cannot contain yourself, you cannot prevent yourself from showing your feelings.

rage[*]
[reidʒ]

n. 격노, 분노; 열광; v. 격노하다
Rage is strong anger that is difficult to control.

leap ^{복습}
[li:p]

v. (심장이) 뛰다, 고동치다; 깡충 뛰다, 뛰어넘다; n. 뜀, 도약
If you leap, you jump high in the air or jump a long distance.

bear ^{복습}
[bɛər]

① v. 참다, 견디다; 가지고 가다 ② n. 곰
If you bear an unpleasant experience, you accept it because you are unable to do anything about it.

royal 복습
[rɔ́iəl]

a. 왕의, 왕위의; 위엄 있는
Royal is used to indicate that something is connected with a king, queen, or emperor, or their family.

sensibility *
[sènsəbíləti]

n. 감수성, 감성; 감각
Sensibility is the ability to experience deep feelings.

defiant *
[difáiənt]

a. 도전적인, 반항적인, 시비조의
If you say that someone is defiant, you mean they show aggression or independence by refusing to obey someone.

stare 복습
[stɛər]

v. 응시하다, 뚫어지게 보다
If you stare at someone or something, you look at them for a long time.

nonetheless *
[nʌnðəlés]

ad. 그럼에도 불구하고, 그래도, 역시
You use nonetheless when saying something that contrasts with what has just been said.

journey 복습
[dʒə́ːrni]

n. 여정, 여행; vi. 여행하다
When you make a journey, you travel from one place to another.

gown 복습
[gaun]

n. 특별한 경우에 입는 여성의) 드레스; (판사의) 법복; 가운
A gown is a dress, usually a long dress, which women wear on formal occasions.

banquet 복습
[bǽŋkwit]

n. 연회; v. 연회를 베풀어 대접하다
A banquet is a grand formal dinner.

ignorant **
[ígnərənt]

a. 무지한, 무식한
If someone is ignorant of a fact, they do not know it.

fate 복습
[feit]

n. 운명, 숙명
A person's or thing's fate is what happens to them.

sparkle **
[spɑːrkl]

v. 반짝이다; 생기 넘치다; n. 반짝거림, 광채
If something sparkles, it is clear and bright and shines with a lot of very small points of light.

outsmart
[àutsmáːrt]

vt. (구어) ~보다 한 수 앞서다, 꾀로 이기다
If you outsmart someone, you defeat them or gain an advantage over them in a clever and sometimes dishonest way.

ruin 복습
[ruːin]

v. 망치다, 못쓰게 만들다; 몰락하다; n. 폐허; 파멸
To ruin something means to severely harm, damage, or spoil it.

still 복습
[stil]

a. 정지한, 움직이지 않는; 조용한, 고요한; ad. 여전히, 아직도; 더욱, 한층
If you stay still, you stay in the same position and do not move.

lick **
[lik]

v. 핥다; n. 한 번 핥기, 핥아먹기
When people or animals lick something, they move their tongue across its surface.

salty *
[sɔ́ːlti]

a. 짠, 소금기 있는 (saltiness n. 소금기가 있음)
Something that is salty contains salt or tastes of salt.

1분에 몇 단어를 읽는지 리딩 속도를 측정해보세요.

$$\frac{535 \text{ words}}{\text{reading time (\quad) sec}} \times 60 = (\quad) \text{ WPM}$$

Build Your Vocabulary

threesome
[θríːsəm]

n. 3인조
A threesome is a group of three people.

apron복습
[éiprən]

n. 앞치마, 에이프런
An apron is a piece of clothing that you put on over the front of your normal clothes and tie round your waist, especially when you are cooking.

tip복습
[tip]

① n. (뾰족한) 끝 ② v. 뒤집어엎다, 기울이다 ③ n. 팁, 사례금
The tip of something long and narrow is the end of it.

feather
[féðər]

n. 깃털, 깃
A bird's feathers are the soft covering on its body.

cease복습
[siːs]

v. 그만두다, 중지하다
If you cease something, you stop it happening or working.

recipe**
[résəpi]

n. 조리법, 요리법
A recipe is a list of ingredients and a set of instructions that tell you how to cook something.

mumble
[mʌmbl]

v. 중얼거리다, 웅얼거리다; n. 중얼거림
If you mumble, you speak very quietly and not at all clearly with the result that the words are difficult to understand.

pantry복습
[pǽntri]

n. 식료품 저장실
A pantry is a small room or large cupboard in a house, usually near the kitchen, where food is kept.

atop복습
[ətáp]

prep. ~의 꼭대기에, 정상에
If something is atop something else, it is on top of it.

flour복습
[fláuər]

n. 밀가루; 분말, 가루
Flour is a white or brown powder that is made by grinding grain, which is used to make bread, cakes, and pastry.

armor복습
[áːrmər]

n. 갑옷, 철갑; vt. ~에게 갑옷을 입히다
In former times, armor was special metal clothing that soldiers wore for protection in battle.

shine복습
[ʃain]

v. (shone–shone) 빛나(게 하)다, 반짝이다; n. 빛, 빛남, 광채
Something that shines is very bright and clear because it is reflecting light.

154

sparkle^{복습}
[spa:rkl]

v. 반짝이다; 생기 넘치다; n. 반짝거림, 광채
If something sparkles, it is clear and bright and shines with a lot of very small points of light.

complicated**
[kámplikèitid]

a. 복잡한, 이해하기 어려운
If you say that something is complicated, you mean it has so many parts or aspects that it is difficult to understand or deal with.

shade^{복습}
[ʃeid]

vt. 그늘지게 하다; n. (시원한) 그늘; 색조, 음영
If you say that a place or person is shaded by objects such as trees, you mean that the place or person cannot be reached, harmed, or bothered by strong sunlight because those objects are in the way.

dapple
[dæpl]

v. 얼룩지게 하다; a. 얼룩진; n. 얼룩
If something dapples, it marks or become marked with spots or patches of a different color.

coal*
[koul]

n. 석탄
Coal is a hard black substance that is extracted from the ground and burned as fuel.

hatred**
[héitrid]

n. 증오, 미움, 원한
Hatred is an extremely strong feeling of dislike for someone or something.

tremendous^{복습}
[triméndəs]

a. 거대한, 대단한; 엄청난, 무서운
You use tremendous to emphasize how strong a feeling or quality is, or how large an amount is.

sorrow*
[sárou]

n. 슬픔, 비통; 후회
Sorrow is a feeling of deep sadness or regret.

empathetic
[èmpəθétik]

a. 감정이입의, 공감할 수 있는
Someone who is empathetic has the ability to share another person's feelings or emotions as if they were their own.

forcible
[fɔ́:rsəbl]

a. 물리력[힘]에 의한, 강제적인 (forcibly ad. 물리력을 동원하여, 강제로)
Forcible action involves physical force or violence.

dungeon^{복습}
[dʌ́ndʒən]

n. 지하 감옥; vt. 지하 감옥에 가두다
A dungeon is a dark underground prison in a castle.

desperate^{복습}
[déspərət]

a. 필사적인; 절망적인, 자포자기의 (desperately ad. 필사적으로)
A desperate situation is very difficult, serious, or dangerous.

empathy
[émpəθi]

n. 감정이입, 공감
Empathy is the ability to share another person's feelings and emotions as if they were your own.

Check Your Reading Speed

1분에 몇 단어를 읽는지 리딩 속도를 측정해보세요.

$$\frac{570 \text{ words}}{\text{reading time ( ) sec}} \times 60 = (\quad) \text{ WPM}$$

Build Your Vocabulary

shed^{복습}
[ʃed]

v. (shed–shed) (빛을) 비추다; 없애다; 흘리다; n. 보관소
To shed light on something means to make it easier to understand, because more information is known about it.

alas^{복습}
[əlǽs]

int. (걱정·슬픔을 나타내어) 아아, 슬프도다!, 불쌍한지고!
Alas is used to express sadness or regret.

good riddance

idiom (~이 없어져서/~을 안 보게 되어) 속이 시원하다
You say 'good riddance' to indicate that you are pleased that someone has left or that something has gone.

rubbish[*]
[rʌ́biʃ]

n. (질이) 형편없는 것, 쓰레기 (같은 것)
If you think that something is of very poor quality, you can say that it is rubbish.

bloody[*]
[blʌ́di]

a. 피투성이의; 피비린내 나는, 유혈의
If you have bloodied part of your body, there is blood on it, usually because you have had an accident or you have been attacked.

stub[*]
[stʌb]

n. (쓰다 남은 물건의) 토막, (수표책 등의) 떼어 주고 남은 쪽
The stub of a cigarette or a pencil is the last short piece of it which remains when the rest has been used.

foul^{복습}
[faul]

a. 악취가 나는, (성격·맛 등이) 더러운 (foul play n. 살인, 폭행; 부정 행위)
Foul play is criminal violence or activity that results in a person's death.

frighten^{복습}
[fraitn]

v. 놀라게 하다, 섬뜩하게 하다; 기겁하다 (frightened a. 겁먹은, 무서워하는)
If something or someone frightens you, they cause you to suddenly feel afraid, anxious, or nervous.

get to one's feet^{복습}

idiom 벌떡 일어서다
If you get or rise to your feet, you stand up.

stick^{복습}
[stik]

① v. (stuck–stuck) 내밀다; 찔러 넣다; 붙이다, 달라붙다; 고수하다
② n. 막대기, 지팡이
If something is sticking out from a surface or object, it extends up or away from it.

pantry^{복습}
[pǽntri]

n. 식료품 저장실
A pantry is a small room or large cupboard in a house, usually near the kitchen, where food is kept.

wring[*]
[riŋ]

v. (손을) 꽉 쥐다; 짜다, 비틀다; 몸부림치다
If someone wrings their hands, they hold them together and twist and turn them, usually because they are very worried or upset about something.

jangle
[dʒæŋgl]

v. 딸랑딸랑 울리다; 귀에 거슬리는 소리를 내다; 시끄럽게 다투다
When objects strike against each other and make an unpleasant ringing noise, you can say that they jangle or are jangled.

despair[복습]
[dispέər]

n. 절망, 자포자기; vi. 절망하다
Despair is the feeling that everything is wrong and that nothing will improve.

comfort[복습]
[kΛmfərt]

n. 위로, 위안; vt. 위로[위안]하다
If you are doing something in comfort, you are physically relaxed and contented, and are not feeling any pain or other unpleasant sensations.

beg[복습]
[beg]

vt. 부탁[간청]하다; 빌다, 구걸하다
If you beg someone to do something, you ask them very anxiously or eagerly to do it.

in earnest

idiom 본격적으로; 진심으로
If you are in earnest, you are sincere in what you are doing and saying.

wail[복습]
[weil]

v. 울부짖다, 통곡하다; n. 울부짖음, 통곡
If someone wails, they make long, loud, high-pitched cries which express sorrow or pain.

sob[*]
[sab]

v. 흐느껴 울다; n. 흐느낌, 오열
When someone sobs, they cry in a noisy way, breathing in short breaths.

slap[**]
[slæp]

v. 찰싹 때리다, 탁 놓다; 철썩 부딪치다; n. 찰싹 (때림)
If you slap someone, you hit them with the palm of your hand.

hem[*]
[hem]

n. (천·옷의) 옷단, 가장자리; vt. 옷단을 대다; 둘러싸다
A hem on something such as a piece of clothing is an edge that is folded over and stitched down to prevent threads coming loose.

apron[복습]
[éiprən]

n. 앞치마, 에이프런
An apron is a piece of clothing that you put on over the front of your normal clothes and tie round your waist, especially when you are cooking.

wipe[복습]
[waip]

vt. 닦다, 닦아 내다; n. 닦기
If you wipe something, you rub its surface to remove dirt or liquid from it.

ferocious[복습]
[fəróuʃəs]

a. 잔인한, 지독한, 사나운
A ferocious animal, person, or action is very fierce and violent.

allow[복습]
[əláu]

v. 허락하다, ~하게 두다; 인정하다
If you allow something to happen, you do not prevent it.

somewhat[*]
[sʌ́mwʌt]

ad. 어느 정도, 약간, 다소
You use somewhat to indicate that something is the case to a limited extent or degree.

dip[*]
[dip]

v. 담그다, 적시다; 가라앉다, 내려가다
If you dip something in a liquid, you put it into the liquid for a short time, so that only part of it is covered, and take it out again.

relieve[복습]
[rilíːv]

vt. (걱정·고통 등을) 덜다, 안도하게 하다, 완화하다 (relieved a. 안도하는)
If something relieves an unpleasant feeling or situation, it makes it less unpleasant or causes it to disappear completely.

slip[*]
[slip]

v. (특히 들키지 않고) 살짝[슬며시] 가다[오다]
If you slip something somewhere, you put it there quickly in a way that does not attract attention.

weep[복습]
[wiːp]

v. 눈물을 흘리다, 울다; 물기를 내뿜다
If someone weeps, they cry.

158

Check Your Reading Speed

1분에 몇 단어를 읽는지 리딩 속도를 측정해보세요.

$$\frac{736 \text{ words}}{\text{reading time ( ) sec}} \times 60 = (\qquad) \text{ WPM}$$

Build Your Vocabulary

throne^{복습}
[θroun]

n. 왕좌, 왕위; vi. 왕위에 앉다, 왕권을 쥐다
You can talk about the throne as a way of referring to the position of being king, queen, or emperor.

slip^{복습}
[slip]

v. (특히 들키지 않고) 살짝[슬며시] 가다[오다]
If you slip something somewhere, you put it there quickly in a way that does not attract attention.

molding^{복습}
[móuldiŋ]

n. 쇠시리(벽·문 등의 윗부분에 돌·목재 등을 띠처럼 댄 장식)
A molding is a strip of plaster or wood along the top of a wall or round a door.

come upon^{복습}

idiom ~을 우연히 만나다[발견하다]
If you come upon something, you meet or encounter it unexpectedly.

council^{복습}
[káunsəl]

n. 의회, 위원회; 회의
A council is a group of people who are elected to govern a local area such as a city or, a county.

honor^{복습}
[ánər]

vt. 존경하다, 공경하다; n. 명예, 영예 (honored a. 명예로운)
To honor someone means to treat them or regard them with special attention and respect.

debate**
[dibéit]

v. 토론하다, 논쟁하다; n. 논쟁, 토론
If people debate a topic, they discuss it fairly formally, putting forward different views. You can also say that one person debates a topic with another person.

matter^{복습}
[mǽtər]

n. 문제, 일; 물질; vi. 중요하다
A matter is a task, situation, or event which you have to deal with or think about, especially one that involves problems.

still^{복습}
[stil]

a. 정지한, 움직이지 않는; 조용한, 고요한; ad. 여전히, 아직도; 더욱, 한층
If you stay still, you stay in the same position and do not move.

fellow^{복습}
[félou]

n. 친구, 동료; 녀석, 사나이
You use fellow to describe people who are in the same situation as you, or people you feel you have something in common with.

makeshift*
[méikʃift]

a. 임시변통의, 일시적인; n. 임시 수단, 미봉책
Makeshift things are temporary and usually of poor quality, but they are used because there is nothing better available.

whisper^{복습}
[hwíspəːr]

v. 속삭이다; n. 속삭임; 속삭이는 소리
When you whisper, you say something very quietly.

Chapter Forty

159

lean ^{복습}
[li:n]

① v. 상체를 굽히다; 기울다; 기대다, 의지하다 ② a. 야윈, 마른
When you lean in a particular direction, you bend your body in that direction.

strain[*]
[strein]

vi. (~얻으려고) 힘껏 노력하다, 애쓰다
If you strain to do something, you make a great effort to do it when it is difficult to do.

make sense ^{복습}

idiom 뜻이 통하다, 도리에 맞다
If something makes sense, it has a meaning that you can easily understand.

utter ^{복습}
[ʌ́tər]

① v. 발언하다, 말하다 ② a. 완전한, 전적인, 절대적인
If someone utters sounds or words, they say them.

pardon ^{복습}
[pa:rdn]

int. 뭐라구요(상대방의 말을 되물을 때 하는 말); n. 용서, 관용; vt. 용서하다
You say 'Pardon?' or 'I beg your pardon?' when you want someone to repeat what they have just said because you have not heard or understood it.

paw ^{복습}
[pɔ:]

n. (갈고리 발톱이 있는 동물의) 발; v. 앞발로 차다
The paws of an animal such as a cat, dog, or bear are its feet, which have claws for gripping things and soft pads for walking on.

telltale
[téltèil]

a. 비밀을 폭로하는; 고자질하는; n. 비밀을 폭로하는 것, 증거; 고자질쟁이
Something that is described as telltale gives away information, often about something bad that would otherwise not be noticed.

thread ^{복습}
[θred]

n. 실, 바느질 실; vt. 실을 꿰다
A thread is a long very thin piece of a material such as cotton, nylon, or silk, especially one that is used in sewing.

trail^{**}
[treil]

n. 지나간 자국, 흔적; v. ~을 뒤쫓다; (보통 땅에 대고 뒤로) 끌다, 끌리다
A trail is a series of marks or other signs of movement or other activities left by someone or something.

fur ^{복습}
[fə:r]

n. 부드러운 털; 모피
Fur is the thick and usually soft hair that grows on the bodies of many mammals.

absence^{**}
[ǽbsəns]

n. 부재, (사람이) 없음; 결석; 결여, 부족
Someone's absence from a place is the fact that they are not there.

whisker ^{복습}
[wískər]

n. (고양이 · 쥐 등의) 수염; 구레나룻
The whiskers of an animal such as a cat or a mouse are the long stiff hairs that grow near its mouth.

tremble ^{복습}
[trembl]

v. 떨(리)다, 진동하다, 흔들리다
If you tremble, you shake slightly because you are frightened or cold.

beat ^{복습}
[bi:t]

v. 치다, 두드리다; 패배시키다, 이기다; n. [음악] 박자, 고동
If you beat a drum or similar instrument, you hit it in order to make a sound.

clasp^{**}
[klæsp]

v. (꽉) 움켜쥐다, 고정시키다, 죄다; n. 걸쇠, 버클; 악수, 포옹
If you clasp someone or something, you hold them tightly in your hands or arms.

community^{복습}
[kəmjúːnəti]

n. 공동[지역] 사회, 공동체; 일반 사회, 대중
The community is all the people who live in a particular area or place.

streak**
[striːk]

v. 기다란 자국을 내다, 줄무늬를 넣다; n. 줄무늬 (streaked a. 줄무늬가 들어간)
If something streaks a surface, it makes long stripes or marks on the surface.

ridiculous^{복습}
[ridíkjuləs]

a. 터무니없는, 웃기는, 우스꽝스러운
If you say that something or someone is ridiculous, you mean that they are very foolish.

perfidy^{복습}
[pə́ːrfədi]

n. (문어) 배신, 배신 행위
Perfidy is the action of betraying someone or behaving very badly toward someone.

renounce^{복습}
[rináuns]

v. (신조·행위 등을 공식적으로) 버리다[그만두다]; (직함·직책 등을) 포기[단념]하다
If you renounce a belief or a way of behaving, you decide and declare publicly that you no longer have that belief or will no longer behave in that way.

sin^{복습}
[sin]

n. 죄, 죄악; v. 죄를 짓다, 나쁜 짓을 하다
A sin is any action or behavior that people disapprove of or consider morally wrong.

repent^{복습}
[ripént]

v. 후회하다, 뉘우치다, 유감으로 생각하다
If you repent, you show or say that you are sorry for something wrong you have done.

face^{복습}
[feis]

v. ~을 마주보다, 향하다; 직면하다; 직시하다
If someone or something faces a particular thing, person, or direction, they are positioned opposite them or are looking in that direction.

slap^{복습}
[slæp]

v. 찰싹 때리다, 탁 놓다; 철썩 부딪치다; n. 찰싹 (때림)
If you slap someone, you hit them with the palm of your hand.

vote^{복습}
[vout]

n. 투표, 투표권; v. 투표하다
A vote is a choice made by a particular person or group in a meeting or an election.

occur^{복습}
[əkə́ːr]

vi. 일어나다, 생기다; 생각이 떠오르다
When something occurs, it happens.

emphatic*
[imfǽtik]

a. 강한, 강조하는, 단호한
An emphatic response or statement is one made in a forceful way, because the speaker feels very strongly about what they are saying.

chorus^{복습}
[kɔ́ːrəs]

n. 일제히 내는 소리; 후렴; 합창, 코러스; vi. 이구동성으로 말하다; 합창하다
When there is a chorus of criticism, disapproval, or praise, that attitude is expressed by a lot of people at the same time.

1分에 몇 단어를 읽는지 리딩 속도를 측정해보세요.

Check Your Reading Speed

1분에 몇 단어를 읽는지 리딩 속도를 측정해보세요.

$$\frac{975 \text{ words}}{\text{reading time ( ) sec}} \times 60 = (\quad) \text{ WPM}$$

Build Your Vocabulary

clutch^{복습}
[klʌtʃ]

v. 부여잡다, 꽉 잡다, 붙들다; n. 붙잡음, 움켜쥠
If you clutch at something or clutch something, you hold it tightly, usually because you are afraid or anxious.

tapestry^{복습}
[tǽpistri]

n. 태피스트리(색색의 실로 수놓은 벽걸이나 실내장식용 비단)
A tapestry is a large piece of heavy cloth with a picture sewn on it using colored threads.

weep^{복습}
[wiːp]

v. 눈물을 흘리다, 울다; 물기를 내뿜다
If someone weeps, they cry.

undertake**
[ʌndərtéik]

v. 시작하다, 착수하다; (일 등을) 맡다, 떠맡다
When you undertake a task or job, you start doing it and accept responsibility for it.

cascade
[kæskéid]

v. 폭포처럼 흐르다; n. 작은 폭포, 폭포처럼 쏟아지는 물
If water cascades somewhere, it pours or flows downward very fast and in large quantities.

puddle
[pʌdl]

n. 웅덩이; 뒤범벅; v. 흙탕물을 휘젓다
A puddle is a small, shallow pool of liquid that has spread on the ground.

exaggerate*
[igzǽdʒəreit]

vt. 과장하다
If you exaggerate, you indicate that something is, for example, worse or more important than it really is.

intent^{복습}
[intént]

① a. 몰두하는, 여념이 없는 ② n. 의지, 의향
If you are intent on doing something, you are eager and determined to do it.

reveal^{복습}
[rivíːl]

vt. 드러내다, 폭로하다, 밝히다
If you reveal something that has been out of sight, you uncover it so that people can see it.

diminish*
[dimíniʃ]

v. (명예·중요성을) 깎아내리다; 줄다, 감소시키다 (diminishment n. 줄임)
If you diminish someone or something, you talk about them or treat them in a way that makes them appear less important than they really are.

terrify*
[térəfài]

vt. 겁나게 하다, 위협하다
If something terrifies you, it makes you feel extremely frightened.

absolute^{복습}
[ǽbsəlùːt]

a. 절대적인, 무조건의; 완전한 (absolutely ad. 절대적으로, 무조건)
Absolute means total and complete.

162

lap*
[læp]

n. 무릎; (경주에서 트랙의) 한 바퀴
If you have something on your lap, it is on top of your legs and near to your body.

mention^{복습}
[ménʃən]

vt. 말하다, 언급하다; n. 언급, 진술
If you mention something, you say something about it, usually briefly.

near-sighted^{복습}
[níər-sàitid]

a. 근시의; 근시안적인, 선견지명이 없는
Someone who is near-sighted cannot see distant things clearly.

unreasonable*
[ʌnríːzənəbl]

a. 불합리한, 부당한, 지나친
If you say that someone is being unreasonable, you mean that they are behaving in a way that is not fair or sensible.

enforce*
[infɔ́ːrs]

vt. 실시하다, 강제하다
If people in authority enforce a law or a rule, they make sure that it is obeyed, usually by punishing people who do not obey it.

drawer^{복습}
[drɔ́ːər]

n. 서랍; 장롱 (not the sharpest knife in the drawer idiom 똑똑하지 못한)
If you say that someone is not the sharpest knife in the drawer, you mean they are not intelligent.

extraordinary^{복습}
[ikstrɔ́ːrdənèri]

a. 놀라운, 비상한
If you describe something as extraordinary, you mean that it is very unusual or surprising.

admirable*
[ǽdmərəbəl]

a. 감탄[칭찬]할 만한, 훌륭한
An admirable quality or action is one that deserves to be praised and admired.

particle*
[páːrtikl]

n. 극소량, 티끌, 입자
A particle of something is a very small piece or amount of it.

address^{복습}
[ədrés]

v. ~에게 말을 걸다; 연설하다; n. 연설; 주소
If you address someone or address a remark to them, you say something to them.

throat^{복습}
[θrout]

n. 목구멍, 목 (clear one's throat idiom 목을 가다듬다, 헛기침하다)
Your throat is the back of your mouth and the top part of the tubes that go down into your stomach and your lungs.

squint^{복습}
[skwint]

v. 눈을 가늘게 뜨고[찡그리고] 보다; n. 사시, 사팔뜨기
If you squint at something, you look at it with your eyes partly closed.

bellow^{복습}
[bélou]

v. (우렁찬 소리로) 고함치다, 큰 소리로 울다; n. 울부짖기, 포효
If someone bellows, they shout angrily in a loud, deep voice.

sniff^{복습}
[snif]

v. 코를 훌쩍이다; 냄새를 맡다, 코를 킁킁거리다; n. 냄새 맡음
When you sniff, you breathe in air through your nose hard enough to make a sound.

royal^{복습}
[rɔ́iəl]

a. 왕의, 왕위의; 위엄 있는
Royal is used to indicate that something is connected with a king, queen, or emperor, or their family.

cloak ^{복습}
[klouk]

n. 소매 없는 외투, 망토; vt. 가리다, 은폐하다
A cloak is a long, loose, sleeveless piece of clothing which people used to wear over their other clothes when they went out.

bend ^{복습}
[bend]

v. (bent–bent) 구부리다, 돌리다; 구부러지다, 휘다; n. 커브, 굽음
When you bend a part of your body such as your arm or leg, or when it bends, you change its position so that it is no longer straight.

enormous ^{복습}
[inɔ́:rməs]

a. 엄청난, 거대한, 막대한
You can use enormous to emphasize the great degree or extent of something.

audible *
[ɔ́:dəbl]

a. 들리는, 들을 수 있는
A sound that is audible is loud enough to be heard.

plop ^{복습}
[plap]

n. 퐁당 (하는 소리); v. 털썩 주저앉다; 퐁당[툭] 하고 떨어지다
A plop is a soft, gentle sound, like the sound made by something dropping into water without disturbing the surface much.

fur ^{복습}
[fə:r]

n. 부드러운 털; 모피
Fur is the thick and usually soft hair that grows on the bodies of many mammals.

dungeon ^{복습}
[dʌ́ndʒən]

n. 지하 감옥; vt. 지하 감옥에 가두다
A dungeon is a dark underground prison in a castle.

rodent ^{복습}
[roudnt]

n. 설치류 동물(쥐·토끼 등)
Rodents are small mammals which have sharp front teeth. Rats, mice, and squirrels are rodents.

clap ^{복습}
[klæp]

v. 박수를 치다; n. 박수 (소리); 쿵[탁] 하는 소리
When you clap, you hit your hands together to show appreciation or attract attention.

illegal ^{복습}
[ilí:gəl]

a. 불법의, 비합법적인
If something is illegal, the law says that it is not allowed.

exist ^{복습}
[igzíst]

v. 존재하다, 실재하다
If something exists, it is present in the world as a real thing.

hum *
[hʌm]

v. 콧노래를 부르다; (벌·기계 등이) 윙윙거리다; n. 윙윙(소리)
When you hum a tune, you sing it with your lips closed.

fortuneteller
[fɔ́:rʧəntèlər]

n. 점쟁이
A fortuneteller is a person who tells you what they think will happen to you in the future, after looking at something such as the lines on your hand.

distant ^{복습}
[dístənt]

a. 먼, (멀리) 떨어져 있는
Distant means very far away.

stare ^{복습}
[stɛər]

v. 응시하다, 뚫어지게 보다
If you stare at someone or something, you look at them for a long time.

dismay ^{복습}
[disméi]

n. 실망, 낙담; 경악, 당황; vt. 낙담[실망]하게 하다
Dismay is a strong feeling of fear, worry, or sadness that is caused by something unpleasant and unexpected.

flood ^{복습}
[flʌd]

v. 가득 차(게 하)다, 쇄도하다, 물밀듯이 밀려들다; 넘치다, 범람하다; n. 홍수; 다수
If feelings or memories flood back, you suddenly remember them very clearly.

knight ^{복습}
[nait]

n. (중세의) 기사
In medieval times, a knight was a man of noble birth, who served his king or lord in battle.

swing ^{복습}
[swiŋ]

v. 휘두르다; (한 점을 축으로 하여) 빙 돌다, 휙 움직이다; n. 휘두르기, 스윙; 흔들기
If something swings in a particular direction or if you swing it in that direction, it moves in that direction with a smooth, curving movement.

armor ^{복습}
[áːrmər]

n. 갑옷, 철갑; vt. ~에게 갑옷을 입히다
In former times, armor was special metal clothing that soldiers wore for protection in battle.

wonder ^{복습}
[wʌ́ndəːr]

n. 경탄할 만한 것, 경이; v. 호기심을 가지다, 이상하게 여기다
If you say that it is a wonder that something happened, you mean that it is very surprising and unexpected.

master ^{복습}
[mǽstər]

n. 대가, 명인, 정통한 사람; vt. 숙달하다, 터득하다
If you say that someone is a master of a particular activity, you mean that they are extremely skilled at it.

Check Your Reading Speed

1분에 몇 단어를 읽는지 리딩 속도를 측정해보세요.

$$\frac{788 \text{ words}}{\text{reading time ( ) sec}} \times 60 = (\quad) \text{ WPM}$$

Build Your Vocabulary

atop^{복습}
[ətáp]

prep. ~의 꼭대기에, 정상에
If something is atop something else, it is on top of it.

spool^{복습}
[spu:l]

n. (실·전선·필름 등을 감는) 릴, 얼레
A spool is a round object onto which thread, tape, or film can be wound, especially before it is put into a machine.

celery^{복습}
[séləri]

n. [식물] 셀러리
Celery is a vegetable with long pale green stalks. It is eaten raw in salads.

sacred^{복습}
[séikrid]

a. 성스러운, 신성한; 종교적인
You can describe something as sacred when it is regarded as too important to be changed or interfered with.

shrug^{복습}
[ʃrʌg]

v. (어깨를) 으쓱하다; n. (양 손바닥을 내보이면서 어깨를) 으쓱하기
If you shrug, you raise your shoulders to show that you are not interested in something or that you do not know or care about something.

pretend^{복습}
[priténd]

v. 가장하다, ~인 체하다; a. 가짜의
If you pretend that something is the case, you act in a way that is intended to make people believe that it is the case, although in fact it is not.

intend^{복습}
[inténd]

vt. ~할 작정이다, 의도하다
If you intend to do something, you have decided or planned to do it.

disagreeable^{복습}
[dìsəgríːəbl]

a. 유쾌하지 못한; 무례한, 무뚝뚝한
Something that is disagreeable is rather unpleasant.

twist^{복습}
[twist]

n. 뒤틀림; 엉킴; 변화; v. 비틀다, 돌리다, 꼬다
A twist in something is an unexpected and significant development.

chamber[*]
[ʧéimbər]

n. (특수한 목적을 위해 설계된) 칸막이 공간; 방, 침실
A chamber is a room designed and equipped for a particular purpose.

maze^{복습}
[meiz]

n. 미로, 미궁; vt. 당혹하게 하다
A maze is a complex system of passages or paths between walls or hedges and is designed to confuse people who try to find their way through it, often as a form of amusement.

jailer^{복습}
[dʒéilər]

n. 교도관, 간수
A jailer is a person who is in charge of a jail and the prisoners in it.

ankle^{복습}
[æŋkl]

n. 발목
Your ankle is the joint where your foot joins your leg.

get lost

phrasal v. 길을 잃다, 헤매다; (명령문) 썩 나가
If you get lost, you do not know where you are or are unable to find your way.

shudder^{복습}
[ʃʌ́dəːr]

vi. 떨다, 몸서리치다; **n.** 떨림, 전율
If you shudder, you shake with fear, horror, or disgust, or because you are cold.

meditative
[méditèitiv]

a. 깊은 생각에 잠긴; 명상적인
Meditative describes things that are related to the act of meditating or the act of thinking very deeply about something.

quest[*]
[kwest]

n. (특히 중세 기사의) 탐구 여행; 탐구, 추구
A quest is a long and difficult search for something.

compel[*]
[kəmpél]

v. ~하지 않을 수 없다; 강요하다, 억지로 ~시키다
If you feel compelled to do something, you feel that you must do it, because it is the right thing to do.

at hand^{복습}

idiom (시간·거리상으로) 가까이에 (있는)
If something is at hand, it is near in distance or time.

chew^{복습}
[ʧuː]

v. 씹다
If a person or animal chews an object, they bite it with their teeth.

leap^{복습}

v. (leapt/leaped–leapt/leaped) 껑충 뛰다, 뛰어넘다; (심장이) 뛰다, 고동치다; **n.** 뜀, 도약
If you leap, you jump high in the air or jump a long distance.

experimental[*]
[ikspèrəméntl]
[liːp]

a. (아이디어·방법 등이) 실험적인
Something that is experimental is new or uses new ideas or methods, and might be modified later if it is unsuccessful.

gnaw^{복습}
[nɔː]

v. 갉아먹다, 물어뜯다; 괴롭히다
If people or animals gnaw something or gnaw at it, they bite it repeatedly.

length^{복습}
[leŋθ]

n. 길이; (무엇이 계속되는) 시간[기간]
The length of something is the amount that it measures from one end to the other along the longest side.

hind^{복습}
[haind]

a. 뒤쪽의, 후방의
An animal's hind legs are at the back of its body.

scent[*]
[sent]

n. 냄새, 향기; **v.** 냄새로 찾아내다, 냄새 맡다; 향기가 나다
The scent of something is the pleasant smell that it has.

wonder^{복습}
[wʌ́ndəːr]

n. 경탄할 만한 것, 경이; **v.** 호기심을 가지다, 이상하게 여기다
If you say that it is a wonder that something happened, you mean that it is very surprising and unexpected.

1분에 몇 단어를 읽는지 리딩 속도를 측정해보세요.

$$\frac{587 \text{ words}}{\text{reading time ( ) sec}} \times 60 = (\quad) \text{ WPM}$$

Build Your Vocabulary

thread^{복습}
[θred]

n. 실, 바느질 실; vt. 실을 꿰다
A thread is a long very thin piece of a material such as cotton, nylon, or silk, especially one that is used in sewing.

lair
[lɛər]

n. 소굴, 은신처; 굴, 집
Someone's lair is the particular room or hiding place that they go to, especially when they want to get away from other people.

innumerable^{복습}
[injú:mərəbl]

a. 셀 수 없는, 무수한
Innumerable means very many, or too many to be counted.

hallway
[hɔ́:lwèi]

n. 복도; 현관
A hallway in a building is a long passage with doors into rooms on both sides of it.

flight^{**}
[flait]

n. (층과 층·층계참 사이의) 계단; (비행기) 여행, 비행
A flight of steps or stairs is a set of steps or stairs that lead from one level to another without changing direction.

allow^{복습}
[əláu]

v. 허락하다, ~하게 두다; 인정하다
If you allow something to happen, you do not prevent it.

perspective[*]
[pərspéktiv]

n. 관점, 시각 (in perspective idiom 올바른 균형으로)
If you put something in perspective, you are able to see or understand its relative importance to everything else.

average^{**}
[ǽvəridʒ]

n. 평균; 표준, 보통 수준
An average person or thing is typical or normal.

weigh^{**}
[wei]

v. 무게[체중]가 ~이다
If someone or something weighs a particular amount, this amount is how heavy they are.

ounce^{복습}
[auns]

n. 온스(무게 단위, 1/16파운드, 28.35그램)
An ounce is a unit of weight used in Britain and the USA. There are sixteen ounces in a pound and one ounce is equal to 28.35 grams.

incredible^{복습}
[inkrédəbl]

a. 놀라운, 믿어지지 않는 (incredibly ad. 믿을 수 없을 정도로, 엄청나게)
If you describe something or someone as incredible, you like them very much or are impressed by them, because they are extremely or unusually good.

quest^{복습}
[kwest]

n. (특히 중세 기사의) 탐구 여행; 탐구, 추구
A quest is a long and difficult search for something.

zip
[zip]

n. 영(零), 무(無); 지퍼; v. 지퍼를 잠그다
Zip sometimes used the same as zero.

nada
[ná:də]

n. 아무것도 없는 것, 무(無)
Nada means nothing.

calculate^{**}
[kǽlkjuleit]

v. 계산하다, 산출하다
If you calculate a number or amount, you discover it from information that you already have, by using arithmetic, mathematics, or a special machine.

odds[*]
[adz]

n. 가능성, 확률; 우세, 승산
You refer to how likely something is to happen as the odds that it will happen.

ridiculous^{복습}
[ridíkjuləs]

a. 터무니없는; 웃기는, 우스꽝스러운
If you say that something or someone is ridiculous, you mean that they are very foolish.

paw^{복습}
[pɔ:]

n. (갈고리 발톱이 있는 동물의) 발; v. 앞발로 차다
The paws of an animal such as a cat, dog, or bear are its feet, which have claws for gripping things and soft pads for walking on.

throb[*]
[θrab]

vi. 욱신거리다; (심장이) 고동치다, 맥이 뛰다; n. 고동, 맥박
If part of your body throbs, you feel a series of strong and usually painful beats there.

somehow^{복습}
[sʌ́mhàu]

ad. 어떻게든지 하여, 어쨌든; 어쩐지, 아무래도
You use somehow to say that you do not know or cannot say how something was done or will be done.

consider^{복습}
[kənsídər]

v. 고려하다, 숙고하다
If you consider something, you think about it carefully.

nasty^{복습}
[nǽsti]

a. 추잡한, 더러운; 못된, 고약한
Something that is nasty is very unpleasant to see, experience, or feel.

despair^{복습}
[dispɛ́ər]

n. 절망, 자포자기; vi. 절망하다
Despair is the feeling that everything is wrong and that nothing will improve.

lean^{복습}
[li:n]

① v. 상체를 굽히다; 기울다; 기대다, 의지하다 ② a. 야윈, 마른
When you lean in a particular direction, you bend your body in that direction.

celery^{복습}
[séləri]

n. [식물] 셀러리
Celery is a vegetable with long pale green stalks. It is eaten raw in salads.

square^{복습}
[skwɛər]

v. (몸을) 똑바로 펴다; 네모지게 하다; n. 정사각형; 광장
If you square up, you pull your shoulders up and back because you feel determined to do something.

stir[*]
[stə:r]

v. 휘젓다, 뒤섞다; 움직이다; n. 휘젓기; 움직임
If you stir a liquid or other substance, you move it around or mix it in a container using something such as a spoon.

beatific
[biːətífik]

a. 기쁨이 넘치는, 더없이 행복해 하는
A beatific expression shows or expresses great happiness and calmness.

halo
[héilou]

n. (그림 등에서 성상의 머리나 몸 주위에 둥글게 그려지는) 후광
A halo is a circle of light that is shown in pictures round the head of a holy figure such as a saint or angel.

instruct^{복습}
[instrʌ́kt]

vt. 지시[명령]하다; 가르치다 (instruction n. 설명, 지시)
If you instruct someone to do something, you formally tell them to do it.

regard**
[rigáːrd]

v. 보다, 대하다; ~으로 여기다; n. 관계, 고려; 존경
If you regard someone in a certain way, you look at them in that way.

dawn*
[dɔːn]

vi. (날이) 새다, 밝아오다; n. 새벽, 동틀 녘
When you say that a particular day dawned, you mean it arrived or began, usually when it became light.

a great deal of^{복습}

idiom 다량의, 많은
If you say that you need or have a great deal of or a good deal of a particular thing, you are emphasizing that you need or have a lot of it.

sneak*
[sniːk]

v. 살금살금 돌아다니다; 슬쩍 넣다[집다]; 고자질하다; n. 밀고자
If you sneak somewhere, you go there very quietly on foot, trying to avoid being seen or heard.

screw**
[skruː]

v. 쥐어짜다; 나사로 죄다, 비틀다; n. 나사
If someone screws something, especially money, out of you, they get it from you by putting pressure on you.

stick^{복습}
[stik]

① v. 붙이다, 달라붙다; 내밀다; 찔러 넣다; 고수하다 (sticking a. 끈적거리는)
② n. 막대기, 지팡이
If you stick one thing to another, you attach it using glue, sticky tape, or another sticky substance.

drip**
[drip]

v. 방울방울[똑똑] 떨어지다; 가득[넘칠 듯이] 지니고 있다
When something drips, drops of liquid fall from it.

frighten^{복습}
[fraitn]

v. 놀라게 하다, 섬뜩하게 하다; 기겁하다 (frightened a. 겁먹은, 무서워하는)
If something or someone frightens you, they cause you to suddenly feel afraid, anxious, or nervous.

1분에 몇 단어를 읽는지 리딩 속도를 측정해보세요.

$$\frac{646 \text{ words}}{\text{reading time ( ) sec}} \times 60 = (\quad) \text{ WPM}$$

Build Your Vocabulary

slump*
[slʌmp]

v. 털썩 앉다; (가치·수량·가격 등이) 급감[급락]하다; n. 급감, 급락; 폭락
If you slump somewhere, you fall or sit down there heavily, for example because you are very tired or you feel ill.

pound^{복습}
[paund]

① v. 쿵쿵 울리다; 마구 치다, 세게 두드리다; n. 타격 ② n. 파운드(무게의 단위) ③ n. 울타리, 우리
If your heart is pounding, it is beating with an unusually strong and fast rhythm, usually because you are afraid.

scent^{복습}
[sent]

n. 냄새, 향기; v. 냄새로 찾아내다, 냄새 맡다; 향기가 나다
The scent of something is the pleasant smell that it has.

swirl
[swəːrl]

vi. 소용돌이치다, 빙빙 돌다
If liquid or flowing swirls, it moves round and round quickly.

inspire**
[inspáiər]

vt. 고무하다, 불어넣다, 영감을 주다 (inspiring a. 감동시키는, 고무적인)
ISomething or someone that is inspiring is exciting and makes you feel strongly interested and enthusiastic.

kettle^{복습}
[ketl]

n. 솥, 냄비; 주전자
A kettle is a metal pot for boiling or cooking things in.

sip^{복습}
[sip]

vt. (음료를) 홀짝거리다, 조금씩 마시다; n. 한 모금
If you sip a drink or sip at it, you drink by taking just a small amount at a time.

swallow^{복습}
[swálou]

v. 삼키다, 목구멍으로 넘기다; (초조해서) 마른침을 삼키다
If you swallow something, you cause it to go from your mouth down into your stomach.

enormous^{복습}
[inɔ́ːrməs]

a. 엄청난, 거대한, 막대한
You can use enormous to emphasize the great degree or extent of something.

sprinkle**
[spriŋkl]

vt. (액체·분말 등을) 뿌리다, 끼얹다; n. 소량, 조금
If you sprinkle a thing with something such as a liquid or powder, you scatter the liquid or powder over it.

embolden
[imbóuldən]

v. 대담하게 하다, 용기를 돋우어 주다
If you are emboldened by something, it makes you feel confident enough to behave in a particular way.

whirl**
[hwəːrl]

v. 빙글 돌다, 선회하다
If something or someone whirls around or if you whirl them around, they move around or turn around very quickly.

shine 복습
[ʃain]

v. (shone–shone) 빛나(게 하)다, 반짝이다; n. 빛, 빛남, 광채
Something that shines is very bright and clear because it is reflecting light.

punish 복습
[pʌ́niʃ]

v. 처벌하다, 벌주다
To punish someone means to make them suffer in some way because they have done something wrong.

smack
[smæk]

v. 쩝쩝거리다, 입맛을 다시다; 맛이 나다; n. 맛, 풍미
If you smack your lips, you open and close your mouth noisily, especially before or after eating, to show that you are eager to eat or enjoyed eating.

paralyze *
[pǽrəlàiz]

vt. 마비시키다; 무력[무능]하게 만들다; 쓸모없게 만들다
If someone is paralyzed by an accident or an illness, they have no feeling in their body, or in part of their body, and are unable to move.

1분에 몇 단어를 읽는지 리딩 속도를 측정해보세요.

$$\frac{560 \text{ words}}{\text{reading time ( ) sec}} \times 60 = (\quad) \text{ WPM}$$

Build Your Vocabulary

stir ^{복습}
[stə:r]

v. 휘젓다, 뒤섞다; 움직이다; n. 움직임; 휘젓기
If you stir a liquid or other substance, you move it around or mix it in a container using something such as a spoon.

opportunity **
[àpərtjú:nəti]

n. 기회
An opportunity is a situation in which it is possible for you to do something that you want to do.

waft
[wæft]

v. 둥둥 떠돌다, 둥실둥실 실어 나르다
If sounds or smells waft through the air, or if something such as a light wind wafts them, they move gently through the air.

whisker ^{복습}
[wískər]

n. (고양이·쥐 등의) 수염; 구레나룻
The whiskers of an animal such as a cat or a mouse are the long stiff hairs that grow near its mouth.

tremble ^{복습}
[trembl]

v. 떨(리)다, 진동하다, 흔들리다
If you tremble, you shake slightly because you are frightened or cold.

goodhearted
[gudhá:rtid]

a. 친절한, 마음씨 고운
Someone is goodhearted is kind or generous.

saucer *
[só:sər]

n. 받침 접시
A saucer is a small curved plate on which you stand a cup.

sniff ^{복습}
[snif]

v. 냄새를 맡다, 코를 킁킁거리다; 코를 훌쩍이다; n. 냄새 맡음
If you sniff something or sniff at it, you smell it by sniffing.

incredible ^{복습}
[inkrédəbl]

a. 놀라운, 믿어지지 않는
If you describe something or someone as incredible, you like them very much or are impressed by them, because they are extremely or unusually good.

creep ^{복습}
[kri:p]

vi. (crept-crept) 살금살금 걷다, 기다; n. 포복
When people or animals creep somewhere, they move quietly and slowly.

bend ^{복습}
[bend]

v. (bent-bent) 구부리다, 돌리다; 구부러지다, 휘다; n. 커브, 굽음
When you bend a part of your body such as your arm or leg, or when it bends, you change its position so that it is no longer straight.

broth ^{복습}
[brɔ:θ]

n. (고기·생선·야채 등을 끓인) 묽은 수프
Broth is a kind of soup. It usually has vegetables or rice in it.

sip ^{복습}
[sip]

vt. (음료를) 홀짝거리다, 조금씩 마시다; n. 한 모금
If you sip a drink or sip at it, you drink by taking just a small amount at a time.

wring ^{복습}
[riŋ]

v. (손을) 꽉 쥐다; 짜다, 비틀다; 몸부림치다
If someone wrings their hands, they hold them together and twist and turn them, usually because they are very worried or upset about something.

gulp[*]
[gʌlp]

n. 꿀꺽꿀꺽 마심; v. 꿀꺽꿀꺽 마시다; (긴장·흥분으로) 꿀꺽 삼키다
If you gulp something, you eat or drink it very quickly by swallowing large quantities of it at once.

damp ^{복습}
[dæmp]

a. 축축한, 습기 있는; n. 습기
Something that is damp is slightly wet.

drip ^{복습}
[drip]

v. 방울방울[뚝뚝] 떨어지다; 가득[넘칠 듯이] 지니고 있다
When something drips, drops of liquid fall from it.

quest ^{복습}
[kwest]

n. (특히 중세 기사의) 탐구 여행; 탐구, 추구
A quest is a long and difficult search for something.

lean ^{복습}
[li:n]

① v. 상체를 굽히다; 기울다; 기대다, 의지하다 ② a. 야윈, 마른
When you lean in a particular direction, you bend your body in that direction.

indicator
[índikèitər]

n. (일의 현황·사정 변화 등을 나타내는) 지표; (속도·압력을 나타내는) 계기[장치]
An indicator is a measurement or value which gives you an idea of what something is like.

indeed ^{복습}
[indi:d]

ad. 실로, 참으로, 과연, 정말
You use indeed to confirm or agree with something that has just been said.

Check Your Reading Speed

1분에 몇 단어를 읽는지 리딩 속도를 측정해보세요.

$$\frac{571 \text{ words}}{\text{reading time ( ) sec}} \times 60 = (\qquad) \text{ WPM}$$

Build Your Vocabulary

peer[*]
[piər]

vi. 응시하다, 자세히 보다; 희미하게 나타나다
If you peer at something, you look at it very hard.

stench^{복습}
[stentʃ]

n. 불쾌한 냄새, 악취
A stench is a strong and very unpleasant smell.

odor^{복습}
[óudər]

n. (불쾌한) 냄새, 악취
An odor is a particular and distinctive smell.

immediately^{복습}
[imí:diətli]

ad. 곧, 바로, 즉시
If something happens immediately, it happens without any delay.

maneuver[*]
[mənú:vər]

v. 교묘히 이동하다; n. 교묘한 조종; 책략, 술책
If you maneuver something into or out of an awkward position, you skillfully move it there.

spool^{복습}
[spu:l]

n. (실·전선·필름 등을 감는) 릴, 얼레
A spool is a round object onto which thread, tape, or film can be wound, especially before it is put into a machine.

exceptional[*]
[iksépʃənl]

a. 극히 예외적인; 특출한 (exceptionally ad. 유난히, 특별히)
Exceptional situations and incidents are unusual and only likely to happen very infrequently.

fate^{복습}
[feit]

n. 운명, 숙명
A person's or thing's fate is what happens to them.

serve^{복습}
[sə:rv]

v. 섬기다, 복무하다; 제공하다, 시중 들다; n. 서브
If you serve your country, an organization, or a person, you do useful work for them.

honor^{복습}
[ánər]

vt. 존경하다, 공경하다; n. 명예, 영예
To honor someone means to treat them or regard them with special attention and respect.

considerable^{**}
[kənsídərəbl]

a. 상당한, 많은 (considerably ad. 꽤, 상당히)
Considerable means great in amount or degree.

accustomed[*]
[əkʌ́stəmd]

a. (~에) 익숙해진, 길들여진
When your eyes become accustomed to darkness or bright light, they adjust so that you start to be able to see things, after not being able to see properly at first.

gloom^{복습}
[glu:m]

n. 어둑어둑함, 어둠; 우울, 침울
The gloom is a state of near darkness.

whisper ^{복습}
[hwíspə:r]

v. 속삭이다; n. 속삭임; 속삭이는 소리
When you whisper, you say something very quietly.

devious
[díːviəs]

a. 비뚤어진, 사악한; 우회하는
If you describe someone as devious, you do not like them because you think they are dishonest and like to keep things secret, often in a complicated way.

a great deal of ^{복습}

idiom 다량의, 많은
If you say that you need or have a great deal of or a good deal of a particular thing, you are emphasizing that you need or have a lot of it.

gusto
[gʌ́stou]

n. 기쁨, 즐거움, 넘치는 활기; 취미, 즐김, 기호
If you do something with gusto, you do it with energetic and enthusiastic enjoyment.

honorable*
[ánərəbl]

a. 명예로운, 고결한
If you describe people or actions as honorable, you mean that they are good and deserve to be respected and admired.

aid**
[eid]

v. 돕다, 지원하다; n. 원조, 지원
To aid someone means to help or assist them.

rescue ^{복습}
[réskjuː]

n. 구출, 구원; vt. 구조하다, 구출하다
Rescue is help which gets someone out of a dangerous or unpleasant situation.

leap ^{복습}
[liːp]

v. (leapt/leaped–leapt/leaped) (심장이) 뛰다, 고동치다; 껑충 뛰다, 뛰어넘다; n. 뜀, 도약
If you leap, you jump high in the air or jump a long distance.

trot*
[trat]

n. 빠른 걸음; v. 빠른 걸음으로 가다; 총총걸음 치다
A trot is a small quick step.

chase**
[ʧeis]

v. 뒤쫓다, 추적하다; 좇다
If you chase someone, or chase after them, you run after them or follow them quickly in order to catch or reach them.

gnarled
[naːrld]

a. 쭈글쭈글한, 울퉁불퉁하고 비틀린
If someone has gnarled hands, their hands are twisted as a result of old age or illness.

delightful ^{복습}
[diláitfəl]

a. 기쁨을 주는, 정말 기분 좋은
If you describe something or someone as delightful, you mean they are very pleasant.

definite*
[défənit]

a. 확실한, 확고한; 분명한, 뚜렷한 (definitely ad. 확실히, 명확히)
If something such as a decision or an arrangement is definite, it is firm and clear, and unlikely to be changed.

detect*
[ditékt]

vt. 발견하다, 간파하다
To detect something means to find it or discover that it is present somewhere by using equipment or making an investigation.

176

whiff
[hwif]

n. 확 풍기는 냄새; (약간의) 조짐
If there is a whiff of a particular smell, you smell it only slightly or only for a brief period of time, for example as you walk past someone or something.

cornucopia
[kɔ̀:rnjukóupiə]

n. (좋은 것들이 가득 찬) 보고
A cornucopia of things is a large number of different things.

scent^{복습}
[sent]

n. 냄새, 향기; v. 냄새로 찾아내다, 냄새 맡다; 향기가 나다
The scent of something is the pleasant smell that it has.

unmistakable
[Ànmistéikəbl]

a. 오해의 여지가 없는, 틀림없는 (unmistakably ad. 틀림없이, 명백하게)
If you describe something as unmistakable, you mean that it is so obvious that it cannot be mistaken for anything else.

1분에 몇 단어를 읽는지 리딩 속도를 측정해보세요.

$$\frac{876 \text{ words}}{\text{reading time ( ) sec}} \times 60 = (\quad) \text{ WPM}$$

Build Your Vocabulary

tremble 복습
[trembl]

v. 떨(리)다, 진동하다, 흔들리다
If you tremble, you shake slightly because you are frightened or cold.

definite 복습
[défənit]

a. 확실한, 확고한; 분명한, 뚜렷한 (definitely ad. 확실히, 명확히)
If something such as a decision or an arrangement is definite, it is firm and clear, and unlikely to be changed.

dire 복습
[daiər]

a. 끔찍한, 불길한; 절박한, 극심한
Dire is used to emphasize how serious or terrible a situation or event is.

ounce 복습
[auns]

n. 온스(무게 단위. 1/16파운드. 28.35그램)
An ounce is a unit of weight used in Britain and the USA. There are sixteen ounces in a pound and one ounce is equal to 28.35 grams.

dungeon 복습
[dándʒən]

n. 지하 감옥; vt. 지하 감옥에 가두다
A dungeon is a dark underground prison in a castle.

sew 복습
[sou]

v. 바느질하다, 꿰매다, 깁다
When you sew something such as clothes, you make them or repair them by joining pieces of cloth together by passing thread through them with a needle.

defend 복습
[difénd]

v. 방어하다, 지키다
If you defend someone or something, you take action in order to protect them.

still 복습
[stil]

a. 정지한, 움직이지 않는; 조용한, 고요한; ad. 여전히, 아직도; 더욱, 한층
If you stay still, you stay in the same position and do not move.

beat 복습
[bi:t]

v. 치다, 두드리다; 패배시키다, 이기다; n. [음악] 박자, 고동
When your heart or pulse beats, it continually makes regular rhythmic movements.

long-lost
[lɔ́:ŋ-lɔ́:st]

a. 오랫동안 보지[소식을 듣지] 못한; 장기간 행방불명인
You use long-lost to describe someone or something that you have not seen for a long time.

**dread*
[dred]

v. 몹시 무서워하다; (안 좋은 일이 생길까 봐) 두려워하다; n. 두려움; 두려운 것
If you dread something which may happen, you feel very anxious and unhappy about it because you think it will be unpleasant or upsetting.

gloom 복습
[glu:m]

n. 어둑어둑함, 어둠; 우울, 침울
The gloom is a state of near darkness.

178

paw ^{복습}
[pɔː]

n. (갈고리 발톱이 있는 동물의) 발; v. 앞발로 차다
The paws of an animal such as a cat, dog, or bear are its feet, which have claws for gripping things and soft pads for walking on.

arm***
[aːrm]

① vt. 무장시키다; n. 무기 (armed a. 무장한, 무기를 가진) ② n. 팔
If you arm someone with a weapon, you provide them with a weapon.

charming*
[ʧɑːrmiŋ]

a. 매력 있는, 매력적인; 마법을 거는
If you say that something is charming, you mean that it is very pleasant or attractive.

surrender*
[səréndər]

v. 항복[굴복]하다, 투항하다; n. 항복, 굴복
If you surrender, you stop fighting or resisting someone and agree that you have been beaten.

locket ^{복습}
[lákit]

n. 로켓(사진 등을 넣어 목걸이에 다는 작은 갑)
A locket is a piece of jewelry containing something such as a picture, which a woman wears on a chain around her neck.

swing ^{복습}
[swiŋ]

v. 휘두르다; (한 점을 축으로 하여) 빙 돌다, 휙 움직이다;
n. 휘두르기, 스윙; 흔들기
If something swings in a particular direction or if you swing it in that direction, it moves in that direction with a smooth, curving movement.

quest ^{복습}
[kwest]

n. (특히 중세 기사의) 탐구 여행; 탐구, 추구
A quest is a long and difficult search for something.

extraordinary ^{복습}
[ikstrɔ́ːrdənèri]

a. 놀라운, 비상한
If you describe something as extraordinary, you mean that it is very unusual or surprising.

inspire**
[inspáiər]

vt. 고무하다, 불어넣다, 영감을 주다 (inspiring a. 고무적인, 감동시키는)
Something or someone that is inspiring is exciting and makes you feel strongly interested and enthusiastic.

humanity*
[hjuːmǽnəti]

n. 인류, 인간; 인간성
All the people in the world can be referred to as humanity.

aid ^{복습}
[eid]

v. 돕다, 지원하다; n. 원조, 지원
To aid someone means to help or assist them.

rescue ^{복습}
[réskjuː]

n. 구출, 구원; vt. 구조하다, 구출하다
Rescue is help which gets someone out of a dangerous or unpleasant situation.

exaggerate ^{복습}
[igzǽdʒəreit]

vt. 과장하다
If you exaggerate, you indicate that something is, for example, worse or more important than it really is.

oversize ^{복습}
[óuvərsaiz]

a. 특대의, 너무 큰
Oversize things are too big, or much bigger than usual.

assist***
[əsíst]

v. 도와주다, 돕다 (assistance n. 도움, 원조)
If you assist someone, you help them to do a job or task by doing part of the work for them.

tremendous^{복습}
[triméndəs]

a. 거대한, 대단한; 엄청난, 무서운
You use tremendous to emphasize how strong a feeling or quality is, or how large an amount is.

deed[*]
[di:d]

n. 행위, 행동; (주택·건물의 소유권을 증명하는) 증서
A deed is something that is done, especially something that is very good or very bad.

dispel
[dispél]

v. (특히 느낌·믿음을) 떨쳐 버리다[없애다]
To dispel an idea or feeling that people have means to stop them having it.

myth[*]
[miθ]

n. (많은 사람들의) 근거 없는 믿음, 신화
A myth is a well-known story which was made up in the past to explain natural events or to justify religious beliefs or social customs.

surround^{복습}
[səráund]

vt. 둘러싸다, 에워싸다; 포위하다
If a person or thing is surrounded by something, that thing is situated all around them.

specific^{복습}
[spisífik]

a. 명확한, 구체적인; 특정의 (specifically ad. 명확하게, 특히)
You use specific to refer to a particular fixed area, problem, or subject.

face^{복습}
[feis]

v. 직면하다; 직시하다; ~을 마주보다, 향하다
If you face or are faced with something difficult or unpleasant, or if it faces you, it is going to affect you and you have to deal with it.

season^{***}
[si:zn]

v. 연마시키다, 단련시키다; 맛을 내다 (seasoned a. 노련한; 양념한)
You can use seasoned to describe a person who has a lot of experience of something.

flour^{복습}
[flauər]

n. 밀가루; 분말, 가루
Flour is a white or brown powder that is made by grinding grain, which is used to make bread, cakes, and pastry.

thwart[*]
[θwɔ:rt]

v. 훼방 놓다, 방해하다; 반대하다
If you thwart someone or thwart their plans, you prevent them from doing or getting what they want.

stare^{복습}
[stɛər]

v. 응시하다, 뚫어지게 보다
If you stare at someone or something, you look at them for a long time.

let go of^{복습}

idiom (쥐고 있던 것을) 놓다, ~에서 손을 놓다
To let go of someone or something means to stop holding them.

zip^{복습}
[zip]

n. 영(零), 무(無); 지퍼; v. 지퍼를 잠그다
Zip sometimes used the same as zero.

nada^{복습}
[ná:də]

n. 아무것도 없는 것, 무(無)
Nada means nothing.

180

1분에 몇 단어를 읽는지 리딩 속도를 측정해보세요.

$$\frac{467 \text{ words}}{\text{reading time (} \quad \text{) sec}} \times 60 = (\quad) \text{ WPM}$$

Build Your Vocabulary

sensation*
[senséiʃən]

n. 감각, 느낌, 기분
A sensation is a physical feeling.

scaly
[skéili]

a. 비늘이 있는, 비늘 모양의
A scaly animal has small pieces of hard skin covering its body.

dependent**
[dipéndənt]

a. 의지하고 있는, 의존적인; ~에 좌우되는
To be dependent on something or someone means to need them in order to succeed or be able to survive.

hideous^{복습}
[hídiəs]

a. 끔찍한, 오싹한, 흉측한 (hideously ad. 소름 끼칠 만큼)
If you say that someone or something is hideous, you mean that they are very ugly or unattractive.

indeed^{복습}
[indí:d]

ad. 실로, 참으로, 과연, 정말
You use indeed to confirm or agree with something that has just been said.

cling^{복습}
[kliŋ]

vi. 매달리다, 달라붙다
If you cling to someone or something, you hold onto them tightly.

nonetheless^{복습}
[nʌnðəlés]

ad. 그럼에도 불구하고, 그래도, 역시
You use nonetheless when saying something that contrasts with what has just been said.

adjust^{복습}
[ədʒʌ́st]

v. 적응하다; (옷매무새 등을) 바로 하다, 조절하다; 조정하다
If you adjust your vision or if your vision adjusts, the muscles of your eye or the pupils alter to cope with changes in light or distance.

shiver^{복습}
[ʃívəːr]

v. (추위·두려움·흥분 등으로) (몸을) 떨다; n. 전율
When you shiver, your body shakes slightly because you are cold or frightened.

litter^{복습}
[lítər]

vt. 어질러 놓다; (새끼를) 낳다; n. 쓰레기, 어질러진 물건; 한 배에서 난 새끼들
If a number of things litter a place, they are scattered untidily around it or over it.

tuft
[tʌft]

n. (머리칼·깃털·실 따위의) 타래, 한 움큼
A tuft of something such as hair or grass is a small amount of it which is growing together in one place or is held together at the bottom.

fur^{복습}
[fəːr]

n. 부드러운 털; 모피
Fur is the thick and usually soft hair that grows on the bodies of many mammals.

knot^{복습}
[nat]

n. 매듭, 얽힘; 나무 마디; v. 매다, 얽히(게 하)다
If you tie a knot in a piece of string, rope, cloth, or other material, you pass one end or part of it through a loop and pull it tight.

thread^{복습}
[θred]

n. 실, 바느질 실; vt. 실을 꿰다
A thread is a long very thin piece of a material such as cotton, nylon, or silk, especially one that is used in sewing.

skeleton*
[skélətn]

n. 뼈대, 골격; 해골
Your skeleton is the framework of bones in your body.

glow^{복습}
[glou]

vi. 빛을 내다, 빛나다; n. 빛, 밝음
If something glows, it produces a dull, steady light.

grin**
[grin]

v. (이를 드러내고) 싱긋 웃다, 활짝 웃다; n. 싱긋 웃음
When you grin, you smile broadly.

skull*
[skʌl]

n. 두개골, 해골
Your skull is the bony part of your head which encloses your brain.

delicate^{복습}
[délikət]

a. 섬세한, 고운; 예민한, 민감한; (음식이) 맛있는, 담백하고 맛좋은
Something that is delicate is small and beautifully shaped.

despair^{복습}
[dispέər]

n. 절망, 자포자기; vi. 절망하다
Despair is the feeling that everything is wrong and that nothing will improve.

negotiate*
[nigóuʃièit]

v. (울타리장애 등을) 뛰어넘다, 넘기다; (조약거래 등을) 협정하다, 협상하다
If you negotiate an area of land, a place, or an obstacle, you successfully travel across it or around it.

horrible**
[hɔ́:rəbl]

a. 끔찍한, 소름 끼치게 싫은; 무서운
You can call something horrible when it causes you to feel great shock, fear, and disgust.

contemplate^{복습}
[kántəmplèit]

v. 응시하다, 눈여겨 보다; 심사숙고하다, 신중히 생각하다
If you contemplate something or someone, you look at them for a long time.

vengeful
[véndʒfəl]

a. 앙심[원한]을 품은; 복수심에 불타는
If you describe someone as vengeful, you are critical of them because they feel a great desire for revenge.

beg^{복습}
[beg]

vt. 부탁[간청]하다; 빌다, 구걸하다
If you beg someone to do something, you ask them very anxiously or eagerly to do it

infringe
[infríndʒ]

v. (법·계약·의무 등을) 어기다, 위반하다; 침해하다
If someone infringes a law or a rule, they break it or do something which disobeys it.

Check Your Reading Speed

1분에 몇 단어를 읽는지 리딩 속도를 측정해보세요.

$$\frac{830 \text{ words}}{\text{reading time ( ) sec}} \times 60 = (\quad) \text{ WPM}$$

Build Your Vocabulary

consider^{복습}
[kənsídər]

v. 고려하다, 숙고하다
If you consider something, you think about it carefully.

occur^{복습}
[əkə́:r]

vi. 일어나다, 생기다; 생각이 떠오르다
When something occurs, it happens.

serve^{복습}
[sə:rv]

v. 제공하다, 시중 들다; 섬기다, 복무하다; n. 서브
When you serve food and drink, you give people food and drink.

chamber^{복습}
[tʃéimbər]

n. (특수한 목적을 위해 설계된) 칸막이 공간; 방, 침실
A chamber is a room designed and equipped for a particular purpose.

chain^{복습}
[tʃein]

v. (사슬로) 묶다; n. 사슬, 쇠줄; 일련
If a person or thing is chained to something, they are fastened to it with a chain.

switch^{복습}
[switʃ]

v. 전환하다, 바꾸다; n. 스위치
If you switch to something different, for example to a different system, task, or subject of conversation, you change to it from what you were doing or saying before.

outfit[*]
[áutfit]

n. 한 벌의 옷, 복장
An outfit is a set of clothes.

sigh^{복습}
[sai]

v. 한숨 쉬다; n. 한숨, 탄식
When you sigh, you let out a deep breath, as a way of expressing feelings such as disappointment, tiredness, or pleasure.

immediately^{복습}
[imí:diətli]

ad. 곧, 바로, 즉시
If something happens immediately, it happens without any delay.

abuse[*]
[əbjú:z]

v. 학대하다; 남용[오용]하다; n. 학대; 남용, 오용
If someone is abused, they are treated cruelly and violently.

biggish
[bígiʃ]

a. 약간 큰, 큰 편인
Something that is biggish is fairly big.

ridiculous^{복습}
[ridíkjuləs]

a. 웃기는, 우스꽝스러운; 터무니없는
If you say that something or someone is ridiculous, you mean that they are very foolish.

blink^{복습}
[bliŋk]

v. 눈을 깜박거리다; (등불·별 등이) 깜박이다; n. 깜박거림
When you blink or when you blink your eyes, you shut your eyes and very quickly open them again.

wipe [복습]
[waip]

vt. 닦다, 닦아 내다; n. 닦기
If you wipe something, you rub its surface to remove dirt or liquid from it.

pile [복습]
[pail]

n. 쌓아 올린 더미; 다수; v. 쌓아 올리다, 쌓(이)다
A pile of things is a mass of them that is high in the middle and has sloping sides.

consign [복습]
[kənsáin]
[spin]

v. 위탁하다, 넘기다, 맡기다; 충당하다, 할당하다
To consign something or someone to a place where they will be forgotten about, or to an unpleasant situation or place, means to put them there.

sentiment [복습]
[séntəmənt]

n. 심정, 감정; 정서, 감상
A sentiment that people have is an attitude which is based on their thoughts and feelings.

spin [복습]

v. 돌다, 회전시키다; (실을) 잣다, (이야기를) 지어내다; (일·이야기 등을) 오래 끌다; n. 회전
If something spins or if you spin it, it turns quickly around a central point.

sob [복습]
[sab]

v. 흐느껴 울다; n. 흐느낌, 오열
When someone sobs, they cry in a noisy way, breathing in short breaths.

squeeze [복습]
[skwi:z]

v. (꼭) 짜다, 쥐다; (억지로) 비집고 들어가다; n. (꼭) 짜기
If you squeeze something, you press it firmly, usually with your hands.

hearty *
[há:rti]

a. 진심 어린, (감정의 정도가) 강한; (마음이) 따뜻한, 다정한 (heartily ad. 진심으로)
Hearty feelings or opinions are strongly felt or strongly held.

instrument [복습]
[ínstrəmənt]

n. 기구, 도구; 악기
An instrument is a tool or device that is used to do a particular task, especially a scientific task.

starve *
[sta:rv]

v. 굶주리다, 굶어죽다
If people starve, they suffer greatly from lack of food which sometimes leads to their death.

chop [복습]
[tʃap]

vt. 자르다, 잘게 썰다; n. 잘라낸 조각, (뼈가 붙은) 토막 고기; 절단
If you chop something, you cut it into pieces with strong downward movements of a knife or an axe.

stuck [복습]
[stʌk]

a. 꽉 끼인, 움직일 수 없는, 곤경에 빠진; v. STICK의 과거·과거분사
If something is stuck in a particular position, it is fixed tightly in this position and is unable to move.

sink [복습]
[siŋk]

v. (sank-sunk) 가라앉히다, 침몰하다; (마음 등이) 가라앉다, 낙심하다
If something sinks, it disappears below the surface of a mass of water.

truthful
[trú:θfəl]

a. 진실의, 사실의; 성실한, 정직한 (truthfully ad. 진실하게)
If a person or their comments are truthful, they are honest and do not tell any lies.

Check Your Reading Speed

1분에 몇 단어를 읽는지 리딩 속도를 측정해보세요.

$$\frac{140 \text{ words}}{\text{reading time (} \quad \text{) sec}} \times 60 = (\quad) \text{ WPM}$$

Build Your Vocabulary

whisper ^{복습}
[hwíspə:r]

v. 속삭이다; n. 속삭임; 속삭이는 소리
When you whisper, you say something very quietly.

dungeon ^{복습}
[dʌ́ndʒən]

n. 지하 감옥; vt. 지하 감옥에 가두다
A dungeon is a dark underground prison in a castle.

bare *
[bɛər]

vt. (신체의 일부를) 드러내다; a. 벌거벗은
If you bare something, you uncover it and show it.

mark ^{복습}
[ma:rk]

n. 표적, 목표물; 표시, 부호; v. 표시하다, 나타내다
If something is off the mark, it is inaccurate or incorrect. If it is on the mark, it is accurate or correct.

1분에 몇 단어를 읽는지 리딩 속도를 측정해보세요.

$$\frac{668 \text{ words}}{\text{reading time ( ) sec}} \times 60 = (\quad) \text{ WPM}$$

Build Your Vocabulary

tip^{복습}
[tip]

① n. (뾰족한) 끝 ② v. 뒤집어엎다, 기울이다 ③ n. 팁, 사례금
The tip of something long and narrow is the end of it.

sideline
[saidlàin]

n. (테니스장 등의) 사이드라인
The sidelines are the lines marking the long sides of the playing area, for example on a football field or tennis court.

slap^{복습}
[slæp]

v. 탁 놓다, 찰싹 때리다; 철썩 부딪치다; n. 찰싹 (때림)
If you slap something onto a surface, you put it there quickly, roughly, or carelessly.

approval^{복습}
[əprúːvəl]

n. 찬성, 동의; 승인
If someone or something has your approval, you like and admire them.

absolute^{복습}
[金bsəlùːt]

a. 절대적인, 무조건의; 완전한 (absolutely ad. 절대적으로, 무조건)
Absolute means total and complete.

delightful^{복습}
[diláitfəl]

a. 기쁨을 주는, 정말 기분 좋은
If you describe something or someone as delightful, you mean they are very pleasant.

anticipate*
[æntísipeit]

vt. 예상하다, 미리 고려하다; 기대하다
If you anticipate an event, you realize in advance that it may happen and you are prepared for it.

shove*
[ʃʌv]

v. 밀치다, 떠밀다, 밀어내다; n. 밀치기
If you shove something somewhere, you push it there quickly and carelessly.

tremble^{복습}
[trembl]

v. 떨(리)다, 진동하다, 흔들리다
If you tremble, you shake slightly because you are frightened or cold.

knight^{복습}
[nait]

n. (중세의) 기사
In medieval times, a knight was a man of noble birth, who served his king or lord in battle.

bow^{복습}
[bau]

① v. 머리를 숙이다, 굽히다 ② n. 활; 곡선
When you bow, you move your head or the top half of your body forward and downward as a formal way of greeting them or showing respect.

whisker^{복습}
[wískər]

n. (고양이·쥐 등의) 수염; 구레나룻
The whiskers of an animal such as a cat or a mouse are the long stiff hairs that grow near its mouth.

186

sniff ^{복습}
[snif]

v. 냄새를 맡다, 코를 킁킁거리다; 코를 훌쩍이다; n. 냄새 맡음
If you sniff something or sniff at it, you smell it by sniffing.

thwart ^{복습}
[θwɔ:rt]

v. 훼방 놓다, 방해하다; 반대하다
If you thwart someone or thwart their plans, you prevent them from doing or getting what they want.

crash^{**}
[kræʃ]

v. 충돌하다, 들이받다, 부딪치다; n. 충돌, 요란한 소리, 굉음
If something crashes somewhere, it moves and hits something else violently, making a loud noise.

chandelier ^{복습}
[ʃændəlíər]

n. 샹들리에(천장에서 내리 드리운 호화로운 장식등)
A chandelier is a large, decorative frame which holds light bulbs or candles and hangs from the ceiling.

moan ^{복습}
[moun]

v. 신음하다, 끙끙대다; 투덜대다; n. 신음; 불평
If you moan, you make a low sound, usually because you are unhappy or in pain.

hiss[*]
[his]

v. 쉬익[쉿] 하는 소리를 내다; n. 쉬[쉿] 하는 소리
To hiss means to make a sound like a long 's'.

miserable ^{복습}
[mízərəbl]

a. 비참한, 초라한, 불쌍한
If you are miserable, you are very unhappy.

appetite[*]
[æpitait]

n. 식욕, 욕구
Your appetite is your desire to eat.

creep ^{복습}
[kri:p]

vi. 살금살금 걷다, 기다; n. 포복
When people or animals creep somewhere, they move quietly and slowly.

drip ^{복습}
[drip]

v. 방울방울[뚝뚝] 떨어지다; 가득[넘칠 듯이] 지니고 있다
When something drips, drops of liquid fall from it.

face ^{복습}
[feis]

v. ~을 마주보다, 향하다; 직면하다; 직시하다
If someone or something faces a particular thing, person, or direction, they are positioned opposite them or are looking in that direction.

aware ^{복습}
[əwéər]

a. 알고 있는, 의식하고 있는, 알아차린
If you are aware of something, you know about it.

fragile[*]
[frædʒəl]

a. 부서지기[깨지기] 쉬운
Something that is fragile is easily broken or damaged.

torment ^{복습}
[tɔ́:rment]

vt. 괴롭히다, 고문하다; n. 고통, 고뇌
If something torments you, it causes you extreme mental suffering.

banquet ^{복습}
[bǽŋkwit]

n. 연회; v. 연회를 베풀어 대접하다
A banquet is a grand formal dinner.

hand over ^{복습}

phrasal v. 건네주다, 넘겨주다
If you hand something over to someone, you pass it to them.

flavor[*]
[fléivər]

n. 맛, 풍미; 정취, 멋, 묘미
The flavor of a food or drink is its taste.

ruin^{복습}
[ruːin]

v. 망치다, 못쓰게 만들다; 몰락하다; n. 폐허; 파멸
To ruin something means to severely harm, damage, or spoil it.

illegal^{복습}
[ilíːgəl]

a. 불법의, 비합법적인
If something is illegal, the law says that it is not allowed.

bend^{복습}
[bend]

v. (bent-bent) 구부리다, 돌리다; 구부러지다, 휘다; n. 커브, 굽음
When you bend a part of your body such as your arm or leg, or when it bends, you change its position so that it is no longer straight.

1분에 몇 단어를 읽는지 리딩 속도를 측정해보세요.

$$\frac{399 \text{ words}}{\text{reading time ( ) sec}} \times 60 = (\quad) \text{ WPM}$$

Build Your Vocabulary

access**
[ǽkses]

n. 접근권, 접촉 기회; 접근; v. 접근하다; 접속하다
If you have access to a building or other place, you are able or allowed to go into it.

dungeon^{복습}
[dʌ́ndʒən]

n. 지하 감옥; vt. 지하 감옥에 가두다
A dungeon is a dark underground prison in a castle.

alas^{복습}
[əlǽs]

int. (걱정·슬픔을 나타내어) 아아, 슬프도다!, 불쌍한지고!
Alas is used to express sadness or regret.

fate^{복습}
[feit]

n. 운명, 숙명
A person's or thing's fate is what happens to them.

mend^{복습}
[mend]

v. 고치다, 회복하다, 개선하다; n. 수선, 개량
If you mend something that is broken or not working, you repair it, so that it works properly or can be used.

crooked^{복습}
[krúkid]

a. 비뚤어진, 구부러진; 부정직한
If you describe something as crooked, especially something that is usually straight, you mean that it is bent or twisted.

seek^{복습}
[siːk]

v. 찾다, 추구하다, 얻으려 하다
When someone seeks something, they try to obtain it.

shed^{복습}
[ʃed]

v. (빛을) 비추다; 없애다; 흘리다; n. 보관소
To shed light on something means to make it easier to understand, because more information is known about it.

release^{복습}
[riliːs]

vt. 놓아주다, 해방시키다, 풀어놓다; n. 석방
If a person or animal is released from somewhere where they have been looked after, they are set free or allowed to go.

atone
[ətóun]

v. 속죄하다
If you atone for something that you have done, you do something to show that you are sorry you did it.

adoring^{복습}
[ədɔ́ːriŋ]

a. 흠모하는
An adoring person is someone who loves and admires another person very much.

glow^{복습}
[glou]

vi. 빛을 내다, 빛나다; n. 빛, 밝음
If something glows, it produces a dull, steady light.

serve^{복습}
[səːrv]

v. 제공하다, 시중 들다; 섬기다, 복무하다; n. 서브
When you serve food and drink, you give people food and drink.

banquet ^{복습}
[bǽŋkwit]

n. 연회; v. 연회를 베풀어 대접하다
A banquet is a grand formal dinner.

kettle ^{복습}
[ketl]

n. 솥, 냄비; 주전자
A kettle is a metal pot for boiling or cooking things in.

honor ^{복습}
[ánər]

n. 명예, 영예; vt. 존경하다, 공경하다
An honor is a special award that is given to someone, usually because they have done something good or because they are greatly respected.

peek
[pi:k]

vi. 살짝 들여다보다, 엿보다; n. 엿봄
If you peek at something or someone, you have a quick look at them.

dusty [*]
[dʌ́sti]

a. 먼지투성이의, 먼지 많은
If a room, house, or object is dusty, it is covered with very small pieces of dirt.

scene ^{복습}
[si:n]

n. 일, 사건, 상황; 장소, 현장; 장면; 무대
You can describe an event that you see, or that is broadcast or shown in a picture, as a scene of a particular kind.

whisper ^{복습}
[hwíspə:r]

v. 속삭이다; n. 속삭임; 속삭이는 소리
When you whisper, you say something very quietly.

cripes ^{복습}
[kraips]

int. 저런, 이것 참
Cripes is an expression of surprise.

unbelievable ^{복습}
[ʌnbilíːvəbl]

a. 믿을 수 없는, 놀라운
You can use unbelievable to emphasize that you think something is very bad or shocking.

thread ^{복습}
[θred]

n. 실, 바느질 실; vt. 실을 꿰다
A thread is a long very thin piece of a material such as cotton, nylon, or silk, especially one that is used in sewing.

master ^{복습}
[mǽstər]

n. 대가, 명인, 정통한 사람; vt. 숙달하다, 터득하다
If you say that someone is a master of a particular activity, you mean that they are extremely skilled at it.

Check Your Reading Speed

$$\frac{88 \text{ words}}{\text{reading time (} \quad \text{) sec}} \times 60 = (\quad) \text{ WPM}$$

Build Your Vocabulary

cup
[kʌp]

vt. 손바닥으로 받다[떠내다]; 두 손을 (컵 모양으로) 동그랗게 모아 쥐다; n. 컵, 잔
If you cup something in your hands, you make your hands into a curved dish-like shape and support it or hold it gently.

jailer
[dʒéilər]

n. 교도관, 간수
A jailer is a person who is in charge of a jail and the prisoners in it.

whisper
[hwíspəːr]

v. 속삭이다; n. 속삭임; 속삭이는 소리
When you whisper, you say something very quietly.

수고하셨습니다!

드디어 끝까지 다 읽으셨군요! 축하드립니다! 여러분은 이 책을 통해 총 32,390개의 단어를 읽으셨고, 1,000개 이상의 어휘와 표현들을 익히셨습니다. 이 책에 나온 어휘는 다른 원서를 읽을 때에도 빈번히 만날 수 있는 필수 어휘들입니다. 이 책을 읽었던 경험은 비슷한 수준의 다른 원서들을 읽을 때 큰 도움이 될 것입니다. 이제 자신의 상황에 맞게 원서를 반복해서 읽거나, 오디오북을 들어 볼 수 있습니다. 혹은 비슷한 수준의 다른 원서를 찾아 읽는 것도 좋습니다. 일단 원서를 완독한 뒤에 어떻게 계속 영어 공부를 이어갈 수 있을지, 도움말을 꼼꼼히 살펴보고 각자 상황에 맞게 적용해 보세요!

리딩(Reading)을 확실하게 다지고 싶다면? 반복해서 읽어 보세요!

리딩 실력을 탄탄하게 다지고 싶다면, 같은 원서를 2~3번 반복해서 읽을 것을 권합니다. 같은 책을 여러 번 읽으면 지루할 것 같지만, 꼭 그렇지도 않습니다. 반복해서 읽을 때 처음과 주안점을 다르게 두면, 전혀 다른 느낌으로 재미있게 읽을 수 있습니다.

처음 원서를 읽을 때는 생소한 단어들과 스토리로 인해 읽으면서 곧바로 이해하기가 매우 힘들 수 있습니다. 전체 맥락을 잡고 읽어도 약간 버거운 느낌이지요. 하지만 반복해서 읽기 시작하면 달라집니다. 일단 내용을 파악한 상황이기 때문에 문장 구조나 어휘의 활용에 더 집중하게 되고, 조금 더 깊이 있게 읽을 수 있습니다. 좋은 표현과 문장을 수집하고 메모할 만한 여유도 생기게 되지요. 어휘도 많이 익숙해졌기 때문에 리딩 속도에도 탄력이 붙습니다. 처음 읽을 때는 '내용'에서 재미를 느꼈다면, 반복해서 읽을 때에는 '영어'에서 재미를 느끼게 되는 것입니다. 따라서 리딩 실력을 더욱 확고하게 다지고자 한다면, 같은 책을 2~3회 정도 반복해서 읽을 것을 권해 드립니다.

리스닝(Listening) 실력을 늘리고 싶다면?
귀를 통해서 읽어 보세요!

많은 영어 학습자들이 '리스닝이 안 돼서 문제'라고 한탄합니다. 그리고 리스닝 실력을 늘리는 방법으로 무슨 뜻인지 몰라도 반복해서 듣는 '무작정 듣기'를 선택합니다. 하지만 뜻도 모르면서 무작정 듣는 일에는 엄청난 인내력이 필요합니다. 그래서 대부분 며칠 시도하다가 포기해 버리고 말지요.

따라서 모르는 내용을 무작정 듣는 것보다는 어느 정도 알고 있는 내용을 반복해서 듣는 것이 더 효과적인 듣기 방법입니다. 그리고 이런 방식의 듣기에 활용할 수 있는 가장 좋은 교재가 오디오북입니다.

리스닝 실력을 향상하고 싶다면, 이 책에서 제공하는 오디오북을 이용해서 듣는 연습을 해 보세요. 활용법은 간단합니다. 일단 책을 한 번 완독했다면, 오디오북을 통해 다시 들어 보는 것입니다. 휴대 기기에 넣어 시간이 날 때 틈틈이 듣는 것도 좋고, 책상에 앉아 눈으로는 텍스트를 보며 귀로 읽는 것도 좋습니다. 이미 읽었던 내용이라 이해하기가 훨씬 수월하고, 애매했던 발음들도 자연스럽게 교정할 수 있습니다. 또 성우의 목소리 연기를 듣다 보면 내용이 더욱 생동감 있게 다가와 이해도가 높아지는 효과도 거둘 수 있습니다.

반대로 듣기에 자신 있는 사람이라면, 책을 읽기 전에 처음부터 오디오북을 먼저 듣는 것도 좋은 방법입니다. 귀를 통해 책을 쭉 읽어보고, 이후에 다시 눈으로 책을 읽으면서 잘 들리지 않았던 부분들을 보충하는 것이지요.

중요한 것은 내용을 따라가면서, 내용에 푹 빠져서 반복해 들어야 한다는 것입니다. 이렇게 연습을 반복해서 눈으로 읽지 않은 책이라도 '귀를 통해' 읽을 수 있을 정도가 되면, 리스닝으로 고생하는 일은 거의 없을 것입니다.

왼쪽의 QR 코드를 인식하여 정식 오디오북을 들어 보세요!
더불어 롱테일북스 홈페이지(www.longtailbooks.co.kr)에서도
오디오북 MP3 파일을 다운로드 받을 수 있습니다.

스피킹(Speaking)이 고민이라면? 소리 내어 읽어 보세요!

스피킹 역시 많은 학습자들이 고민하는 부분입니다. 스피킹이 고민이라면, 원서를 큰 소리로 읽는 낭독 훈련(Voice Reading)을 해 보세요!

'소리 내어 읽는 것이 말하기에 정말로 도움이 될까?'라고 의아한 생각이 들 수도 있습니다. 하지만 인간의 두뇌 입장에서 봤을 때, 성대 구조를 활용해서 '발화'한다는 점에서는 소리 내어 읽기와 말하기에 큰 차이가 없다고 합니다. 소리 내어 읽는 것은 '타인의 생각'을 전달하고, 직접 말하는 것은 '자신의 생각'을 전달한다는 차이가 있을 뿐, 머릿속에서 문장을 처리하고 조음기관(혀와 성대 등)을 움직여 의미를 만든다는 점에서 같은 과정인 것이지요. 따라서 소리 내어 읽는 연습을 꾸준히 하는 것은 스피킹 연습에 큰 도움이 됩니다.

소리 내어 읽기를 하는 방법은 간단합니다. 일단 오디오북을 들으면서 성우의 목소리를 최대한 따라 하며 같이 읽어 보세요. 발음뿐 아니라 억양, 어조, 느낌까지 완벽히 따라 한다고 생각하면서 소리 내어 읽습니다. 따라 읽는 것이 조금 익숙해지면, 옆의 누군가에게 이 책을 읽어 준다는 생각으로 소리 내어 계속 읽어 나갑니다. 한 번 눈과 귀로 읽었던 책이기 때문에 보다 수월하게 진행할 수 있고, 자연스럽게 어휘와 표현을 복습하는 효과도 거두게 됩니다. 또 이렇게 소리 내어 읽은 것을 녹음해서 들어 보면 스스로에게도 좋은 피드백이 됩니다.

최근 말하기가 강조되면서 소리 내어 읽기가 크게 각광을 받고 있기는 하지만, 그렇다고 소리 내어 읽기가 무조건 좋은 것만은 아닙니다. 책을 소리 내어 읽다 보면, 무의식적으로 속으로 발음을 하는 습관을 가지게 되어 리딩 속도 자체는 오히려 크게 떨어지는 현상이 발생할 수 있습니다. 따라서 빠른 리딩 속도가 중요한 수험생이나 고학력 학습자들에게는 소리 내어 읽기가 적절하지 않은 방법입니다. 효과가 좋다는 말만 믿고 무턱대고 따라 하기보다는 자신의 필요에 맞게 우선순위를 정하고 원서를 활용하는 것이 좋습니다.

라이팅(Writing)까지 욕심이 난다면? 요약하는 연습을 해 보세요!

원서를 라이팅 연습에 직접적으로 활용하는 데에는 한계가 있지만, 적절히 활용하면 원서도 유용한 라이팅 자료가 될 수 있습니다.

특히 책을 읽고 그 내용을 요약하는 연습은 큰 도움이 됩니다. 요약 훈련의 방식도 간단합니다. 원서를 읽고 그날 읽은 분량만큼 혹은 책을 다 읽고 전체 내용을 기반으로, 책 내용을 한번 요약하고 나의 느낌을 영어로 적어보는 것입니다.

이때 그 책에 나왔던 단어와 표현을 최대한 활용하여 요약하는 것이 중요합니다. 영어 표현력은 결국 얼마나 다양한 어휘로 많은 표현을 해 보았느냐가 좌우하게 됩니다. 이런 면에서 내가 읽은 책을, 그 책에 나온 문장과 어휘로 다시 표현해 보는 것은 매우 효율적인 방법입니다. 책에 나온 어휘와 표현을 단순히 읽고 무슨 말인지 아는 정도가 아니라, 실제로 직접 활용해서 쓸 수 있을 만큼 확실하게 익히게 되는 것이지요. 여기에 첨삭까지 받을 수 있는 방법이 있다면 금상첨화입니다.

이러한 '표현하기' 연습은 스피킹 훈련에도 그대로 적용될 수 있습니다. 책을 읽고 그 내용을 3분 안에 다른 사람에게 영어로 말하는 연습을 해 보세요. 순발력과 표현력을 기르는 좋은 훈련이 될 것입니다.

꾸준히 원서를 읽고 싶다면? 뉴베리 수상작을 계속 읽어 보세요!

뉴베리 상이 세계 최고 권위의 아동 문학상인 만큼, 그 수상작들은 확실히 완성도를 검증받은 작품이라고 할 수 있습니다. 특히 '쉬운 어휘로 쓰인 깊이 있는 문장'으로 이루어졌다는 점이 영어 학습자들에게 큰 호응을 얻고 있습니다. 이렇게 '검증된 원서'를 꾸준히 읽는 것은 영어 실력 향상에 큰 도움이 됩니다.

아래에 수준별로 제시된 뉴베리 수상작 목록을 보며 적절한 책들을 찾아 계속 읽어 보세요. 꼭 뉴베리 수상작이 아니더라도 마음에 드는 작가의 다른 책을 읽어 보는 것 또한 아주 좋은 방법입니다.

• 영어 초보자도 쉽게 읽을 만한 아주 쉬운 수준. 소리 내어 읽기에도 아주 적합. Sarah, Plain and Tall*(Medal, 8,331단어), The Hundred Penny Box (Honor, 5,878단어), The Hundred Dresses*(Honor, 7,329단어), My Father's Dragon (Honor, 7,682단어), 26 Fairmount Avenue (Honor, 6,737단어)

- 중·고등학생 정도 영어 학습자라면 쉽게 읽을 수 있는 수준. 소리 내어 읽기에도 비교적 적합한 편.

Because of Winn-Dixie*(Honor, 22,123단어), What Jamie Saw (Honor, 17,203단어), Charlotte's Web (Honor, 31,938단어), Dear Mr. Henshaw (Medal, 18,145단어), Missing May (Medal, 17,509단어)

- 대학생 정도 영어 학습자라면 무난한 수준. 소리 내어 읽기에 적합하지 않음.

Number The Stars*(Medal, 27,197단어), A Single Shard (Medal, 33,726단어), The Tale of Despereaux*(Medal, 32,375단어), Hatchet*(Medal, 42,328단어), Bridge to Terabithia (Medal, 32,888단어), A Fine White Dust (Honor, 19,022단어), Jennifer, Hecate, Macbeth, William McKinley and Me, Elizabeth (Honor, 23,266단어)

- 원서 완독 경험을 가진 학습자에게 적절한 수준. 소리 내어 읽기에 적합하지 않음.

The Giver*(Medal, 43,617단어), From the Mixed-Up Files of Mrs. Basil E. Frankweiler (Medal, 30,906단어), The View from Saturday (Medal, 42,685단어), Holes*(Medal, 47,079단어), Criss Cross (Medal, 48,221단어), Walk Two Moons (Medal, 59,400단어), The Graveyard Book (Medal, 67,380단어)

뉴베리 수상작과 뉴베리 수상 작가의 좋은 작품을 엄선한 「뉴베리 컬렉션」에도 위 목록에 있는 도서 중 상당수가 포함될 예정입니다.

★ 「뉴베리 컬렉션」으로 이미 출간된 도서

어떤 책들이 출간되었는지 확인하려면, 지금 인터넷 서점에서 뉴베리 컬렉션을 검색해 보세요.

뉴베리 수상작을 동영상 강의로 만나 보세요!

영어원서 전문 동영상 강의 사이트 영서당(yseodang.com)에서는 뉴베리 컬렉션 『Holes』, 『Because of Winn-Dixie』, 『The Miraculous Journey of Edward Tulane』, 『Wayside School 시리즈』 등의 동영상 강의를 제공하고 있습니다. 뉴베리 수상작이라는 최고의 영어 교재와 EBS 출신 인기 강사가 만난 명강의! 지금 사이트를 방문해서 무료 샘플 강의를 들어 보세요!

'스피드 리딩 카페'를 통해 원서 읽기 습관을 길러 보세요!

일상에서 영어를 한마디도 쓰지 않는 비영어권 국가에서 살고 있는 우리가 영어 환경에 가장 쉽고, 편하고, 부담 없이 노출되는 방법은 바로 '영어원서 읽기'입니다. 언제 어디서든 원서를 붙잡고 읽기만 하면 곧바로 영어를 접하는 환경이 만들어지기 때문이지요. 하루에 20분씩만 꾸준히 읽는다면, 1년에 무려 120시간 동안 영어에 노출될 수 있습니다. 이러한 이유 때문에 영어 교육 전문가들이 영어 원서 읽기를 추천하는 것이지요.

하지만 원서 읽기가 좋다는 것을 알아도 막상 꾸준히 읽는 것은 쉽지 않습니다. 그럴 때에는 13만 명 이상의 회원을 보유한 국내 최대 원서 읽기 동호회 〈스피드 리딩 카페〉 (cafe.naver.com/readingtc)를 방문해 보세요.

원서별로 정리된 무료 PDF 단어장과 수준별 추천 원서 목록 등 유용한 자료는 물론, 뉴베리 수상작을 포함한 다양한 원서의 리뷰와 정보를 무료로 확인할 수 있습니다. 특히 함께 모여서 원서를 읽는 '북클럽'은 중간에 포기하지 않고 원서 읽기 습관을 기르는 데 큰 도움이 될 것입니다.

Book the First (Chapter One to Chapter Fifteen)

1. C   This story begins within the walls of a castle, with the birth of a mouse. A small mouse. The last mouse born to his parents and the only one of his litter to be born alive. The mouse mother held a handkerchief to her nose and then waved it in front of her face. She sniffed. "I will name him. Yes. I will name this mouse Despereaux, for all the sadness, for the many despairs in this place. Now, where is my mirror?"

2. B   "The last one," said the father. "And he'll be dead soon. He can't live. Not with his eyes open like that."

3. D   He said nothing in defense of himself. How could he? Everything his aunt and uncle said was true. He was ridiculously small. His ears were obscenely large. He had been born with his eyes open. And he was sickly. He coughed and sneezed so often that he carried a handkerchief in one paw at all times. He ran temperatures. He fainted at loud noises. Most alarming of all, he showed no interest in the things a mouse should show interest in.

4. C   While his larger, older siblings ate, Despereaux stood with his head cocked to one side, holding very still. "Do you hear that sweet, sweet sound?" he said.

5. D   His brother Furlough took him on a tour of the castle to demonstrate the art of scurrying.

6. B   "Um," said Despereaux, "it would ruin the story."

7. A   Despereaux's brothers and sisters soon abandoned the thankless task of trying to educate him in the ways of being a mouse. And so Despereaux was free.

8. A   But . . . the music, the music. The music made him lose his head and act against the few small mouse instincts he was in possession of, and because of this he revealed himself; and in no time at all, he was spied by the sharp-eyed Princess Pea.

9. B   The Princess Pea looked down at Despereaux. She smiled at him. And while her father played another song, a song about the deep purple falling over sleepy garden walls, the princess reached out and touched the top of the mouse's head. Despereaux

stared up at her in wonder. The Pea, he decided, looked just like the picture of the fair maiden in the book in the library. The princess smiled at Despereaux again, and this time, Despereaux smiled back. And then, something incredible happened: The mouse fell in love.

10. B   And, executing a classic scurry, Furlough went off to tell his father, Lester Tilling, the terrible, unbelievable news of what he had just seen.

11. A   "Yes," said Lester, "the drum." He held it up high above his head, first to the north and then to the south, and then to the east and the west. He lowered it and turned his back to his wife and closed his eyes and took a deep breath and began to beat the drum slowly, one long beat with his tail, two staccato beats with his paws.

12. D   "He cannot, he simply cannot be my son," Lester said. "You," said Lester. "This is your fault. The French blood in him has made him crazy." . . . "He will be the end of us all," he shouted, "sitting at the foot of a human king. Unbelievable! Unthinkable!"

13. C   "Mice are rodents," said the king. He adjusted his crown. "They are related to . . . rats. You know how we feel about rats. You know of our own dark history with rats."

14. A   Despereaux, seeing her tears, broke the last of the great, ancient rules of mice. He spoke. To a human.

15. D   "We have no choice," said the Head Mouse. "He must go to the dungeon." He pounded his fisted paw on the table. "He must go to the rats. Immediately. Members of the council, I will now ask you to vote. Those in favor of Despereaux being sent to the dungeon, say 'aye.'"

16. B   The only noise came from Lester. He was crying. . . . Reader, can you imagine your own father not voting against your being sent to a dungeon full of rats? Can you imagine him not saying one word in your defence?

17. A   And Furlough found his brother in the library, standing on top of the great, open book, his tail wrapped tightly around his feet, his small body shivering.

18. D   Despereaux turned to him. "Do you know what love is?" he said. "Huh?" "Love."

19. C   "Yes, sir," said Despereaux. He raised his voice. "But . . . I broke the rules for good reasons. Because of music. And because of love."

20. C   "No," said Despereaux. And this time, he did not whisper the word. "I am not sorry. I will not renounce my actions. I love her. I love the princess."

21. A   Lying on the floor with the drum beating and the mice shouting and the threadmaster calling out, "Make way, make way," Despereaux had a sudden, chilling thought: had some other mouse eaten the words that spoke the truth? Did the knight and the fair maiden actually not live happily ever after?

22. B   "Be brave, friend," whispered the threadmaster. "Be brave for the princess."

23. C   But his mother, who had an excellent sense of dramatic timing, beat him to it; she executed a beautiful, flawless swoon, landing right at Despereaux's feet. . . . At the last moment, Antoinette came out of her faint and shouted one word to her child.

24. D   *Adieu* is the French word for farewell. . . . But, reader, there is no comfort in the word "farewell", even if you say it in French. "Farewell" is a word that, in any language, is full of sorrow. It is a word that promises absolutely nothing.

25. A   Together the three mice traveled down, down, down. The thread around Despereaux's neck was tight. He felt as if it was choking him. He tugged at it with one paw. "Don't touch the thread," barked the second hood. "Yeah," echoed the first hood, "don't touch the thread." They moved quickly. And whenever Despereaux slowed down, one of the two hoods poked him in the shoulder and told him to keep moving.

26. B   The voice was terribly familiar to Despereaux. "Furlough?" he said. "What?" said the first hood irritably. Despereaux shuddered. His own brother was delivering him to the dungeon.

27. C   He cleared his throat. He let go of his tail. He stood up straighter. "Once upon a time," he said out loud to the darkness. He said these words because they were the best, the most powerful words that he knew and just the saying of them comforted him.

28. A   That voice, the loudest voice that Despereaux had ever heard, could only, he assumed, belong to the world's largest rat.

29. D   "The answer to that question, mouse, is Gregory. You are talking to Gregory the jailer, who has been buried here, keeping watch over this dungeon for decades, for centuries, for eons. For eternities. You are talking to Gregory the jailer, who, in the richest of ironies, is nothing but a prisoner here himself."

30. C   "Why would you save me, then?" "Because you, mouse, can tell Gregory a story. Stories are light. Light is precious in a world so dark. Begin at the beginning. Tell Gregory a story. Make some light."

Book the Second (Chapter Sixteen to Chapter Twenty-three)

1. B   From that moment on, Roscuro showed an abnormal, inordinate interest in illumination of all sorts. He was always, in the darkness of the dungeon, on the lookout for light, the smallest glimmer, the tiniest shimmer. His rat soul longed inexplicably for it; he began to think that light was the only thing that gave life meaning, and he despaired that there was so little of it to be had.

2. A   "The meaning of life," said Botticelli, "is suffering, specifically the suffering of others. Prisoners, for instance. Reducing a prisoner to weeping and wailing and begging is a delightful way to invest your existence with meaning."

3. D   "Give him his small comforts," shouted a voice at the top of the stairs, and a red cloth was thrown into the light. The cloth hung suspended for a moment, bright red and glowing, and then the door was slammed shut again and the light disappeared and the cloth fell to the floor. It was Gregory the jailer who bent to pick it up.

4. C   "Listen," said Botticelli, "this is what you should do: go and torture the prisoner. Go and take the red cloth from him. The cloth will satisfy your craving for something from that world. But do not go up into the light. You will regret it."

5. A   The man cleared his throat. "I'm here for stealing six cows, two Jerseys and four Guernseys. Cow theft, that's my crime."

6. B   What a disappointment it was! Looking at it, Roscuro knew that Botticelli was wrong. What Roscuro wanted, what he needed, was not the cloth, but the light that had shone behind it.

7. C   Roscuro had never seen happy people. He had known only the miserable ones. Gregory the jailer and those who were consigned to his domain did not laugh or smile or clink glasses with the person sitting next to them.

8. A   And the little princess! How lovely she was! How much like light itself. Her gown was covered in sequins that winked and glimmered at the rat. And when she laughed, and she laughed often, everything around her seemed to glow brighter.

9. D   There was, in the banquet hall, a most beautiful and ornate chandelier. The crystals that hung from it caught the light of the candles on the table and the light from the face of the laughing princess. They danced to the rhythm of the minstrels' music, swaying back and forth, twinkling and beckoning. What better place to view all this glory, all this beauty?

10. C   *Rat.* He had never before been aware of what an ugly word it was. $Rat. In the middle of all that beauty it immediately became clear that it was an extremely distasteful syllable.

11. D   "There is a rat in my soup" were the last words she uttered. She clutched her chest and fell over backward. Her royal chair hit the floor with a thump, and the banquet hall exploded.

12. D   He looked back. And he saw that the princess was glaring at him. Her eyes were filled with disgust and anger. "Go back to the dungeon" was what the look she gave him said. "Go back into the darkness where you belong." This look, reader, broke Roscuro's heart.

13. B   And the queen was still dead, of course, when Roscuro encountered the queen's royal soup spoon lying on the floor. . . . "I will have something beautiful," he said aloud. "I am a rat, but I will have something beautiful. I will have a crown of my own." He picked up the spoon. He put it on his head.

14. A   "Yes," said Roscuro. "I will have something beautiful. And I will have revenge. Both things. Somehow."

15. B   For instance (if, reader, you will indulge me, and allow me to continue this meditation on consequences), because the queen died while eating soup, the heartbroken king outlawed soup; and because soup was outlawed, so were all the instruments involved in the making and eating of soup: spoons and bowls and kettles. These things were collected from all the people of the Kingdom of Dor, and they were piled in the dungeon.

16. C   And speaking of consequences, the same evening that Despereaux stood inside the castle hearing music for the first time, outside the castle, in the gloom of dusk, more consequences drew near. A wagon driven by a king's soldier and piled high with spoons and bowls and kettles, was making its way to the castle. And beside the soldier there sat a young girl with ears that looked like nothing so much as pieces of cauliflower stuck on either side of her head.

Book the Third (Chapter Twenty-four to Chapter Thirty-four)

1. C   With that said, here begins a short history of the life and times of Miggery Sow, a girl born into this world many years before the mouse Despereaux and the rat Chiaroscuro, a girl born far from the castle, a girl named for her father's favorite prize-winning pig.

2. C   She squeezed Mig's hand once, twice, and then she died, leaving Mig alone with her father, who, on a market day in spring soon after his wife's death, sold his daughter into service for a handful of cigarettes, a red tablecloth, and a hen.

3. D   Another unfortunate fact of life with Uncle was that he very much liked giving Mig what he referred to as "a good clout to the ear." In fairness to Uncle, it must be reported that he did always enquire whether or not Mig was interested in receiving the clout.

4. A   The less Mig heard, the less she understood. The less she understood, the more things she did wrong; and the more things she did wrong, the more clouts to the ear she received, and the less she heard. This is what is known as a vicious circle. And Miggery

Sow was right in the center of it.

5. B   When Mig turned seven years old there was no cake, no celebration, no singing, no present, no acknowledgement of her birthday at all other than Mig saying, "Uncle, today I am seven years old." And Uncle saying in return, "Did I ask ye how old you were today? Get out of my face before I give ye a good clout to the ear." A few hours after receiving her birthday clout to the ear, Mig was out in the field with Uncle's sheep when she saw something glittering and glowing on the horizon.

6. D   Mig did not wave back; instead, she stood and watched, open-mouthed, as the perfect, beautiful family passed her by.

7. B   "I saw some human stars today." "How's that?" "I saw them all glittering and glowing, and there was a little princess wearing her own crown and riding on a little white, tippy-toed horse."

8. C   "I would like . . . ," said Mig shyly. "I wish to be one of them princesses." "Har," laughed Uncle. "Har. An ugly, dumb thing like you? You ain't even worth the enormous lot I paid for you. Don't I wish every night that I had back that good hen and that red tablecloth in place of you?"

9. A   In the evening, spring or winter, summer or fall, Mig stood in the field as the sun set, hoping that the royal family would pass before her again.

10. B   "No matter," said the soldier. "It is against the law to own another. Now, you will hand over to me, if you please, your spoons, your bowls, your kettle, and your girl. Or if you choose not to hand over these things then you will come with me to be imprisoned in the castle dungeon. Which will it be?"

11. D   On her first day on the job as a castle servant she was sent to deliver a spool of red thread to the princess.

12. A   "I am making a history of the world, my world," said the Pea, "in tapestry. See? Here is my father, the king. And he is playing the guitar because that is something he loves to do and does quite well. And here is my mother, the queen, and she is eating soup because she loved soup."

13. C   At the castle, for the first time in her young life, Mig had enough to eat. And eat she did. She quickly became plump and then plumper still. She grew rounder and rounder and bigger and bigger. Only her head stayed small.

14. B   "You are being sent to the dungeon. You are to take the jailer his noonday meal. That will be your duty from now on."

15. D   The terrible foul odor of the dungeon did not bother Mig. Perhaps that is because, sometimes, when Uncle had been giving her a good clout to the ear, he had missed his mark and delivered a good clout to Mig's nose instead. This had happened

often enough that it interrupted the proper workings of Mig's olfactory senses. And so it was that the overwhelming stench of despair and hopelessness and evil was not at all discernible to her, and she went happily down the twisting and turning stairs.

16. A   "Yes, yes," whispered the rat, "a lovely song. Just the song I have been waiting to hear." And Roscuro quietly fell in step beside Miggery Sow.

17. B   "Here," said Mig, staring hard at him, "you forgot the bones." "Not forgotten. Chewed." "Gor," said Mig, staring at Gregory with respect. "You eats the bones. You are most ferocious."

18. D   Roscuro, hidden beneath Mig's skirts, rubbed his front paws together. "Warn her all you like, old man," he whispered. "My hour has arrived. The time is now, and your rope must break. No nib-nib-nibbling this time, rather a serious chew that will break it in two. Yes, it is all coming clear. Revenge is at hand."

19. A   That great, unusual, portentous thing is this: Roscuro's voice was pitched perfectly to make its way through the tortuous path of Mig's broken-down, cauliflower ears. That is to ay, dear reader, Miggery Sow heard, perfect and true, every single word he rat Roscuro uttered.

20. C   "There is, my dear, a way to make that happen. I believe hat there is a way to make that dream come true." "You mean that I could be the Princess Pea?" "Yes, Your Highness," said Roscuro. And he swept the spoon off his head and bowed deeply at the waist. "Yes, your most royal Princess Pea."

Book the Fourth (Chapter Thirty-five to Chapter Fifty-two) & Coda

1. A   "Back to the light," that was what Gregory whispered to him when he wrapped Despereaux in his napkin and placed him on the tray. And then Mig, after her conversation with Roscuro, carried the tray into the kitchen, and when she saw Cook she shouted, "It's me, Miggery Sow, back from the deep downs."

2. D   She reached over and took hold of the napkin and gave it a good shake, and Despereaux tumbled out of the napkin and landed right directly, plop, in a measuring cup full of oil. . . . But the mouse tail, covered as it was in oil, was slick and difficult to hold onto and Mig, in reaching for the knife, loosened her grip, and Despereaux fell to the floor. . . . "I got the little meecy's tail, though," said Mig. She bent over and picked up Despereaux's tail and held it up, proudly displaying it to Cook.

3. B   So Despereaux wept with joy and with pain and with gratitude. He wept with exhaustion and despair and hope. He wept with all the emotions a young, small

mouse who has been sent to his death and then been delivered from it in time to save his beloved can feel.

4. C   The knight stopped swinging his sword. He looked at Despereaux. "You know me," he said. "No," said Despereaux, "I don't." "You do," said the knight. He slowly took the armor off his head and revealed . . . nothing, no one. The suit of armor was empty.

5. C   In her hand she carried a candle. And in the pockets of her apron were two very ominous things. In the right pocket, hidden in case they should encounter anyone on the stairs, was a rat with a spoon on his head and a cloak of red around his shoulders. In the left pocket was a kitchen knife, the same knife that Miggery Sow had used to cut off the tail of a certain mouse. These were the things, a rat and a knife and a candle, that Mig carried with her as she climbed up, up, up the stairs.

6. A   The rat's real plan was, in a way, more simple and more terrible. He intended to take the princess to the deepest, darkest part of the dungeon. He intended to have Mig put chains on the princess's hands and her feet, and he intended to keep the glittering, glowing, laughing princess there in the dark.

7. B   She was asleep and dreaming of her mother, the queen, who was holding out a spoon to her and saying, "Taste this, my sweet Pea, taste this, my darling, and tell me what you think." The princess leaned forward and sipped some soup from the spoon her mother held out to her. "Oh, Mama," she said, "it's wonderful. It's the best soup I have ever eaten."

8. D   "Do you know me, Princess?" "No," she said, lowering her head, "I don't know you." But, reader, she did know him. He was the rat who had fallen in her mother's soup. And he was wearing her dead mother's spoon on his head! The princess kept her head down. She concentrated on containing the rage that was leaping up inside of her.

9. C   You are able to think: "Oh, poor Mig, she wants to be a princess so badly and she thinks that this is the way. Poor, poor Mig. What must it be like to want something that desperately?" That, reader, is empathy.

10. D   And now you have a small map of the princess's heart (hatred, sorrow, kindness, empathy), the heart that she carried inside her as she went down the golden stairs and through the kitchen and, finally, just as the sky outside the castle began to lighten, down into the dark of the dungeon with the rat and the serving girl.

11. A   "And more foul play. Gregory dead!" shouted Cook. "Poor old man, that rope of his broken by who knows what and him lost in the dark and frightened to death because of it. It's too much."

12. D   And so, the small mouse who had been dipped in oil, covered in flour and relieved of his tail slipped out of the pantry and past the weeping ladies. He went to find

the king.

13. B   Despereaux looked at his father and saw an old mouse whose fur was shot through with grey. How could that be? Despereaux had been gone only a few days, but his father seemed to have aged many years in his absence.

14. C   Only one mouse said nothing. That mouse was Despereaux's father. Lester Tilling had turned his head away from the other members of the Mouse Council; he was trying to hide his tears. He was crying, reader, because he had been forgiven.

15. C   Despereaux found the king in the Pea's room, sitting on his daughter's bed, clutching the tapestry of her life to his chest. He was weeping. Although "weeping," really, is too small a word for the activity that the king had undertaken. Tears were cascading from his eyes. A small puddle had formed at his feet. I am not exaggerating. The king, it seemed, was intent on crying himself a river.

16. B   "I cannot hear you! And anyway, what you say is wrong because you are a rodent and therefore a liar." He started to hum again. And then he stopped and said, "I have hired fortunetellers. And a magician. They are coming from a distant land. They will tell me where my beautiful daughter is. They will speak the truth. A mouse cannot speak the truth."

17. D   "Yes, like a maze. And I have to find my way to her, wherever she is hidden, and then I have to lead her back out again, and the only way to do that is with the thread. Gregory the jailer tied a rope around his ankle so that he would not get lost." As the mouse said this he shuddered, thinking of Gregory and his broken rope, dying, lost in the darkness. "I," said Despereaux, "I . . . I will use thread."

18. A   "There's something else. Something that belongs with the thread." Hovis went into a corner and came back with a needle. "You can use it for protection." "Like a sword," said Despereaux. "Like a knight would have."

19. D   He gnawed off a length of thread and used it to tie the needle around Despereaux's waist. "Like so." . . . That night Despereaux rolled the thread from the threadmaster's lair, along innumerable hallways and down three flights of stairs. . . . He was nothing but two ounces of mouse pushing a spool of thread that weighed almost as much as he did. . . . And he still had a very, very long way to go, into the kitchen and down the many stairs of the dungeon . . .

20. A   But he had to go through Cook's kitchen to get to the dungeon door.

21. B   Despereaux put his head up in the air. He sniffed. He sniffed some more. He had never in his life smelled anything so lovely, so inspiring. With each sniff he took, he felt himself growing stronger, braver.

22. D   "A mouse," said Cook. "A mouse in my kitchen." Despereaux closed his eyes.

He prepared for his death. He waited, reader. And waited. And then he heard the sound of laughter. He opened his eyes and looked at Cook. "Ho," said Cook. "Ho-hee. For the first time in my life, I am glad to see a mouse in my kitchen. . . ."

23. A   "Mouse," said Cook, "would you like some soup?" And then, without waiting for an answer, she took a saucer and spooned some soup into it and set it on the kitchen floor.

24. C   "Too much garlic?" said Cook, wringing her fat hands. "No," said Despereaux. "It's perfect." Cook smiled. "See?" she said. "There ain't a body, be it mouse or man, that ain't made better by a little soup." Despereaux bent his head and sipped again, and Cook stood over him and smiled, saying, "It don't need a thing, then? Is that what you're saying? It's just right?"

25. B   "I will tell myself a story," said Despereaux. "I will make some light. Let's see. It will begin this way: Once upon a time. Yes. Once upon a time, there was a mouse who was very, very small. Exceptionally small. And there was a beautiful human princess whose name was Pea. And it so happened that this mouse was the one who was selected by fate to serve the princess, to honour her and to save her from the darkness of a terrible dungeon."

26. A   But the spool had a head start. And it was faster. It flew down the dungeon stairs, leaving Despereaux far behind. When it came to the end of the stairs, it rolled and rolled, until finally, lazily, it came to a stop right at the gnarled paw of a rat.

27. D   He stood very still. "I'll go back," he said. But he didn't move. "I have to go back." He took a step backward. "But I can't go back. I don't have a choice. I have no choice." He took one step forward. And then another. "No choice," his heart beat out to him as he went down the stairs, "no choice, no choice, no choice."

28. B   Botticelli did not want to be of service. Far from it. You know what Botticelli wanted. He wanted others to suffer. Specifically, he wanted this small mouse to suffer. How best to do that? Why, take him right directly to what he wanted. The princess. Let him see what his heart desired, and then, and only then, faced with what he loved, would Despereaux die. And at the end of it all, how tasty the mouse would be . . . seasoned with hope and tears and flour and oil and thwarted love!

29. A   He saw that the floor of the dungeon was littered with tufts of fur, knots of red thread and the skeletons of mice. Everywhere there were tiny white bones glowing in the darkness. And he saw, in the dungeon tunnels through which Botticelli led him, the bones of human beings too, grinning skulls and delicate finger bones, rising up out of the darkness and pointing toward some truth best left unspoken. Despereaux closed his eyes.

30. C   Botticelli called out to the other rats. "Mine," he said. "This little treasure is all

mine, gentlemen and ladies. Please, I beg you. Do not infringe on my discovery."

31. B   "How do I look?" Mig asked, smiling at him. "Ridiculous," he said. "Laughable." Mig stood, blinking back tears. "You mean I don't look like a princess?" she said to the rat. "I mean," said Roscuro, "you will never look like a princess, no matter how big a crown you put on your tiny head. You look exactly like the fool you are and always will be. Now, make yourself useful and chain the princess up. Dress-up time is over."

32. A   "What do you want, Mig?" the princess said softly. "Eh?" shouted Mig. "What do you want, Miggery Sow?!" the princess shouted. "Don't ask her that," said Roscuro. "Shut up. Shut up." But it was too late. The words had been said; the question, at last, had been asked. The world stopped spinning and all of creation held its breath, waiting to hear what it was that Miggery Sow wanted.

33. D   The Princess Pea heard her name. She looked up. "Despereaux," she whispered. And then she shouted it, "Despereaux!" Reader, nothing is sweeter in this sad world than the sound of someone you love calling your name.

34. A   Mig said, "Don't worry, Princess. I will save the meecy." She took the kitchen knife. She aimed to cut off the rat's head, but she missed her mark.

35. C   And the smell of soup crashed through his soul like a great wave, bringing with it the memory of light, the chandelier, the music, the laughter, everything, all the things that were not, would never, could never be available to him as a rat. Roscuro. And he began to cry.

36. B   I think, reader, that she was feeling the same thing that Despereaux had felt when he was faced with his father begging him for forgiveness. That is, Pea was aware suddenly of how fragile her heart was, how much darkness was inside it, fighting, always, with the light. She did not like the rat. She would never like the rat, but she knew what she must do to save her own heart. And so here are the words that the princess spoke to her enemy. She said, "Roscuro, would you like some soup?"

37. C   Roscuro, reader, told the princess about the prisoner who had once owned a red tablecloth, and the princess saw to it that the prisoner was released. And Roscuro led the man up out of the dungeon and to his daughter, Miggery Sow. Mig, as you might have guessed, did not get to be a princess. But her father, to atone for what he had done, treated her like one for the rest of his days.

38. D   And what of Despereaux? Did he live happily ever after? Well, he did not marry the princess, if that is what you mean by happily ever after. Even in a world as strange as this one a mouse and a princess cannot marry. But, reader, they can be friends. And they were. Together, they had many adventures. Those adventures, however, are another story, and this story, I'm afraid, must now draw to a close.